Football Fortunes

Football Fortunes

The Business, Organization, and Strategy of the NFL

FRANK P. JOZSA, JR.

Foreword by JOHN MAXYMUK

McFarland & Company, Inc., Publishers

Jefferson, North Carolina, and London

LIBRARY OF CONGRESS CATALOGUING-IN-PUBLICATION DATA

Jozsa, Frank P., 1941–
   Football fortunes : the business, organization and strategy of
the NFL / Frank P. Jozsa, Jr. ; foreword by John Maxymuk.
      p.   cm.
   Includes bibliographical references and index.

   ISBN 978-0-7864-4641-4
   softcover : 50# alkaline paper ∞

   1. National Football League.   2. Football — Economic aspects —
United States.   I. Title.
   GV955.5.N35J69   2010
   796.332'64 — dc22   2010003175

British Library cataloguing data are available

Cover photograph ©2010 Neustockimages

Manufactured in the United States of America

*McFarland & Company, Inc., Publishers
   Box 611, Jefferson, North Carolina 28640
   www.mcfarlandpub.com*

To my son Jeff,
an Indianapolis Colts fan

Acknowledgments

While studying the business of the National Football League (NFL), I have received expert advice and assistance from several people, some of whom had provided me with information in connection with the publication of my previous books and articles about the sports industry.

Among the employees at Pfeiffer University's campuses in Charlotte and Misenheimer, North Carolina, I am especially grateful to the director of information support services, Frank Chance, and his part-time evening librarian, Theresa Frady. The library director and assistant professor of library science, Lara Little, forwarded me the titles of numerous sports books and other readings. The administrative director of Pfeiffer's School of Graduate Studies, Michael Utsman, provided me with technical support, and also suggested that I discuss the change in broadcasting NFL games from the ABC, CBS, FOX, and NBC networks to cable outlets like ESPN and the NFL Network.

Others who contributed in some way to my research include Rutgers University reference librarian John Maxymuk, who wrote this book's foreword, and University of Michigan sport management professor and author Rodney Fort, who explained the differences between small, midsized, and large sports markets, and posted on his website the home attendances and other related business data of teams in each professional sport.

My friend Bill Focht suggested that I discuss such topics about the NFL as public finance and stadium development, player behavior, parity between teams, expansion in foreign countries, and the league's status as a non-profit corporation. Loras College professor of economics and diehard Chicago Cubs fan Laddie Sula offered comments about labor relations and the salaries of players within the sports industry. Former Pittsburgh Steelers strong safety Donnie Shell contacted some NFL officials for information that I needed about teams.

I had excellent cooperation from staff at the public library in Fort Mill, South Carolina, and from reference/interlibrary loan librarian Page Hendrix of the York County Library. Finally, my companion, Maureen Fogle, and I shared a computer, desk, and printer in an office of her house while our dog, Lucy, alerted me to feed her, take timeouts, and go for walks.

I appreciate and wholeheartedly thank those cited above, and acknowledge their contributions to the creation of this book.

Table of Contents

List of Tables

Foreword

by John Maxymuk

When George Hals and the other founding members of the American Professional Football Association sat on the running boards in Ralph Hay's Canton Hupmobile showroom in 1920, it is doubtful that he or any of his fellow sports pioneers foresaw the day when the league they formed would grow to become the multibillion-dollar business empire the National Football League is today. At the time, not only was professional football dwarfed by major league baseball, it was also the poor, neglected stepchild of college football. While the game itself has changed dramatically in the ensuing decades in order to propagate its appeal as America's national game, today's NFL is also the product of lengthy progression of smart and innovative business decisions. In this book, economics professor Frank Jozsa examines these astute business practices in detail to determine how the NFL became such a financial and cultural success in this country as well as what the future holds for the league.

We have come a long way from the early days of myriad town teams dotted throughout very minor markets in the Midwest to the dominant position the NFL holds in the current sports industry. Indeed, even in recent years as the market shares and ratings of other major sports have declined — some due to various problems on and off the field — the NFL glides imperviously on. Jozsa, a former college baseball and basketball player, makes the point that perhaps one reason the NFL has adapted so well to change over time is that it has sharpened its edge against more competitor leagues (five different American Football Leagues, the Continental Football League, World Football League and United States Football League) than any other sport.

In this, his ninth book, Jozsa examines why and when the NFL decided to contract, expand or merge to better compete for market share and earnings. He explores why and when the league has relocated franchises in response to changes in local economies and other commercial factors. The author details the sound business strategies that have allowed the NFL to continue to increase revenues and manage its expenses to steadily increase the financial value of its franchises, particularly regarding television contracts, revenue sharing and a salary cap. He points out the importance of the location, financing and benefits of team stadiums and the development of markets across ethnic groups and throughout economic hard times to ensure the continued growth of the league.

Finally, Jozsa looks at the success of several important subsidiaries to the league: NFL Properties, NFL Films, NFL Network, and the separate entity that is the Super Bowl, as well as estimating the league's prospects for international expansion. He also addresses the two most prominent missteps of the league — the failure of the NFL's World Football League in Europe and the inability to field a successful franchise in Los Angeles, the nation's second-largest market.

This work should appeal to several groups. The current and prospective owners of professional football franchises as well as officials of the NFL and other professional sports leagues will find a solid overview of effective business practices in the industry. Likewise, advertisers, marketers, promoters affiliated with the NFL and decision makers in the vital broadcast markets will find a thorough examination of what works in their field. College and university professors who teach either undergraduate or graduate classes in sports administration, management, and marketing or business organization and strategy should find it useful as a textbook or for reference.

Many people have commented that the NFL became such a capitalist success in large part due to the socialist practices of revenue sharing, but that is somewhat misguided. The NFL is an amalgamation of franchise operations of the same brand. The teams are not competing financially as much against each other as they are partners in competing against other sports and, at times, other football leagues. As the costs and revenue streams have expanded in recent years, there has been increasing pressure for teams to forego "league think" for a more individualistic approach. How the league responds to this challenge will be central to the success or failure of new commissioner Roger Goodell, particularly with the possibility of the disappearance of the salary cap in 2010. How that plays out may provide Professor Jozsa with enough material for another book.

John Maxymuk • *Rutgers University, Camden, New Jersey*

John Maxymuk is the author of *Uniform Numbers of the NFL: All-Time Rosters, Facts and Figures* (McFarland, 2005) and *Strong Arm Tactics: A History and Statistical Analysis of the Professional Quarterback* (McFarland, 2008).

Preface

Since completing a doctoral degree in 1977 at Georgia State University and while authoring eight books on the business and economics of professional team sports between the late 1990s and 2009, I continued to research topics about successful organizations such as the National Football League (NFL). Numerous readings have discussed different aspects of professional football and especially the problems of the NFL. Many of these publications, however, simply (if interestingly) describe the history of the league and thus provide data and other information about its regular seasons and postseasons, and the performances of teams, coaches and players. In other words, they focus on and report various NFL events, statistics, and years of play.

In contrast to — but respectful of — those volumes, the present work evaluates other factors to analyze the business, organization, and strategy of the NFL. There are no prior publications, for example, that focus upon the matters of league expansions and mergers, team territories and relocations, franchise organizations and operations, football stadiums and markets, and NFL domestic and foreign affairs. Indeed, according to my research of the sports literature, each of these has a major relationship to the development of the league in America and thus of professional football.

To examine the growth of the NFL and provide some reasons for its popularity between 1920 and the early 2000s, I constructed a number of tables that reflected something interesting with respect to each chapter's theme. These tables, for example, include such information as the names of new franchises in the league and those teams that had folded, or relocated and survived, and the administrative offices within NFL clubs and the titles of officials and their jobs. Other tables address professional football stadiums in metropolitan areas, existing and potential markets of current or expansion NFL teams, and the responsibilities of league and team vice presidents, managers, directors, and other executives.

Based on the variety of topics within, readers will learn how and why

3

the NFL has thrived as a professional league in the United States. That is, they will understand the business importance of leadership and management, organizational structure, and company strategy. Furthermore, this book provides a 14-part statistical appendix, detailed notes, an extensive bibliography, and an index.

In sum, this book is unique because it analyzes the business that is the NFL.

Introduction

Most of the successful organizations in American professional team sports emerged during the twentieth century. As of 2009, these different groups include the 109-year-old major league baseball (MLB), 93-year-old National Hockey League (NHL), 90-year-old National Football League (NFL), 61-year-old National Basketball Association (NBA), and 14-year-old Major League Soccer (MLS).

Despite such internal issues as franchise owner lockouts and player scandals and strikes, and such external problems as economic downturns and military conflicts, the teams within these leagues continued to perform in games during regular seasons and in various types of postseason tournaments. Consequently, at least four professional sports leagues and their teams have been important to American culture and the history of this nation during most of the past century.[1]

The professional sports leagues have helped their teams to exploit local and regional consumer markets, to provide entertainment for spectators, and to secure sufficient cash flows. For various reasons, some leagues previously based in the United States ultimately folded because their clubs had financial difficulties or inadequate leadership — or just showed poor performances against opponents.

Since the late 1800s, some of these failures in each professional sport were the Union Association (1884), Players League (1890), and Federal League (1914–1915) in baseball; the World Hockey Association (1972–1979), National Hockey Association (1909–1917), and Western Professional Hockey League (1996–2001); the All-America Football Conference (1946–1949), American Football League (1960–1969), and World Football League (1974–1975); the United States Basketball League (1985–2007), American Basketball Association (1967–1976), and World Basketball League (1988–1992); and, the United Soccer Association (1967), North American Soccer League (1968–1975), and Women's United Soccer Association (2001–2003). Because these leagues no

5

longer exist, the present work does not discuss the commercial aspects and histories of these former sports organizations.[2]

Between the 1970s and early 2000s the NFL gradually became the dominant professional sports league in America and almost in the world. Indeed, the majority of its teams surpassed those in MLB, NBA, NHL, and MLS, with thousands more fans in a majority of sports markets within metropolitan areas of the United States. Other leagues' decline in market shares, profits, and television ratings relative to the NFL resulted from a number of business, demographic, economic, and social factors.

Each of the professional sports leagues experienced to some degree short-term, intermediate, or long-term deficiencies or hardships. Within MLB, it was lockouts, strikes, and the cancellation of the 1994 baseball season and postseason, abuse of illegal substances by several popular ballplayers, and a lack of parity and competition among some teams in divisions of the American League (AL) and National League (NL). Within the NBA, it was excessive increases in ticket prices to home games, inflated salaries of players and their irresponsible and sometimes illegal behavior. Within the NHL, it was the players strike in 2004, low television ratings of teams' regular season and postseason games, and unpredictable changes in value of the Canadian dollar. And within MLS, it was some clubs' inability to attract more sponsors and establish partnerships, inadequate exposure of soccer matches on national television networks and local satellite and cable channels, and the inferior quality of teams' stadiums, which made it difficult to attract spectators.

In my opinion, unless these four U.S.-based professional leagues implement innovations and marketing reforms and thereby become significantly more efficient as organizations, the NFL will attract additional sports fans and thus increase its market share at the expense of the other leagues. As a result, football franchises should experience growth in revenues and profits.

Rather than discuss and predict the future of all professional team sports and the sports industry, this work focuses on the NFL, and analyzes when, why and how the league and various teams adapted to changing circumstances and challenged other leagues, and how it became the most well-respected and wealthiest organization in American sports history. (The Premier League in England is the only other professional sports organization in the world that rivals the NFL in power, prestige, and market value.)

National Football League

Readers, including but not limited to football fans, sports executives and students studying sports administration and marketing, will find interesting business, cultural and historical insights into the emergence, growth and lasting success of the NFL. First, the book describes how the league has changed in composition since it began in 1920. Readers will understand why the organization occasionally adjusted the number of teams and agreed to their locations in order to compete for fans and revenue with MLB and the NHL, and then later with the NBA and MLS.

Second, readers learn that various consumer markets for professional sports changed throughout the twentieth century. Thus, the NFL expanded in a number of metropolitan areas in response to changes in local economies. Third, readers will realize that various qualitative factors — besides the adoption of a salary cap system and revenue-sharing agreement among the league's franchises — also contributed to the evolution of the NFL, including such intangibles as foresight, intuition and luck.

Fourth, the book reveals why football — rather than professional baseball, basketball, ice hockey, or outdoor soccer — has better met the entertainment demands of sports fans and therefore become increasingly popular, even during economic slowdowns and despite the deomographic changes within American society. Fifth, readers will recognize the consequence of business matters in a sports organization's struggle to survive and thrive. In other words the NFL and its officials, including team owners and general managers, have interdependently made practical and prudent decisions based on realistic financial and managerial strategies.

Besides these five issues there are other interesting characteristics that distinguish the league's history, policies and structure from those of MLB, the NBA, the NHL, and MLS. The game itself had relatively upper-class origins, for example, developing from rugby played on campuses by college students in the eastern U.S. during the mid–1800s. In the 1890s, some amateur football teams organized and became the game's first professionals.

Another major difference between the NFL and other professional sports leagues is that since the early 1900s, the NFL faced more competitive and professional rival organizations than did other sports leagues. Indeed, baseball's Federal League, the American Basketball Association, the World Hockey Association, and National Professional Soccer League were relatively inferior organizations in comparison to the market power of the American Football League, which mounted a serious challenge during the 1960s.

As of early 2009, the NFL had successfully played 89 consecutive regular seasons and 43 Super Bowls, while MLB and the NHL had to cancel a season or more because of owner lockouts or player strikes. The NFL experienced its most serious labor-management troubles during two years: In 1982, a 57-day players' strike reduced the number of regular season games from 224 to 126, and in 1987, a 24-day players' strike resulted in 14 games being cancelled. Moreover, the Super Bowl — unlike the World Series, NBA Championship, Stanley Cup, or MLS Cup — has become a national obsession and de facto holiday, and the premier event in American professional sports. The television and radio ratings for the four other major professional sports' championships have remained level or moderately declined in recent years while the number of viewers has expanded for the Super Bowl, played between winners of the NFL's American and National Football Conferences (respectively, the AFC and NFC).

The NFL's annual preseason, regular season, and postseason are distinct, making it easy for fans to keep up with a particular team as the season progresses and therefore maintain their interest. Although the lengths of these three periods are comparable with other professional sports, the fact that there are relatively few professional football games means fans have more time between games to discuss and measure team performances, and division rank, and standing in the league as a whole.

Baseball, basketball, ice hockey, and outdoor soccer are more popular sports than American-style football in the majority of foreign countries, and the NFL's opportunities for the placement of teams into metropolitan areas beyond North America is spatially limited. The failure in 2007 of NFL Europa (formerly the NFL Europe League), after competing in cities there for several years, suggests that the NFL must revise its international strategy. For example, the league may need to invest more financial capital and marketing resources into basic amateur programs to teach people in Asia, Europe, and elsewhere how to play the game. Otherwise, the league must locate any of its new teams within the U.S., or potentially, in Canada or Mexico.

In part, the NFL has prospered because it adopted a salary cap and implemented a revenue-sharing system for the benefit of all of the league's teams. Because of these policies, such small-market franchises as the Buffalo Bills, Cincinnati Bengals, and Kansas City Chiefs have a realistic chance each season of winning a division title, conference championship, and perhaps a Super Bowl. Among the other major sports leagues, there are advantages and greater opportunities for clubs located in large metropolitan areas. Some improvements in parity have occurred since the late 1990s among teams in MLB and somewhat between clubs in the NBA, NHL and MLS. It appeared, therefore, that aspects of the NFL's business model were copied and applied by officials in America's other professional sports leagues.

A number of books and articles that touch upon business aspects and the corporate history of the NFL are worthy of mention. Several titles merit brief summaries because they include one or more of the topics discussed in this book. The bibliography lists other books on professional football, the NFL, various seasons and specific teams.[3]

Peter King's *Football: A History of the Professional Game* was published in 1994 and includes many unique illustrations and classic photographs. King, a noted author in the field, discusses developments in professional football from the early 1920s to the mid–1990s. Each chapter covers a decade, and includes stories about teams and their players.

In 1999 sportswriter Will McDonough's *The NFL Century: The Complete Story of the National Football League, 1920–2000* was published. This was an updated edition of his *75 Seasons: The Complete Story of the National Football League, 1920–1995*, which appeared in 1994. It begins with an overview of the meeting of a group of mildly successful but optimistic American businesspersons in Canton, Ohio, and their planning the formation of a new football league. *The NFL Century* describes the impressive and profitable growth of the sport, which was based in part on these planners' decisions, determination and foresight. The main focus of the book, however, is the NFL's growth in popularity during the period from the early 1970s into the mid– to late 1990s. In addition, the book features quotes, original illustrations, and photographs of teams and players.

In *America's Game: The Epic Story of How Pro Football Captured a Nation* (20009), former journalist Michael MacCambridge explains how the NFL expanded from a struggling regional organization in the 1940s to surpass major league baseball in popularity and eventually become the nation's most profitable sports league. In addition to stories about prominent football coaches, players and teams, MacCambridge details the vision and business decisions of NFL leaders, including former commissioner Pete Rozelle and team owners Al Davis, George Allen and Lamar Hunt, exploring how each of them was in part responsible for the league's success. MacCambridge discusses the goals and effects of NFL Properties and NFL Films, and he relates details about television negotiations and internal bickering among groups of NFL executives. MacCambridge also examines race relations, stadium construction and financing, and the relocation of franchises. *America's Game* is a detailed and expansive history of the NFL and its ascent.

Mark Yost's *Tailgating, Sacks, and Salary Caps: How the NFL Became the Most Successful Sports League in History* was published by Kaplan Business in 2006, and essentially provides a financial history of the NFL. It covers such topics as the league's merchandising rights, media and fantasy games, television contracts, and attempts by the NFL to broaden its market by attracting and convincing women to be dedicated football fans. Case studies examine ways in which team owners came up with methods to generate money, from their stadiums and other sources, revenue they were not required to share with other league franchises. Yost supports the NFL's revenue sharing system and salary cap, the league's draft system and the way in which it equitably schedules games among teams whose win-loss record varied from best to worst in the previous season. The author praises former commissioners Bert Bell and Pete Rozelle for their efforts to achieve greater competitive balance within conferences, and for their reaction to threats from competing pro football organizations. According to one reviewer, the book makes it clear that "The richest professional sports league in the most capitalistic nation on the planet got that way by applying principles that would have been recognizable to that unheralded gridiron pioneer, V.I. Lenin."

In 2007, former NFL offensive lineman–turned–university professor Michael Oriard authored the insightful *Brand NFL: Making and Selling America's Favorite Sport*. Oriard exposed the business practices that helped the NFL become popular and profitable during the twentieth century, and emerge as the country's premier professional sport. More specifically, he analyzes the league's labor-management relations, its image on television, racial issues, and the frequent erratic and detrimental behavior of many players. Furthermore, he discusses the media's fascination with the Super Bowl, and the costs to taxpayers of financing the construction of new stadiums, thereby subsidizing operations of the league's franchises. Because of Oriard's personal experience and his detailed research, *Brand NFL* is an important reference for observers of American culture, and for fans of football in particular. A reviewer in *Publishers Weekly* wrote, "Oriard has fashioned a riveting examination of how a violent sport has become a staggering mainstream American success."[4]

The bibliography lists several other works that discuss one or more of the subjects covered within. With respect to league expansions and mergers in Chapter 1 and team territories and relocations in Chapter 2, there are such books as my *American Sports Empire* and *Big Sports, Big Business*, and my and John Guthrie's *Relocating Teams and Expanding Leagues in Professional Sports*. Regarding franchise organizations and operations in Chapter 3, readers should see such recent articles as "The 2004 Team Valuations," Michael K. Ozanian's "Selective Accounting" and David Romer's "Do Firms Maximize? Evidence From Professional Football," and, on the Internet, "NFL Team Valuations."[5]

For information about football stadiums and markets in Chapter 4, there are several interesting articles, including Robert Baade's "Professional Sports as a Catalyst For Metropolitan Economic Development," Steve Cameron's "Politically Correct? Rarely When It Comes to Facilities," and Matthew Futterman's "Jets to Auction Seats on eBay." In relation to Chapter 5's domestic and foreign affairs, several publications discuss the league's organization and its strategies. Three relevant media guides, for example, are the *2008 NFL Record & Fact Book*; David Boss and Bob Oates, Jr.'s *First Fifty Years*; and the *NFL International: A Winning Partnership*. Information about the business of broadcasting NFL games and other events appears in "A Political Football," Adam Duerson's "TV Watch," and Matthew Futterman's "NFL Games Go Wireless" and "NFL Seeks Balance in Cable Fray."[6]

Several books listed in the bibliography focus on the economic performance and structure of the NFL. Four of these titles are: Paul Downward and Alistair Dawson's *The Economics of Professional Team Sports*; John Fizel's *Handbook of Sports Economics Research*; Roger G. Noll's *Government and the Sports Business*; and James Quirk and Rodney D. Fort's *Pay Dirt*. The commercialization and entrepreneurial activities and programs associated with the league are topics covered in Brad R. Humphreys and Dennis R. Howard's *The Business of Sports*, my own *Sports Capitalism*, Jon Morgan's *Glory For Sale*, and Phil Schaaf's *Sports, Inc.* Information from these and additional sources was crucial in this effort to interpret the successful development of the NFL as a b usiness entity.[7]

Organization

Chapter 1, "League Expansions and Mergers," relates when and why the NFL approved the entry of new teams into the league, provides tabular data relative to these clubs' home attendance figures and their success at winning division titles, conference championships, and Super Bowls. The short- and long-term business implications and effects of expansions and mergers by the NFL are important parts of this chapter.

Chapter 2 provides characteristics of NFL team's home territories, and reveals why several of these clubs moved from one U.S. metropolitan area to another. In tables, the chapter reports the home attendances and win-loss records of each team for specific seasons prior to and after relocation. This discussion, in turn, includes the reasons for whether and where these teams moved again, merged, or folded. Specific commercial aspects relative to team territories and relocations within the NFL are examined as well.

Chapter 3 concentrates on the organization and operation of NFL franchises. For example, the chapter includes such topics as the amounts and sources of teams' revenues and expenses, and their operating incomes and values as business enterprises. Tables relate the ticket prices and fan cost indexes of NFL clubs during various years. There is information about the various offices and officials of franchises and the positions held by their top executives, including vice presidents, managers, and directors. The chapter also explores the reasons some teams operate more efficiently and profitably than others.

Chapter 4 identifies different football stadiums and markets that teams have occupied during the current and previous NFL seasons. It examines the ages, capacities, types of financing, and benefits of these facilities. In addition, the chapter highlights the economics of the newest stadiums, such as those in Dallas for the Cowboys, New York for the Giants and Jets, and Indianapolis for the Colts. From a business perspective, the chapter compares and ranks the markets and qualities of various NFL stadiums.

Chapter 5 focuses on some of the NFL's most important domestic and foreign affairs as well as a few of its special events. In general, it focuses on the league's exhibition and preseason games in foreign countries, including the former American Bowls and current International Series, and within the U.S.—most importantly, the Super Bowl. The chapter evaluates the success or failure of these events, and furthermore, it explains why they have (or have not) contributed to the success of the league and the sport. Concerning the role of NFL Properties, Inc., NFL Films, and the NFL Network, Chapter 5 emphasizes their promotion and commercial effect, and what they accomplish for the league.

The appendices contain additional tables of data, statistics, and information related to the league, markets, and performances of former and current NFL teams. These tables elaborate upon and clarify specific topics discussed within the text.

I hope readers find this to be an important and useful examination of the business of professional football, and of the NFL's 90 years in American culture.

1

League Expansions
and Mergers

Before the 1890s, American football games were played primarily between college teams located in the central and eastern portions of the United States and among sports clubs that belonged to amateur and sandlot leagues.

From the early 1890s to 1900s, such professional football teams as the Alleghany Athletic Association, Latrobe Athletic Association, and Morgan Athletic Club organized and competed in regular seasons and tournaments. As a result, the sport became increasingly popular among athletes and fans, especially in areas of western Pennsylvania and northeast Ohio.[1]

While these events occurred, league officials and professional teams adopted new rules designed to attract athletes and spectators both. In addition to assigning payments for players, the forward pass became legal, point values were determined for field goals and touchdowns, and popular teams won championships, which, in turn, caused the sport to prosper. The resultant growth in popularity led the sport to spread into cities and rural communities west of Ohio.

Even so, there was much confusion within professional football leagues throughout the mid– to late 1910s. Players frequently moved from one team to another for an increase in salary; many outstanding athletes on college football teams decided to join professional clubs; and general inflation in the economy made it very difficult for team owners to even operate their franchises, much less earn a profit.

During those early years, professional football urgently needed a business-oriented and reputable organization to implement and enforce standardized regulations regarding team conduct. The ambiguous and unruly environment led to the formation of a league administration and a new managerial organization in the sport.

American Professional Football Association

At a meeting held on August 20, 1920, in the Jordan and Hupmobile automobile showroom in Canton, Ohio, the representatives of four professional football teams formed the American Professional Football Conference (APFC). One month later, ten officials representing football teams from the states of Illinois, Indiana, New York, and Ohio met in Canton and changed the APFC's title to the American Professional Football Association (APFA).[2]

In addition, they also elected football's greatest athlete, Jim Thorpe, to be president of the new league, established a membership fee of $100 per team (which reportedly none of them paid), and permitted each club to set its schedule of games. Thus, the APFA opened in late 1920, fielding a few competitive teams in a limited number of markets, and reflecting growing interest in — and the economic feasibility of— organized pro football.

Table 1.1 provides information about the AFPA's only two regular seasons. First, from 1920 to 1921, the APFA increased from 14 to 21 teams, or by 50 percent, with nine clubs added as new members. Although the Chicago Tigers and Detroit Heralds folded after their first season in the league, franchises from Indiana, Kentucky, Michigan, Minnesota, New York, Ohio, Washington, D.C., and Wisconsin joined the APFA in its second year of operation. Nonetheless, five (or approximately 55 percent) of these new expansion teams failed in 1921 while the Evansville Crimson Giants, Green Bay Packers, Louisville Brecks, and Minneapolis Marines continued to exist as NFL teams one or more years.

Second, the table reveals that teams that performed below average in 1920 tended to fold one year later. In contrast to that group, the inferior Brecks, Marines, Columbus Panhandles, Hammond Pros, and Rochester Jeffersons survived after 1921 despite ranking tenth or worse in their performance. Within a few years, however, all of these franchises disbanded due to internal corruption, insufficient gate receipts, and other financial reasons. Interestingly, market size was not a decisive facgtor: the large-market New York Giants and Washington Senators and small-market Muncie Flyers and Tonawanda Kardex all failed after 1921.

Surprisingly the only original APFA franchise to play in consecutive seasons from 1920 to 2008 was the Chicago Cardinals. Although the franchise relocated twice and had not won any championships until its National Football Conference title in 2008-2009 (the Cardinals lost in Super Bowl XLIII), its longevity was, in part, due to the early leadership of Charles Bidwill, who purchased the club in 1932 for $50,000. After his death in 1947, various members of the Bidwill family continued to be the franchise's majority owner. The next most experienced teams listed in the table, which have existed for almost 90 years, are the Green Bay Packers and Chicago Staleys (renamed Bears in 1922). In the end, these are among the most profitable franchises in professional football.

TABLE 1.1 AMERICAN PROFESSIONAL FOOTBALL ASSOCIATION CHARACTERISTICS OF TEAMS, 1920–1921

	Performance		
Teams	1920	1921	History
Akron Pros	1st	3rd	Orig. franchise in NFL
Buffalo All-Americans	3rd	2nd	Orig. franchise in NFL
Canton Bulldogs	8th	4th	Orig. franchise in NFL
Chicago Cardinals	4th(t)	9th	Orig. franchise in NFL
Chicago Tigers	11th(t)	NA	Disbanded in 1920
Cincinnati Celts	NA	13th(t)	Disbanded in 1921
Cleveland Tigers/Indians	10th	11th	Disbanded in 1921
Columbus Panhandles	13th	17th	Orig. franchise in NFL
Dayton Triangles	6th	8th	Orig. franchise in NFL
Decatur Staleys→Chicago Staleys	2nd	1st	Renamed Bears in NFL
Detroit Heralds	9th	NA	Disbanded in 1920
Detroit Tigers	NA	16th	Disbanded in 1921
Evansville Crimson Giants	NA	6th(t)	Orig. franchise in NFL
Green Bay Packers	NA	6th(t)	Orig. franchise in NFL
Hammond Pros	11th(t)	13th(t)	Orig. franchise in NFL
Louisville Brecks	NA	19th(t)	Orig. franchise in NFL
Minneapolis Marines	NA	13th(t)	Orig. franchise in NFL
Muncie Flyers	14th	19th(t)	Disbanded in 1921
New York Giants	NA	19th(t)	Disbanded in 1921
Rochester Jeffersons	7th	10th	Orig. franchise in NFL
Rock Island Independents	4th(t)	5th	Orig. franchise in NFL
Tonawanda Kardex	NA	18th	Disbanded in 1921
Washington Senators	NA	12th	Disbanded in 1921

Note: "NA" means "not applicable" since a team with that name did not play in the league during the 1920 or 1921 season, such as the Cincinnati Celts in 1920 and Chicago Tigers in 1921. The (t) is a tie in performance between teams. While nine new clubs joined the APFA in 1921, the Staleys moved from Decatur to Chicago after the 1920 season. The Cleveland Tigers team was renamed Cleveland Indians in 1921. The American Professional Football Association was renamed National Football League (NFL) in 1922.

Source: 2008 NFL Record & Fact Book.

During early to mid–1921, the APFA's new president, Joe Carr, reorganized the league. He implemented a number of significant reforms that disciplined yet rewarded teams by stabilizing, standardizing, and unifying their operations. That is, Carr moved the APFA's headquarters from Canton to Columbus, Ohio, drafted a new constitution and bylaws, and provided territorial rights for the league's franchises. In addition, he restricted the movements of players from one club to another, developed specific criteria for membership in the league, discouraged APFA teams from competing against nonleague opponents, and established official standings so that a team became the official champion after each season. These changes, in turn, contributed to an expansion of the league in 1921, when the Chicago Staleys were officially awarded the championship.

In January 1922, the Green Bay Packers withdrew from the APFA after the club admitted using players with college eligibility. Having promised to obey the APFA's rules and then repurchasing its former franchise rights from the league, Packers owner Earl "Curly" Lambeau declared bankruptcy. Because of this financial problem, Green Bay business executives arranged a $2,500 loan to bail out the club and established a nonprofit organization to operate it, with Lambeau appointed head coach and manager. Six months later, the Chicago Staleys renamed themselves the Chicago Bears and the APFA revised its title to become the National Football League (NFL). America's elite professional football league was prepared to open the 1922 regular season with 18 member teams.

The next two sections of this chapter discuss when, where, and how the NFL expanded from 1922 through 2008. To that end, I identified the league's new teams and also researched and examined their performances during regular seasons and, if they qualified, in postseasons. Consequently, these sections reveal which of the league's expansion clubs failed in 1922, which teams continued to perform after one or more years, and why they succeeded or failed. Further analysis examines the merger of the NFL with another U.S.-based football league in 1950, and again in 1970.

NFL Expansion Franchises

As indicated previously in Table 1.1, nine new clubs joined the APFA in 1921 and four (44 percent) became members of the NFL in 1922. These four were the Evansville Crimson Giants, Green Bay Packers, Louisville Brecks, and Minneapolis Marines. To recap, although the Packers have remained solvent and played in the league through 2009, the Evansville Crimson Giants folded before 1923. The Brecks suspended operations in 1924-25 but changed its nickname to Louisville Colonels in 1926 and then canceled itself as a franchise one year after suspension of play in 1927. Meanwhile, the Marines played three seasons in the NFL but failed in 1928, after discontinuing operations during the league's 1925–1927 seasons.[3]

Other than those four former APFA clubs, Table 1.2 lists the different franchises that became members of the league after its name changed to National Football League (designated NFL) in early 1922. As denoted in the table, columns three through six show their number of seasons and various types of performances. To highlight some historical facts about each of these NFL teams, I rearranged the periods of expansion into ten-year increments, beginning with the 1920s and ending in the early 2000s.

1920s

In column two of Table 1.2 (pages 18–19), there are 20 franchises listed that became new members of the NFL during the 1920s. As a group, their number of seasons ranged from one to 84 years and championships won in divisions, conferences, and other tournaments from zero to seven. The following section contains some historical information about their formation and/or development while in the league.

Four clubs entered the NFL in 1922. These were the Milwaukee Badgers, Oorang Indians, Racine Legion, and Toledo Maroons. During its five regular seasons, the Badgers used a large number of African American players since Milwaukee in 1922 was one of America's most integrated cities. In 1925, however, the NFL fined the team $500 for using some high school athletes in a football game against the Chicago Cardinals. Unfortunately, one year later, the franchise went bankrupt and subsequently released its players to other NFL teams.

Established in tiny LaRue, Ohio, by Oorang dog kennel owner Walter Lingo, the Indians franchise was a travelling team of Native American players that included NFL Hall of Famers Jim Thorpe and Joe Guyon. Lingo, however, focused on promoting his kennel and presenting glamorous pregame and halftime shows for spectators rather than playing competitively in games. Indeed, the Indians won four and lost 16 in 1922-23. When many sports fans in the LaRue area decided not to attend home games because of the team's poor quality, players partying and drinking, and boredom from the shows, Lingo withdrew his financial support, which forced the Indians to disband in early 1924.

Originally titled the Racine Regulars and formed as an independent semiprofessional team in 1915, this franchise — which became known as Racine Legion until, in 1926, it was renamed the Racine Tornadoes — existed for four years as a member of the NFL. After three mediocre regular seasons and low attendances at its home games, the club became inactive in 1925. After reentering the league one year later, the team performed poorly and decided to fold its operation and disband. In contrast to the Badgers, Indians and Legion, the Toledo Maroons scheduled weak opponents to play against during the 1922–23 NFL seasons. When the champion Canton Bulldogs humiliated and defeated the Maroons, 28–0, in a regular season game, the franchise disappointed its fans in Toledo and thus withdrew from the league in 1923.

TABLE 1.2 NATIONAL FOOTBALL LEAGUE PERFORMANCE
OF EXPANSION FRANCHISES, 1922–2008

			Performance		
Year	Franchise	Seasons	Division Titles	Conference Championships	Other
1922	Milwaukee Badgers	5	NA	NA	0
1922	Oorang Indians	2	NA	NA	0
1922	Racine Legion	4	NA	NA	0
1922	Toledo Maroons	2	NA	NA	0
1923	Cleveland Indians	3	NA	NA	1
1923	Duluth Kelleys	5	NA	NA	0
1923	St. Louis All-Stars	1	NA	NA	0
1924	Frankford Yellow Jackets	8	NA	NA	1
1924	Kansas City Blues	3	NA	NA	0
1924	Kenosha Maroons	1	NA	NA	0
1925	Detroit Panthers	2	NA	NA	0
1925	New York Giants	84	15	10	7
1925	Pottsville Maroons	4	NA	NA	0
1925	Providence Steam Roller	7	NA	NA	1
1926	Brooklyn Lions	3	NA	NA	0
1926	Hartford Blues	1	NA	NA	0
1926	Los Angeles Buccaneers	1	NA	NA	0
1927	New York Yankees	2	NA	NA	0
1928	Detroit Wolverines	1	NA	NA	0
1929	Staten Island Stapletons	4	NA	NA	0
1930	Portsmouth Spartans	4	0	NA	0
1931	Cleveland Indians	1	NA	NA	0

Year	Franchise	Seasons	Division Titles	Conference Championships	Other
1932	Boston Braves	5	1	NA	0
1933	Cincinnati Reds	2	0	NA	0
1933	Philadelphia Eagles	76	11	3	3
1933	Pittsburgh Pirates	76	19	7	6
1937	Cleveland Rams	8	1	NA	1
1944	Boston Yanks	5	0	NA	0
1952	Dallas Texans	1	NA	0	0
1960	Dallas Cowboys	49	19	10	5
1961	Minnesota Vikings	48	17	4	0
1966	Atlanta Falcons	43	3	1	0
1967	New Orleans Saints	43	3	0	0
1976	Seattle Seahawks	33	1	1	0
1976	Tampa Bay Buccaneers	33	6	1	1
1995	Carolina Panthers	14	3	1	0
1995	Jacksonville Jaguars	14	2	0	0
1999	Cleveland Browns	10	0	0	0
2002	Houston Texans	7	0	0	0

Note: Year is these teams' first season in the NFL. Franchise is each team's initial nickname. Seasons include those of teams while they were located at their original sites and also of those that had changed their nicknames. Some examples of the latter teams were the Cleveland Indians/Bulldogs, Duluth Kelleys/Eskimos, Kansas City Blues/Cowboys, Boston Braves/Redskins, Cincinnati Reds/St. Louis Gunners, and Pittsburgh Pirates/Steelers. Clubs that had reentered the league after missing one or more seasons, such as the Canton Bulldogs, Racine Tornadoes, and Louisville Colonels, were not expansion franchises. Performance lists each team's division and conference titles and includes a column labeled "Other," which is the total of teams' victories in Super Bowls (1967–2008) and their number of wins in NFL championships prior to Super Bowls (1922–1966). "NA" is "not applicable" because NFL divisions and/or conferences did not exist for these teams.

Source: *2008 NFL Record & Fact Book* and "NFL Teams Playoff Histories."

During 1923-24, the NFL expanded again by adding six new clubs. The Cleveland Tigers/Indians had played two seasons in the APFA and then disbanded in late 1921. Two years later, however, wealthy jeweler Samuel H. Deutsch formed a new football franchise named the Cleveland Indians and entered it into the NFL. Deutsch then purchased the Canton Bulldogs in 1923 for approximately $2,500 and merged the Indians and Bulldogs franchises to create the Cleveland Bulldogs, who won a championship in 1924. Other than the Indians/Bulldogs, a team named after the Kelley-Duluth hardware store in Minnesota joined the NFL in 1923. After two winning seasons as the Duluth Kelleys and subsequent to being renamed Duluth Eskimos in 1926, the franchise became a traveling team in 1927. That year, the Eskimos won only one game and dropped out of the league.

In addition to the entry of the Cleveland Indians and Duluth Kelleys in 1923, the St. Louis All-Stars played one season in the NFL while based at Sportsman's Park in Missouri. Because the team was not competitive and failed to excite football fans in the St. Louis area, it quit operating after the 1923 season. One year later, another NFL expansion club, the Frankford Yellow Jackets, began play. Located in the northeast Philadelphia area, this franchise played a grueling and competitive schedule of games, winning 14 of them and a league title in 1926. Nevertheless, five years later, the Yellow Jackets failed to finish its regular season because of financial problems associated with the Great Depression. When this occurred, the market area of America's third-largest city did not host another NFL club until the Philadelphia Eagles began to compete in 1933.

The Kansas City Blues and Kenosha Maroons also joined the NFL in 1924. Renamed the Kansas City Cowboys in 1925, this franchise had to play all its games in stadiums of other cities. After three dismal-to-mediocre years, the Missouri-based Cowboys ceased operating in late 1926. Meanwhile, the City of Kenosha in Wisconsin purchased the Toledo franchise in 1924 and played one season in the league. After the team lost games to the Yellow Jackets, Badgers, Kelleys and Buffalo Bisons and finishing sixteenth without winning again, local sports journalists criticized the Maroons for its inferior performances and low attendances while playing at home in Nash Field. After the Maroons cancelled some regular season games, several players left the team, which then dissolved as a franchise. In short, nine (90 percent) of the NFL's expansion teams of 1922–24 had survived five seasons or fewer while the Frankford Yellow Jackets competed in eight campaigns and even won a championship in 1926.

In 1925, four additional new clubs entered the NFL. Five years after the APFA's Detroit Heralds failed in 1920 and four following the Detroit Tigers demise in 1921, the Detroit Panthers performed in the NFL for two seasons. After it finished third in 1925 and twelfth one year later, the club had to suspend its operations in 1927. Along with the entry of the Panthers in Detroit, rich businesspersons Tim Mara and Billy Gibson purchased an NFL expansion franchise in 1925 for $500 and based it in New York City. Despite some initial financial troubles, the New York Giants became profitable within a few years and also finished 11–1–1 in 1927 and won its first NFL championship. Even though Tim Mara died in 1959 and his sons and grandsons inherited the franchise from him, the Giants have been one of the most prosperous teams in NFL history and, as indicated in the next major section of this chapter, have won a number of championships.

The Pottsville Maroons and Providence Steam Roller also became original NFL members in 1925. One year earlier, a Pottsville Eleven team won the Anthracite Football League's title after a local surgeon named John Streigel had purchased it for $1,500. While performing with the nickname Maroons in the NFL, this Pennsylvania-based Pottsville franchise was a very popular attraction for sports fans and a rival of the nearby Frankford Yellow Jackets. Furthermore, some visiting clubs prospered because they ignored the Pennsylvania blue laws and collected large amounts of gate receipts by scheduling the Maroons on Saturday and Yellow Jackets on Sunday. When the Maroons' performances declined in 1927-28 and its revenues fell during home games at little Minersville Park, the franchise moved from Pottsville to Boston and play in 1929.

Formed in the state of Rhode Island to be a member of the Independent Football League during 1916–24, the Providence Steam Roller played a majority of its home game for seven years while in the NFL at the Cyclodome, which was a 10,000-seat stadium built for bicycle races. After mediocre seasons in 1925–27, a Steam Roller club finished 8–1–2 in games and won a league championship in 1928. However, three years later, the franchise had to suspend its operations due to financial troubles caused by the Great Depression. Of the 14 expansion clubs that began play in the NFL during the 1922 to 1925 seasons, the only survivor by 1932 was the New York Giants.

Between 1926 and 1929 inclusive, the NFL expanded by six franchises. As denoted in column three of Table 1.2, their number of seasons varied from one to four. First, an American Football League (AFL) team named the Brooklyn Horsemen struggled financially because it lost a series of games to opponents. As a result, the Horsemen withdrew from the AFL in November 1926 and then merged its operations with the Brooklyn Lions of the NFL. After finishing fourteenth in the league and failing to establish a fan base while located at Commercial Field in Brooklyn, the Lions ceased to perform in mid– to late 1926.

Second, the Hartford Blues played one season in the NFL. Its home stadium was an 8,000-seat facility named the Velodrome, which was built for outdoor bicycle races. Because of bad weather conditions in Hartford and scheduling conflicts, the Blues had to cancel a few home games. These problems, in turn, disturbed football fans in the Hartford area and contributed significantly to the team's suspension after three wins and seven losses in 1926.

Third, a travelling team based in Chicago, Illinois, named the Los Angeles Buccaneers performed in the 1926 NFL season. Interestingly, the team recruited and used players who had enrolled in colleges within California. Despite winning six (or two-thirds) of its games, the Buccaneers could not generate enough money from gate receipts to exist more than one year in the league.

Fourth, the NFL awarded New York Giants owner Tim Mara the rights to a franchise, which previously was property assigned to the defunct Brooklyn Lions. In turn, Mara leased these rights to Red Grange's agent, C.C. Pyle, who formed a new team in 1927 and named it the New York Yankees. Nonetheless, a condition of the lease was that the Yankees could play only a few games at home in New York's Yankee Stadium; the others would be at the opponent's field. This agreement lasted for two years. However, without enough gate receipts to survive from its home games, the Yankees had to disband after the 1928 NFL season.

The final new teams that joined the NFL during the 1920s were the Detroit Wolverines and Staten Island Stapletons. According to one source, the Wolverines made several thousand dollars while playing a season in the league. In early 1929, however, Tim Mara decided to purchase the Wolverines in order to acquire the rights to a player for his Giants team. Anyway, because of this transaction, the Wolverines franchise became inactive and forced it to leave the NFL.

When football's New York Yankees folded in 1928, the club's franchise returned to Tim Mara, who then reissued it to the current owner of the Stapletons, Dan Blaine. Despite hiring an excellent player named Ken Strong, Blaine's team finished at or below .500 during four NFL seasons. After winning only two games in 1932, the Stapletons suspended operations in the league but continued to schedule games with independent clubs located in the New York area. In 1935, Blaine surrendered his franchise to the NFL. Thus, other than the New York Giants, each NFL expansion team of the 1920s had terminated operations before 1933.

1930s

During the 1930s, the following seven franchises became new members of the NFL. After Ohio's Portsmouth Spartans performed as an independent professional football team in 1929, the Portsmouth NFL Corporation sold $25,000 of stock to investors so that the Spartans could enter the league in 1930. Nevertheless, despite excellent regular seasons in 1931–32, the club declared itself bankrupt in 1933. One year later, executive George Richardson bought the franchise from the team's owners for $15,000 and moved it to a large sports market in southeast Michigan where the club was renamed Detroit Lions.

Following admission of the Spartans in 1930, the NFL sponsored the entry of an expansion team in 1931 named the Cleveland Indians. Although the Indians played only road games, the league intended that it would eventually exist at home somewhere in the Cleveland area. When the NFL could not find a group to buy this franchise, the Indians folded after finishing the season at 2–8–0.

In 1932, a syndicate headed by George Marshall purchased an NFL expansion franchise for approximately $8,000 and named it the Boston Braves. This team won an Eastern Division title in 1936 but then lost by a score of 21–6 in the NFL championship game to the Green Bay Packers of the Western Division. Because of that defeat and a lack of fan support, resulting in poor attendance at home games, Marshall moved his club from Boston to Washington, D.C., in 1937.

Meanwhile, in 1933, the Cincinnati Reds began to compete against others in the league's Western Division. That year, the team scored a total of only 38 points in ten games. When it started the 1934 season with eight consecutive losses, the Reds franchise failed to pay its membership dues and was suspended by the NFL. As a result, an independent professional team nicknamed the St. Louis Gunners purchased the Reds for about $25,000 and relocated the franchise to eastern Missouri.

Also in 1933, the NFL expanded by adding the Philadelphia Eagles and Pittsburgh Pirates. These franchises were purchased from the league for about $2,500 each by groups that were led, respectively, by Bert Bell and Lud Wray of the Eagles, and Art Rooney and A. McCool of the Pirates. After being sold and then exchanged between their owners, the two clubs merged in 1943. As the Phil-Pitt Steagles, it finished 5–4–1 in the NFL's Eastern Division.

In 1944, this arrangement dissolved and the Eagles remained in the Eastern Division while Pittsburgh (renamed Steelers) merged with the Chicago Cardinals. As such, the Card-Pitt combination played in the league's Western Division. After the mid–1940s, the Eagles had different owners, while Art Rooney's son, Dan, took control of the Steelers during the late 1980s. As denoted by their performances in Table 1.2, both of these franchises won several championships. Thus, they have significantly contributed to the competitiveness, image, and prosperity of the NFL for more than 75 years.

After playing one season in the AFL, the Cleveland Rams replaced the former St. Louis Gunners to become a new expansion team in the NFL's Western Division in 1937. Indeed, a syndicate then headed by Homer Marshman paid a fee of $10,000 for the franchise. During several years in the league — but excluding 1943 when it had to suspend operations because of a shortage of players — the Rams tended to finish in fourth or fifth of its division. When the team improved to 9–1 in the league's regular season and defeated the

Washington Redskins to win a championship in 1945, the Rams incurred financial losses that had accumulated to $82,000 since 1941. As a result of these deficits, small attendances at home games in Cleveland Stadium, and problems of competing for sports fans with the popular Cleveland Browns of the All-American Football Conference (AAFC), Rams owner Dan Reeves decided to move his club from Cleveland to Los Angeles in 1946.

1940s

After the NFL expanded by 27 teams since 1922 and because of economic issues associated with the Great Depression and World War II, the NFL added only one club in the 1940s. This franchise named itself the Boston Yanks. It played home games at Fenway Park when the Boston Red Sox were on the road or not playing or at the Manning Bowl in Lynn, Massachusetts, to avoid any schedule conflicts. In 1945, Ted Collins' Boston Yanks merged with owner Dan Topping's Brooklyn Tigers. When the NFL revoked Topping's franchise in 1946, his players joined the Yanks. After ranking third or worse in the NFL's Eastern Division for three consecutive seasons, Collins transferred his team from Boston to New York in 1949.

1950s

Because of the merger in 1950, New York Bulldogs owner Ted Collins relinquished his team's rights in exchange for his purchasing and operating the NFL's New York Yankees. However, after the Yankees had a financial loss of $1 million in the 1951 season, Collins returned his franchise to the NFL and received $100,000 for the players' contracts.

The next year, a syndicate from Texas led by Giles and Connell Miller purchased the franchise from the NFL for $300,000 and moved it from New York to Dallas to play in the league's National Conference with the nickname Texans. Besides its pathetic performance, the team incurred a financial loss of $250,000 in five games and bankrupted before the 1952 season had ended. In fact, less than 18,000 fans from the Dallas area attended the Texans' game played in the 75,000-seat Cotton Bowl against the New York Giants.

Some football historians have suggested that the club's failure occurred, in part, because of racism in the South and the behavior of activists in the civil rights movement, including African Americans. If true, perhaps thousands of football fans in the Dallas area may have boycotted Texans home games due to the team's black players. Nonetheless, the Dallas Texans franchise returned its operation to the NFL before the season concluded and then was cancelled by the league in late 1952.

1960s

Between 1960 and 1969 inclusive, four new football franchises entered the NFL. These teams were the Dallas Cowboys in 1960, Minnesota Vikings in 1961, Atlanta Falcons in 1966, and New Orleans Saints in 1967. Following are some facts and other information that describe their formation, entry into the league, and history.

For decades, the Washington Redskins dominated the market for professional football for sports fans who lived in the Southeast. Consequently, Redskins owner George Marshall adamantly resisted efforts by the NFL to place a team anywhere in the northeast Texas area. When a group of investors in Texas purchased the rights to Washington's fight song "Hail to the Redskins" and then threatened that the song would not be played at Redskins home games, Marshall dropped his opposition to an expansion. This, in turn, caused the league to allow the existence of a new franchise at a stadium in Dallas. Even so, Marshall's resistance resulted in a bitter rivalry in regular season and postseason games between the Redskins and its adversary in north Texas.

Executives Clint Murchison and Bedford Wynne paid the NFL a fee of $600,000 in 1960 for the right to own and operate a new franchise in Texas. To that end, these men made a number of shrewd management decisions. One, they hired Tex Schramm as general manager, Gil Brandt as director of player personnel, and Tom Landry as head coach of this franchise. Two, they rejected such nicknames as Stars and Rangers, and instead, chose Cowboys to identify their sports business. Third, they marketed the Cowboys as "America's Team," even though the club struggled until the mid– to late 1960s when it made a few playoff appearances and won some division titles and conference championships. After playing 12 seasons in the Cotton Bowl and 38 in Texas Stadium, the Cowboys will compete in 2009 and thereafter in a new $1 billion stadium located in Arlington, Texas.

In 1921, a professional football team named the Minneapolis Marines played in the APFA, and then for another three seasons in the NFL. After suspending operations for four years, this team was renamed Minneapolis Red Jackets when it returned to the league in 1929. Thirty years later, the newly established AFL awarded three business officials a franchise. Rather than play in that league, these entrepreneurs forfeited their membership and accepted the offer to own an expansion franchise in the NFL, beginning with the 1961 season. After paying a fee of $600,000 to the NFL, the new owners officially named their team Minnesota Vikings, which partly reflected the area's status as a center of Scandinavian American culture.

Occasionally nicknamed the Vikes and sometimes known as the "Purple People Eaters," the club played for 21 years in Metropolitan Stadium, and since 1982, in the Hubert H. Humphrey Metrodome. During the early 2000s, its syndicate of owners lobbied local and Minnesota legislators to approve the construction and financing of a new stadium somewhere in the Minneapolis–St. Paul area. According to these Vikings executives, the 27-year-old Metrodome was obsolete relative to the stadiums occupied by clubs in the league's North Division of the National Conference, which included the Chicago Bears, Detroit Lions, and Green Bay Packers. The discussions among these groups and others will continue until this NFL franchise receives a new facility in which to play its home games.

Between the early 1970s and mid–1990s, there were several disputes among the Vikings owners about the distribution and control of voting rights and the franchise's shares of stock. Undoubtedly, this friction contributed to the team's underperformance in the league, especially during the 1980s. The Vikings did not win a National Conference championship after 1976, although it shared and/or earned division titles during the late 1970s and in 1980 and again in 1989.

During the early 1960s, there were no AFL or NFL clubs located in the Southeast. Regionally, the Houston Oilers (AFL) and Dallas Cowboys (NFL) existed in the Southwest and the Washington Redskins (NFL) in the East-to-Southeast. Rather than transfer a struggling NFL team from its home in a current city, and thus counterbalance the AFL's approval of a team for Miami, Florida, and a decision by Major League Baseball that allowed the Braves to move from southeast Wisconsin to northern Georgia in 1966, the NFL authorized an expansion team for the growing and diverse Atlanta metropolitan area.

As a result, the league charged business entrepreneur Rankin Smith Sr. and his partners a fee of $8.5 million to own and operate a new NFL club in Atlanta. This ownership group officially named their franchise the Falcons, who played games at home for a total of 26 years in Atlanta-Fulton County Stadium and since 1992 in the Georgia Dome. For more about the development of this franchise, the next major section of this chapter discusses the Falcons' performances in its divisions and conferences of the league.

In the mid–1960s, a Congressional committee in Washington, D.C., headed by Louisiana representative Hale Boggs, evaluated the antitrust implications of a proposed merger between the AFL and NFL. During October of 1966, Boggs' committee and Congress approved the leagues' merger and passed legislation to exempt it from antitrust action. Then in December, NFL commissioner Pete Rozelle announced that the league had awarded an expansion franchise and placed it in New Orleans to play in 1967.

Subsequent to the merger, and after a review of applications from all bidders, the NFL allocated the new franchise in New Orleans to Houston oilman John Mecom Jr. for a fee of $8 million. Mecom, in turn, nicknamed his team the Saints as a tribute to the famous jazz anthem titled "When the Saints Go Marching In." After performing the 1967 season as a member of the Eastern Conference's Capitol Division and then the next two years in the Century Division, the NFL transferred Mecom's franchise in 1970 to the National Conference's Western Division. It remained there until 2002, when it joined the South Division.

In 1985, multimillionaire Tom Benson purchased this NFL franchise from Mecom for $70 million, which included for the Saints a renegotiated contract to use the Louisiana Superdome and a $15 million local guarantee by the State of Louisiana. For performances of the Saints during the club's history of regular seasons and postseasons, the reader is urged to consult the next major section of this chapter.

1970s

A group of business and community leaders in Washington State formed the Seattle Professional Football, Inc., in 1972 to pursue and obtain an NFL expansion franchise for the city. Two years later the league awarded a franchise to this group of investors, headed by executive Lloyd W. Nordstrom. As such, they paid the NFL an expansion fee of $16 million. Then in 1975, a name-the-team contest took place in Seattle that attracted thousands of entries. From more than 1,500 different names, the club's owners selected Seattle Seahawks (a seahawk being a mythical bird).

Other events affected this franchise before its first NFL preseason game in August 1976. For example, majority stockholder Lloyd W. Nordstrom died of a heart attack; former University of Washington executive John Thompson was hired as general manager, and he recruited and signed Minnesota Vikings assistant coach Jack Patera to be the team's initial head coach; and, the Kingdome became the team's field for its home games. Unlike other NFL expansion teams, the Seahawks had to switch from one conference to another in 1977 and again in 2002. In retrospect, the NFL had implemented its realignment in 1977 so that expansion teams would play each other twice and every other franchise once during their first two seasons. Meanwhile, the realignment in 2002 occurred to balance the league by assigning four teams to each of four divisions within the two conferences.

As part of its plan to expand in the mid–1970s, the NFL decided to add a fifth team to the American Conference's Western Division. To inform fans of that event, in 1974 the league originally awarded construction company entrepreneur Tom McCloskey the exclusive right to establish an expansion franchise and to locate and operate it in Tampa, Florida. However, when the NFL discovered that McCloskey had severe financial problems, Hugh Culverhouse, a wealthy tax attorney from Jacksonville, replaced him. To identify the franchise, a name-the-team contest took place and, as a result, the nickname "Buccaneers" was chosen in honor of the annual Gasparilla Pirate Festival in Tampa. Since its first game in 1976, the Buccaneers performed at home in Tampa Stadium (renamed Houlihan's Stadium in 1996) for a total of 22 years and then in Raymond James Stadium, beginning in 1998.

1990s

Between the late 1980s and early 1990s, local business leaders, some prominent civilians, and popular current and former politicians in Charlotte as well as the states of North and South Carolina formed various groups to convince the NFL that the population in the city's metropolitan area would support a new professional football team. These groups consisted of such individuals as previous Baltimore Colts player Jerry Richardson, Senator Jesse Helms of North Carolina, Governor Carroll Campbell Jr. of South Carolina, and executives from different banks, manufacturers, and retail corporations. Besides successfully hosting preseason football games in the region, Richardson and others in his group praised the success of the National Basketball Association's Charlotte Hornets.

During 1992, the NFL released a list of five metropolitan areas that it considered potential sites for an expansion team. Other than Charlotte, these places were Baltimore, Jacksonville, Memphis and St. Louis. When a conflict occurred between players and the league, NFL team owners decided to delay a vote on expansion until sometime in late 1993. To promote its bid in June of that year, an investment group named Richardson Sports announced that the sale of permanent seat licenses (PSLs) would primarily finance the construction of a new 70,000-seat football stadium near downtown Charlotte. Later, all of the club seats and luxury boxes in the stadium sold out within 24 hours for the team's 1995 season.

Because of these efforts, the NFL awarded its twenty-ninth franchise to Charlotte and, more specifically, to Richardson's group. Football fans in the Carolinas rejoiced when majority owner Jerry Richardson appeared on television and thanked the thousands of people who had purchased club seats, luxury boxes, and PSLs. Although the Carolina Panthers franchise played its home games in the 1995 season at Memorial Stadium in Clemson, South Carolina, Ericsson Stadium in Charlotte was built without public money and initially opened in August 1996 for a preseason game between the Panthers and Chicago Bears.

Since Florida hosted two NFL clubs and contained outstanding football programs at three colleges, Jacksonville was not considered a prime site for a new expansion franchise. Indeed, the city's television market in the early 1990s ranked below those located in Baltimore, Charlotte, Memphis, and St. Louis. Moreover, the group that represented Jacksonville's bid for a franchise had internal conflicts, organizational problems, and power struggles. In fact, some members left the group during 1990–1992 while others challenged and disagreed with decisions made by the organization's leaders.

After these matters were resolved, shoe magnate J. Wayne Weaver became head of a group named Touchdown Jacksonville! Despite Weaver's experience and leadership, there were some significant issues for his group to discuss and settle. One major problem was the failure of the Jacksonville City Council to approve a financial package to renovate the Gator Bowl. The council's action, unfortunately, meant that depositors received refunds for season tickets to future NFL games and Touchdown Jacksonville! closed its downtown office.

Within a few months, Weaver's group and city officials renegotiated with each other and agreed to a new financial deal. As such, this agreement contributed to the successful sale of club seats for the prospective expansion team's games played in the Gator Bowl. Impressed by these expenditures and the level of support from football fans in northeast Florida, the NFL selected Jacksonville in November 1993 to be the league's thirtieth franchise and not Baltimore, Memphis, or St. Louis.

The NFL's announcement triggered a campaign in Jacksonville for Weaver's staff to aggressively sell season tickets to Jaguars games played in the league's 1995 regular season and perhaps thereafter. Within weeks, more than 50,000 were sold. In addition, during early 1994, the city's current football stadium was demolished and replaced with a reinforced concrete superstructure. Originally named Jacksonville Municipal Stadium in 1995-96 and changed one year later to Alltel Stadium, this facility has continued to be the home field of the 14-year-old Jacksonville Jaguars.

About three months after Cleveland Browns owner Art Modell signed an agreement to move his team from northern Ohio to Baltimore, Maryland, and compete there in home games during the league's 1996 regular season, the NFL announced that it awarded an expansion team to the City of Cleveland. The team would play a schedule of home games somewhere in the Cleveland area, beginning in 1999. The league decided to deactivate the former Browns franchise during 1996–1998, after which a new stadium would open in Cleveland to host the NFL's thirty-first team. Besides those conditions, the league also authorized the City of Cleveland to retain the Browns' heritage and some records, which included the club's name and logo, and its colors, history of regular season and postseason games, memorabilia, and trophies.

In order to fulfill its commitment and obligation to the City of Cleveland, the league formed a trust. This organization, in turn, had several tasks to accomplish. These responsibilities included the design and construction of a local football stadium for Browns games, and the sale of club seats, luxury suites, PSLs, and season tickets at the stadium. Furthermore, the trust was assigned to reorganize Browns fan clubs across the U.S., organize and market shows about professional football on radio stations and television networks throughout Ohio, and launch a countdown campaign to celebrate Cleveland's new team.

In 1998-1999, the NFL sold the rights for an expansion franchise in Cleveland to banking mogul Al Lerner for $520 million. According to reports in the media, this was the highest price ever paid for a new team in the history of professional sports. Interestingly, when Cleveland Browns Stadium opened in the summer of 1999 for a preseason game, approximately 72,000 fans attended. In its initial NFL season, the Browns finished 2–14 in the American Conference's Central Division. Even so, three years later the club qualified for the playoffs as a wild card but lost 36–33 in a game played against the Pittsburgh Steelers.

2000s

For 37 years of the twentieth century, Houston hosted a professional football team that had existed within the AFL or NFL. Nonetheless, in the spring of 1996, Houston Oilers owner Bud Adams received permission from the NFL to move his team from southeast Texas to Nashville, Tennessee. After this relocation occurred, a syndicate led by businessman Bob McNair and Steve Patterson formed Houston NFL Holdings, which was a group organized to attract an NFL team into their city, in part, by advertising and promoting a proposal to construct a new domed football stadium.

Since it had previously awarded Cleveland a new franchise nicknamed the Browns, NFL commissioner Paul Tagliabue announced that areas in Houston, Los Angeles, and Toronto were the three most attractive sites to host another expansion team in the league. Provided an ownership group and stadium deal successfully organized and proved superior, it appeared that the NFL preferred Los Angeles as a prime location and not Houston or Toronto. However, while visiting officials in Los Angeles during April-May 1999, a committee of NFL owners determined that a proposed business complex that included a new or renovated football stadium for an expansion team did not meet their requirements, including the cost, location, and structure.

Because of these and other deficiencies, Houston reportedly outbid Los Angeles by more than $150 million for the rights to the NFL's thirty-second franchise. Consequently, NFL team owners voted unanimously to award Houston the league's newest club and to host Super Bowl XXXVIII in 2004. With Bob McNair as its chair, chief executive officer and majority owner, the new team named itself Texans and opened the 2002 season by defeating the Dallas Cowboys 19–10 before a sellout crowd in Houston's 71,100-seat Reliant Stadium.

Between 1922 and 2002 inclusive, 39 expansion franchises joined the NFL. In fact, the 1980s was the only decade in which this elite professional football league did not permit the entry of at least one new club. During these ten years, there were such interesting events as a competitive challenge to the NFL monopoly by the United States Football League; the adoption and implementation of numerous rule changes by the NFL; football players strikes in 1982 and 1987; an antitrust trial against the NFL from the Los Angeles Coliseum Commission and the league's Oakland Raiders; negotiation of new NFL business contracts with television broadcast and cable networks; the relocation of three NFL franchises; and the replacement of Commissioner Pete Rozelle by Paul Tagliabue. In short, the league experienced these challenges during the 1980s and overcame them to become America's most popular and prosperous professional sports organization.[4]

In the next section, I highlight and discuss performances of the league's different expansion clubs during eight decades, and those of other NFL teams. As such, this historical information includes — as available in the literature — such data as their home game attendances and various championships, players, regular seasons and postseasons, and/or other characteristics that specifically relate to them. After this section concludes, I examine the circumstances, effects, and results of merging the NFL and AAFC in 1950 and the NFL and AFL in 1970. Finally, there is a summary of this chapter followed by the notes.

Team Performances

1920–1929

In 1921, nine new clubs entered the APFA (see Table 1.1). Within this group, the Evansville Crimson Giants and Green Bay Packers each won three games and tied for sixth while the Louisville Brecks and a first franchise of the New York Giants finished in a tie for nineteenth with the second-year but winless Muncie Flyers. As such, these four expansion teams finished the regular season far behind such tough competitors as the Chicago Staleys, Akron Pros, and Canton Bulldogs. Even so, three of these new teams survived to play the next season in the NFL, but the New York Giants folded because of inferior players and insufficient support from sports fans in their home market.[5]

Between 1922 and 1929 inclusive, three expansion teams won a title in consecutive seasons. These were the Frankford Yellow Jackets in 1926, New York Giants (new franchise) in 1927, and Providence Steam Roller in 1928. Despite their championships, some financial problems from the Great Depression caused the Yellow Jackets and Steam Roller clubs to fail in 1931. Meanwhile, the Giants finished second in 1929–1930. Besides these three clubs, the only expansion franchise of the early-to-mid 1920s that existed after 1929 was the Staten Island Stapletons. In short, the majority of new NFL teams disbanded during the 1920s because professional football was not popular entertainment for sports fans and other households within their local markets. Furthermore, APFA and NFL team owners had little or no experience in operating football enterprises that would generate enough revenues to earn a profit.

When the 1920s ended, the most prosperous franchises in the NFL tended to be those located in large-to-very large areas, among them the Chicago Bears, Chicago Cardinals, and New York Giants. Alternatively, the Green Bay Packers had established a home in northeast Wisconsin within a small market. Although expansion was not an overwhelming or successful strategy for the NFL during the 1920s, it started a trend for entrepreneurs in football and other professional sports to establish new teams despite an imminent stock market crash and collapse of the nation's economy.

1930–1939

During these ten NFL seasons, seven expansion franchises formed and joined the league. The Portsmouth Spartans — while located in a very small-market within Ohio — played three consecutive seasons above .500. However, when sports fans in the Portsmouth area did not enthusiastically attend the team's games at its home stadium, the Spartans franchise left Portsmouth in 1934 and relocated to Detroit, Michigan. Next, the Cleveland Indians won two and lost eight games in 1931 and placed eighth in the league. The Indians, however, experienced financial troubles since it did not play any home games in Cleveland. After the NFL was unable to attract anyone from Cleveland or elsewhere to invest in and assume ownership of this failing franchise, the Indians terminated operations before the league's 1932 season.

The Boston Braves (renamed Redskins in 1933) ranked somewhere between first and fifth in the league during 1932–1935. Moreover, the team's total attendance at Fenway Park in Boston was less than 70,000 in 1936 despite the Braves winning the league's Eastern Division title before losing in a championship game 21–6 to the Green Bay Packers. Because a popular football team named the Boston Shamrocks won the American Football League's first title in 1936, and lacking support of fans at the Redskins home games in Boston, this NFL franchise moved to Washington, D.C., in 1937.

Organized one year after the Braves had formed in Boston, the expansion Cincinnati Reds established NFL records in 1933 and 1934 when the team scored, respectively, a total of 38 points in ten games and then 10 points in eight games. Furthermore, this NFL club scored no points in 12 (or 66 percent) of its contests. Based on its attendances in Cincinnati — which was below 40,000 in 1934 — and also not paying its annual membership fees to the league, the Reds franchise was suspended by the NFL.

Meanwhile in 1933, the Philadelphia Eagles and Pittsburgh Pirates (renamed Steelers in 1940) became new franchises and competed in the NFL. Both teams were relatively unproductive between 1933 and 1939 inclusive; that is, they did not win an Eastern Division title and each tended to finish fourth and/or fifth every season. In fact, the Eagles did not claim its first division title until 1947 and the Steelers until 1972. Yet these NFL teams became gradually popular, profitable, and well established, at least in their hometowns, during the 1930s and in years thereafter.

In retrospect, the most dominant professional football team of the 1930s was the Green Bay Packers, an organization that joined the APFA in 1921. Although the franchise drew much fewer fans to its home games in Green Bay than did such big-city clubs as the Chicago Bears, Detroit Lions and New York Giants, some of head coach Earl "Curly" Lambeau's Packers teams featured Hall of Fame running back Don Hutson on offense and several all-star players on defense. So while the Packers thrived in tiny Green Bay, it was before 1939 that such new NFL teams as the Portsmouth Spartans, Cleveland Indians, Boston Braves, and Cincinnati Reds had to terminate their franchises or relocate to another metropolitan area within the U.S.

The seventh and final NFL expansion team of the 1930s was the Cleveland Rams. While assigned to the league's Western Division and playing its home games in three different stadiums, the Rams finished fourth or fifth in the division for five consecutive years and third in 1942. After suspending its operations in 1943, the Rams placed fourth in 1944. One year later, however, the club defeated the Washington Redskins 15–14 and won an NFL championship. On average, the Rams' attendance in Cleveland was approximately 70,000 per season. But due to small gate receipts from its home games and the inability to attract more sports fans from the same market area as the popular Cleveland Browns of the AAFC, Rams owner Dan Reeves made a decision to move his franchise from northern Ohio to Los Angeles in 1946.

In short, the Boston Braves, Green Bay Packers, and New York Giants were the only previous new or current expansion teams that qualified for and appeared in NFL championship games during the 1930s. Therefore, in 1939, the league's ten teams included five of the 27 that had their first seasons in years after 1920. In other words, 50 percent of the NFL members consisted of expansion franchises, another four moved from sites in other cities, and the Chicago Cardinals began to perform in 1920 as an original member of the APFA. Consequently, this distribution of ten franchises indicates, in part, that the NFL had stabilized its operations and attained some form of market equilibrium with the number and location of its teams after existing as a league for 20 years.

1940–1949

Between 1940 and 1943 inclusive, a number of significant events occurred in the professional football industry. In 1940, for example, a six-team rival organization to the NFL named the American Football League formed; the Columbus Bullies won the league's first championship. In 1941, the NFL changed its bylaws to provide playoffs if any teams in a division tied during the regular season and also implemented sudden-death overtime if a playoff game was tied after four quarters had been completed. In 1942, World War II caused shortages that depleted the rosters of NFL clubs. And in 1943, the league adopted free substitution of players during games and mandated the wearing of helmets. It also approved a ten-game regular season schedule.

Then in 1944, the NFL authorized the entry of a new franchise named the Boston Yanks. Owned by singer Kate Smith's manager, Ted Collins, the Yanks finished third, fourth, or fifth in the league's Eastern Division during five consecutive seasons. Although the club's attendances in games played at Fenway Park averaged about 95,000 per season, some of its most talented players joined the military, limiting the Yanks to only nine wins from 1946–48. As a result of these and other issues, Collins moved his team in 1949 from eastern Massachusetts to the Polo Grounds in New York City. As such, it would be four years before another expansion team penetrated a conference of the NFL.

1950–1959

When New York Yanks owner Ted Collins sold his club back to the NFL in early 1952, the league eventually awarded a new franchise to a group of business executives from Dallas, Texas, that had previously purchased the Yanks' assets. Located for a few games at home in the Cotton Bowl and later at a football stadium in Hershey, Pennsylvania, the Dallas Texans averaged approximately 15 points per game, finished 1–11–0, and ranked sixth in the National Conference. After its season, the owners cancelled the Texans franchise. As of 2009, this is the last NFL team to play at least one regular season and fail to operate.

Although the NFL ceased to expand for a number of years, the following are a few matters that influenced its operation after 1952. First, Philadelphia U.S. District Court Judge Allan K. Grim upheld the league's policy of blacking out home games. Second, the NFL Players Association organized and became active in 1956. Third, the Columbia Broadcasting System (CBS) became the first network to broadcast some NFL regular season games into selected television markets within the U.S. Fourth, a group of wealthy sports entrepreneurs met in Chicago and announced their formation of the American Football League. Fifth, NFL commissioner Bert Bell died of a heart attack in 1959 at Franklin Field in Philadelphia during a game played between the city's Eagles and Pittsburgh Steelers.

1960–1969

As explained in the previous section of this chapter, the NFL expanded by four teams during the 1960s. Undoubtedly, the most successful of these franchises is the Dallas Cowboys. In fact, Cowboy teams have won 19 division and 10 conference titles, and five Super Bowls through the league's 2008-2009 season. More specifically, the club's greatest performances were in the early-to-mid 1990s and least impressive during the late 1980s.

The Cowboys accomplishments happened, in part, because of such coaches as Tom Landry, Jimmy Johnson and Barry Switzer, and players Emmitt Smith, Troy Aikman and Michael Irvin. In 2008, the franchise's estimated market value exceeded $1 billion, and in 2009, the Cowboys played its games at home in a fabulous new stadium that provided the franchise with millions of dollars from advertising, concessions, merchandise sales, and other amenities. To be sure, Cowboys owner/president/general manager Jerry Jones is determined to win additional titles and championships since this stadium will generate increasingly more revenues for head coach and defensive coordinator Wade Phillips to improve his roster of players on offense, defense, and special teams.

After the Cowboys joined the Western Conference, the NFL expanded again in 1961 by placing the Minnesota Vikings in that conference but switching the Cowboys to the Eastern Conference. Although much less lucrative than the Cowboys, the Vikings have performed satisfactorily throughout the years. Based in some NFL seasons on the leadership of such former head coaches as Bud Grant, Jerry Burns and Dennis Green, and the talents of players like quarterback Fran Tarkenton, receiver Cris Carter and field goal specialist Fred Cox, the franchise appeared in 25 years of playoffs, during which it successfully won 17 division and four conference titles between 1961 and 2008 inclusive. However, it has been more than 30 years since the club won a conference championship and played in a Super Bowl.

For the Vikings to marginally improve in the league and increase its revenue and economic value, the club's owner/chairman Zygi Wilf and his coaching staff need to make smarter decisions in drafting college players and in trading its unproductive athletes in exchange for skilled players on other NFL teams. Furthermore, the Vikings perform at home in a 27-year-old stadium named the Hubert H. Humphrey Metrodome. As an asset, this facility is inferior to Ford Field of the Lions in Detroit and Soldier Field of the Bears in Chicago, and perhaps to Lambeau Field of the Packers in Green Bay.

If Wilf and government officials in the Minneapolis-St. Paul area negotiate and then agree to jointly finance the construction of a modern single- or multi-purpose stadium, the Vikings may earn enough cash flows from the facility to significantly raise the team's payroll and bid for outstanding free agents and veterans. Otherwise, the Vikings will continue to be moderately competitive against rival clubs in the National Conference's North Division but not in winning more championships.

Five years following entry of the Minnesota Vikings, the league expanded again and assigned owner Rankin Smith's Atlanta Falcons to play in the Eastern Conference. Since the late 1960s, this franchise has been mediocre in its performances during regular seasons. In nine playoff appearances through 2008, the Falcons won three division titles and one conference championship. Among the club's 16 head coaches, Leeman Bennett and Wade Phillips had more victories than defeats while the others varied in wins from zero by Jim Hanifan in 1989 to 52 by Dan Reeves in 1997–2003. During previous seasons, the Falcons greatest players and record holders included quarterback Steve Bartkowski, running back Gerald Riggs, and field goal kicker Morten Andersen.

This franchise has struggled to win championships for several reasons. Besides the incompetence and inconsistency of various head coaches, general managers and owners, one of the team's most talented players was sentenced to prison during the mid–2000s. Quarterback Michael Vick financed and scheduled illegal dogfights and sponsored others at or near his residence in Virginia. For Vick, who knowingly committed this crime, it was irresponsible, selfish, and extraordinarily stupid. In the end, he paid millions for lawyers and in court costs, and greatly diminished any hope of the Falcons to win their division in 2007-2008.

In 2008, the Falcons drafted Boston College quarterback Matt Ryan in the first round. As a result, Ryan performed above owner/chief executive officer Arthur M. Blank's expectations as a rookie. If he continues to improve as a quarterback and thereby avoids major injuries, the club will effectively compete in the National Conference's South Division and thus challenge the Carolina Panthers, New Orleans Saints, and Tampa Bay Buccaneers for a title. This improvement in performance, in turn, will attract more fans from the Atlanta area to Falcons games played in the Georgia Dome. As a business enterprise, however, Blank's franchise ranked below average in 2008 relative to other NFL clubs in operating income, revenue, and market value. Even so, because of new head coach Mike Smith and such assistants as special team coordinator Keith Armstrong, offensive coordinator Mike Mularkey and defensive assistant Joe Danna, the Falcons may win more games and perhaps upgrade the team's balance sheet and earnings statement.

One year after agreeing to merge with the AFL and implementing an internal realignment, the NFL expanded to 16 franchises when the New Orleans Saints joined the Capitol Division of the Eastern Conference. After Saints teams had performed below expectations for 17 years, current owner/ president Tom Benson purchased the club for $70 million from John Mecom Jr. Since 1985, the Saints have appeared in six playoffs and won three division titles. During this era, the club's most productive head coaches were Jim Mora and Sean Payton, who guided such players as quarterback Drew Brees, running back Deuce McAllister, and receiver Eric Martin.

In recent years, problems from the destruction caused by Hurricane Katrina have negatively affected the Saints' attendances at the Louisiana Superdome and thus influenced the franchise's cash flow. Indeed, it is extremely doubtful whether Benson and his coaching staff can motivate quarterback Brees, running back Reggie Bush, and other Saints players enough to win another South Division title and a National Conference championship and Super Bowl. I was wrong.

For his part, Benson has lobbied various local politicians and state offices in Louisiana for support to finance and build a new football stadium in the New Orleans area. As of early 2009, these efforts have failed and therefore not resulted in any commitments to use public money for the construction of a new facility. In my opinion, the next major strategy that Benson will adopt is to threaten the Saints' fans and sponsors as well as politicians and the media of his intention to move his franchise to another city, such as Los Angeles, Portland, or San Antonio. If the New Orleans business environment does not completely recover from the effects of Hurricane Katrina, the NFL may authorize Benson to relocate his team to a potentially more profitable site.

1970–1979

After adding four new teams during the 1960s and a group from the AFL in 1970, the NFL waited a number of years to expand again. This plan became a reality, however, when the Seattle Seahawks and Tampa Bay Buccaneers became the league's twenty-seventh and twenty-eighth franchises in 1976. Each located in relatively small-to-midsized metropolitan areas, these clubs have experienced difficulties and disappointments while competing in the NFL. The Seahawks, for example, won only two division titles between 1976 and 2003 but finished first in the National Conference's West Division during 2004–2007. It was executive vice president of football operations and head coach Mike Holmgram who taught quarterback Matt Hasselbeck, running back Shaun Alexander, and receiver Bobby Engram how to be efficient on offense, make big plays for first downs, and score touchdowns.

Because of Holmgram's retirement in 2009, chairman Paul Allen will hire a replacement. That decision may or may not cause the Seahawks to win more games at Qwest Field against its opponents, especially in the West Division. Besides a new coach, two other factors are important to the future prosperity of this professional football club. The first is how quickly Seattle's economy recovers from a housing crisis and the U.S. recession of 2007–2009. Since prices of homes in the Seattle area did not decline as much as in other regions of America during the recession, the operating income and revenue of the Seahawks should remain relatively stable, at least in the short run, after 2009.

The second factor to consider is the National Basketball Association Supersonics' departure from Seattle to Oklahoma City in 2008. In other words, the Seahawks may benefit from the Supersonics' movement because basketball fans in Seattle may gradually switch their support to the Seahawks and/or perhaps major league baseball's Mariners. Alternatively some fans will abandon games involving professional team sports and decide to participate in personal activities like amateur bowling, golf, and tennis. On the other hand, they may invest their disposable income and time into non-sports events, such as movies, museums, and family trips to places beyond Seattle. In short, the Seahawks will not likely dominate the West Division's Arizona Cardinals, St. Louis Rams and San Francisco 49ers after the NFL's 2009 regular season.

The other NFL franchise that originated in 1976 was the Tampa Bay Buccaneers. This expansion team played one season in the American Conference's

Western Division, from 1977 to 2001 in the National Conference's Central Division, and since 2002 in the latter conference's South Division. Through 2008, the Buccaneers had won six division titles and a conference championship and Super Bowl in the league's 2002-2003 season. The club's most successful coach has been Jon Gruden followed by Tony Dungy and John McKay. Meanwhile, during five playoff appearances in the 2000s, the team played competitive football because of quarterback Brad Johnson and fullback Mike Alstott, and a stingy defense led by all-pro players Derrick Brooks, Ronde Barber, and Warren Sapp.

The Buccaneers majority owner and its president, Malcolm Glazer, also owns England's most prominent soccer club, Manchester United. Despite Glazer's interest and investment overseas, Tampa Bay has talented players at skilled positions. As such, the team will continue to be a threat each season to others in the National Conference's South Division. As a commercial enterprise, the team's operating income and market value have increased in recent years primarily because of a significant demand for professional football among populations located in west-central Florida. If the player payroll expands, the Buccaneers should qualify for the playoffs and compete for a conference championship within a few seasons. That opportunity depends, in part, on the business and strategy of the division's Atlanta Falcons, Carolina Panthers, and New Orleans Saints.

1990–1999

Throughout years of the late 1980s and early 1990s, the NFL as an organization became more prosperous from advertising campaigns, sponsorships, television contracts, and new stadiums. As a result, the majority of its teams experienced growth in their home attendances at games, revenues, and market values. Because of this economic momentum, the league expanded during the 1990s and placed two new clubs in the Southeast and another one into the Upper Midwest. In retrospect, this was a clever and profitable decision by league officials and the current owners of several franchises. To explain, the following are some facts about the performances of these three NFL expansion teams of the 1990s.

The Carolina Panthers played in the National Conference's Western Division in 1995–2001 and in the conference's South Division since 2002. Within 14 seasons, the franchise had appeared in four playoffs and won three division titles, and in 2003, a conference championship. Because of his straightforward attitude, excellent football experience, and thorough preparation for games, John Fox has been the team's most consistent and productive head coach. Likewise, such players as quarterback Jake Delhomme, receiver Steve Smith, and kicker John Kasay have played competitively and thus contributed their talents to many of the club's victories. Meanwhile, the Panthers owner/founder Jerry Richardson and his sons Mark and Jon have been leaders and admired within the local community because they dedicated themselves to operate their franchise to win games and entertain fans while also earning maximum profits for the team.

In early 2009, Jerry Richardson received a heart transplant at a hospital in Charlotte. Before this medical procedure and during recovery, Richardson thanked those who prayed for him and, in turn, newspaper sports journalists praised his character, leadership, and spirit. Many observers expect, therefore, that supervision of the franchise will transfer primarily to general manager Marty Hurney. As a result, those decisions and plans will determine the Panthers success in regular seasons and whether or not the team wins more titles and championships as a member of the National Football Conference.

Similar to assignment and reassignment of the Panthers, the Jacksonville Jaguars performed in the American Conference's Central Division for seven years and then in the conference's South Division beginning in 2002. For several reasons the club has underperformed yet won its division in the NFL's 1998 and 1999 regular seasons. These titles were due to former head coach Tom Coughlin and players like quarterback Mark Brunell, running back Fred Taylor, and receiver Jimmy Smith. To win more regular season games, however, the Jaguars need to outscore such outstanding competitors as the Indianapolis Colts and Tennessee Titans, and defeat the Houston Texans.

Although the Jaguars have a solid fan base in the Jacksonville area, chairman/chief executive officer Wayne Weaver needs to improve his franchise as a business. This effort will require additional investments in advertising and marketing campaigns to boost its image and reputation, attract more partners and sponsors, and sell large quantities of the team's merchandise. Nevertheless, an immediate and important goal is for a Jaguars team to win an American Conference championship and a Super Bowl. If these latter events occur, the club's revenue and economic value will increase despite its relatively small television market and the area's mediocre population size.

After three years without professional football for sports fans located in northern Ohio, the NFL approved an expansion team nicknamed the Browns to invade the Cleveland metropolitan area and compete in 1999 and thereafter. As a member of the American Conference's Central Division for three seasons and then the North Division since 2002, Browns teams have struggled to win games, especially against the Pittsburgh Steelers and Baltimore Ravens. Cleveland, however, finished 9–7 in 2002 with a better conference record than the Denver Broncos, Miami Dolphins, and New England Patriots. In a wild-card playoff game, the Browns lost 36–33 to the Steelers.

To be successful, the Browns must win a division and conference title but also improve its business as an enterprise. If owner Randy Lerner hires an experienced coach who motivates his players, the club will generate more operating income and revenue from its stadium and other operations. In turn, senior vice president/general manager Phil Savage may then reinvest these funds into the franchise's community relations programs, human resources, and marketing services.

It will be awhile, however, before the Browns are able to challenge and consistently defeat the Steelers and Ravens in regular season games. Nonetheless, a series of lucky draft choices or key trades of its players may turn around the Browns and make the team a threat in every game against the conference's North Division. Certainly, the great football tradition established by previous Cleveland Browns clubs is an incentive for Lerner and his coaching staff to remember and instill in the franchise's players.

2000–2009

Six years after the Oilers departed to Memphis, the Houston Texans became the NFL's latest expansion team. Assigned to the American Conference's South Division, the club has tended to finish most regular seasons in fourth place behind the Colts, Jaguars, and Titans. In fact, Texans head coaches Dom Capers and Gary Kubiak won 32 and lost 64 games in total during 2002–2007. To be competitive on offense, these coaches depended primarily on quarterback David Carr, running back Domanick Williams, and receiver Andre Johnson.

If chairman/chief executive officer Robert McNair and general manager Rick Smith adopt incentives that successfully encourage and further support coach Kubiak's strategies, the Texans will eventually qualify for the playoffs and perhaps win a division title. However, if the Colts' Peyton Manning and the Titans' Kerry Collins continue to excel as a quarterback of their respective team, the Texans may not finish above third in the South Division for years. From a business perspective, however, the Texans are fortunate. Eight-year-old, 71,100-seat Reliant Stadium in Houston is a modern football facility that provides abundant cash flows for the league's newest franchise. Indeed these amounts, combined with generous revenue sharing from a multibillion-dollar television contract, will supply McNair and his staff enough financial capital to operate the Texans franchise within the state's most populated city and largest sports market.

This discussion concludes the previous section about performances of the league's various new teams since they began to play in regular seasons. From the nine new APFA clubs in 1921 and four NFL expansion teams in

1922 to the Houston Texans in 2002, there were more that failed after one or more seasons than had survived.

In contrast to those and other years of expansion, there were two specific periods when the NFL significantly increased in size. In the next section, I discuss these eras and the histories of clubs that transferred from two other professional football organizations into the NFL. With this information, the readers of *Football Fortunes* will realize how an elite American-based football league became the world's most valuable organization in team sports.

League Mergers

NFL-AAFC Merger

During 1946–1949, the AAFC consisted of several professional football teams. As a group, these organizations existed in small, midsized, and large metropolitan areas or sports markets. Respectively, the Buffalo Bisons/Bills and Miami Seahawks played at home in stadiums within the smallest areas; the Baltimore Colts, Cleveland Browns, and San Francisco 49ers existed in midsized urban settings; and the Brooklyn Dodgers, Chicago Rockets/Hornets, Los Angeles Dons, and New York Yankees each played at home in the three largest sports markets within America.[6]

After the AAFC and NFL agreed to merge in December 1949, the AAFC's Dodgers/Yankees (who combined operations after the league's 1948 season) and the Bills, Hornets, and Dons disbanded while the Browns, Colts, and 49ers transferred out of the AAFC to play in the NFL's 1950 regular season. As such, the next few paragraphs highlight the performances of these three clubs during their years while in the AAFC and NFL.

Baltimore Colts

When the Miami Seahawks pulled out of the AAFC in 1947, the Baltimore Colts replaced that franchise. In three seasons, the Colts won ten games, lost 29, and tied two. Moreover, the franchise was sold and resold again in 1948-1949. After a payment of $150,000 to Washington Redskins owner George Marshall for invasion of his territory, the Colts entered the NFL in 1950. That season the team finished 1–11–0 and incurred financial losses of approximately $106,000. Consequently, in 1951, Colts owner Abraham Watner returned his club to the NFL and sold its players for $50,000 to other franchises in the league.

Before relocating from Baltimore to Indianapolis in 1984, the Colts had existed in the NFL for 32 years (1950, 1953–83). Given these numerous seasons, the franchise won five division and conference titles, a league championship in 1958, and 12 years later, Super Bowl V. The club's most prominent head coaches included Webb Ewbank, Don Shula and Ted Marchibroda, and such excellent players were quarterback Johnny Unitas, lineman Gino Marchetti, and running back Lenny Moore.

Being relatively popular and successful as a team in the NFL, the Colts attendances at Baltimore's Memorial Stadium averaged more than 400,000 per season for nine years, from 1963 to 1971. When this average declined after the late 1970s, owner Robert Irsay was unable to persuade government officials in the Baltimore area to use public money and construct a new stadium for his franchise to play its home games. As a result, Irsay moved the Colts to Indianapolis after the team participated in the 1983 NFL season and finished 7–9–0 in the American Conference's Eastern Division. In Chapter 2, I discuss in more detail the demographic, financial, and sport-specific reasons for the movement of the Colts from Baltimore to Indianapolis.

Cleveland Browns

As an original member of the AAFC, the Cleveland Browns dominated many aspects of the league during four regular seasons and postseasons. Indeed, the franchise won 87 percent of its games and four championships, and had the highest average home attendance at 47,500 among all AAFC teams and those clubs in the NFL. In 1950, the Browns merged with the AAFC's Buffalo Bills and then entered the American Conference of the NFL. Between 1950 and 1995 inclusive, the Browns appeared in 23 playoffs, won nine division and 11 conference titles, and four NFL championships. The team's most accomplished head coaches included Paul Brown, Blanton Collier and Marty Schottenheimer, and its outstanding athletes were quarterbacks Otto Graham and Brian Sipe, running backs Jim Brown and Marion Motley, receivers Ozzie Newsome and Mac Speedie, and field goal kickers Lou Groza and Matt Stover.

After business executive Art Modell acquired a major part of the franchise from minority owners during the early 1970s, the Browns won fewer titles. Moreover, although attendances at Cleveland Municipal Stadium remained above the league's average for a while, the number of spectators fell from 600,000 per season in 1979–81 to less than 550,000 for a few years. Attendances at the stadium rebounded during the late 1980s and early 1990s.

Modell's confrontation with Cleveland officials and his controversial comments in the media about using taxpayer funds to renovate the dilapidated and outmoded Municipal Stadium created tension within this Ohio community, especially among its football fans and corporate sponsors. After relations further deteriorated between these groups, Modell endorsed an agreement of the league in late 1995 for him to move the Browns from Cleveland to Baltimore. In February 1996, the NFL officially approved the club's relocation. For more details regarding the business aspects of this move, see the next chapter of *Football Empire*.

San Francisco 49ers

Anthony Morabito and two minority owners organized this franchise and in 1946 they entered it into the AAFC. While playing in the league's Western Division, the 49ers had the second highest average attendance at 37,450 and finished second to the Cleveland Browns in four regular seasons. With San Francisco's lucrative sports market, expanding population and job growth, as well as the club's excellent performances in the AAFC, the 49ers agreed to join the NFL's National Conference in 1950.

Between 1950 and 2008 inclusive, several 49ers teams played competitively in many regular season and postseason games. In 22 playoff appearances, the franchise won 17 division and five conference titles, plus five Super Bowls. To earn these championships, there were contributions from such football experts as head coaches Bill Walsh, George Seifert and Steve Mariucci and such talented players as quarterbacks Joe Montana and Steve Young, receiver Jerry Rice, and defensive back Ronnie Lott. Walsh and these four athletes are members of the NFL Hall of Fame.

Since 1999, most 49ers teams have struggled to qualify for the playoffs and win a championship. In six seasons, for example, the club finished third or fourth in the National Conference's Western Division. Instead of the 49ers, it was the Arizona Cardinals, St. Louis Rams, or Seattle Seahawks that won the majority of titles in the division. To some extent, the 49ers' inferior performances have undermined the franchise's image and its fan base in the San Francisco area. Therefore, co-owners Denise DeBartolo and John York must somehow challenge head coach Mike Singletary and his staff to improve the performances of quarterbacks Shaun Hill and Alex Smith, runner/receiver Frank Gore, and other members of the team. Otherwise, the 49ers will continue to flounder as a football organization and perhaps as a business enterprise.

NFL-AFL Merger

For ten years, the AFL and its franchises existed as an independent professional football organization in various cities across America. As such, different teams in that league played their home and away games in stadiums located within such small areas as Buffalo and Kansas City, within midsized places like Boston and Miami, and within large markets such as Los Angeles and New York. Collectively the AFL teams' attendances per game varied from 40,100 in 1960 to 54,400 in 1969. Furthermore, three teams won two league's championships while another three failed to win even one title. Relative to their home sites, the Texans moved from Dallas to Kansas City in 1963 and the Chargers shifted from Los Angeles to San Diego in 1961. Moreover, the AFL increased in size when it added the Miami Dolphins in 1966 and two years later the Cincinnati Bengals. During its tenth and final season, the AFL included ten franchises.

In retrospect, the AFL and NFL engaged in costly economic conflicts about such issues as inflation of players salaries, allocation of television contracts, and invasion of each other's markets. When Congress passed a law permitting them to unite legally, the leagues merged as football enterprises in 1970. That year, ten former AFL clubs and the NFL's Baltimore Colts, Cleveland Browns, and Pittsburgh Steelers established themselves as competitors in a newly organized American Football Conference (AFC). In contrast, the National Football Conference (NFC) consisted of 13 teams that had played in the NFL's 1969 season.

Both in the short and long run, this merger significantly affected the NFL's fan base and market power, and it influenced the total number of games its clubs played during regular seasons and in postseasons. More specifically, from 1969 to 1970, the league's paid attendance in regular seasons increased by 56 percent and in postseasons by 182 percent while the total number of games played rose by 75 (65 percent). In 2007, the NFL's total paid attendance for 256 regular season games was 17.3 million and 792,000 for 12 postseason games. Thus, between 1969 and 2007 inclusive, the NFL's paid attendance per game increased by 24 percent during regular seasons and by 22 percent in postseasons.

Besides these specific changes in teams attendances, this alliance affected the NFL's business model in other ways. For example, new regional rivalries occurred within each division of the AFC and NFC. In the former conference, these included games between the Boston (renamed New England) Patriots and New York Jets of the Eastern Division, Cleveland Browns and Pittsburgh Steelers of the Central Division, and Denver Broncos and Kansas City Chiefs of the Western Division. Within the same three divisions of the NFC, competition intensified between the Philadelphia Eagles and Washington Redskins, Chicago Bears and Detroit Lions, and Los Angeles Rams and San Francisco 49ers.

The decision by the NFL to merge in 1970 and then expand during the 1970s, 1990s, and in 2002 created different challenges among various teams and therefore affected the business environments of each of them and the league. To illustrate, a number of football fans demanded to attend games of

the Seattle Seahawks and 49ers in the Northwest/West, Tampa Bay Buccaneers and Miami Dolphins in Florida, the Atlanta Falcons, Carolina Panthers, and/or Jacksonville Jaguars in the South/Southeast, Cincinnati Bengals
and Cleveland Browns in the Midwest, and Houston Texans and Dallas Cowboys in the Southwest. Consequently, growth of the NFL caused the sport of
football to become more popular regionally and financially lucrative for most
of the league's franchises.

Since the merger of these elite football leagues in 1970, a few former AFL
clubs have been very prominent and successful, and thus they appreciated by
hundreds of millions of dollars in market value for their respective owners.
Listed In order of winning NFL titles and championships, four of these franchises are the Oakland/Los Angeles/Oakland Raiders, Boston/New England
Patriots, Miami Dolphins, and Denver Broncos (see Appendix C).

Based on 39 years of performances, the Raiders ranked second among
the ten clubs from the AFL in the number of NFL playoff appearances and
division titles and in a tie for first in winning three Super Bowls. Meanwhile,
the Patriots tied for first in winning conference titles and Super Bowls; the
Dolphins were first in playoff appearances and division titles; and the Broncos tied for first in winning AFC championships. Inversely, the worst performers in the group of ten have been the Cincinnati Bengals, Houston/
Tennessee Oilers/Titans, and New York Jets.

Due to reorganization in 1970, NFL teams realized a substantial increase
in their exposure on television and earned income from other sources. During the 1970s, for example, NFL commissioner Pete Rozelle negotiated contracts with three television networks to broadcast for four years all regular
season and postseason games of the league plus other games in the preseason;
in the 1980s, NFL franchise owners adopted a resolution that encouraged
their teams to schedule and play a series of preseason games overseas beginning in 1986, with one game each year to be held in Western Europe and/or
Japan; in the 1990s, NFL International Week featured six playoff teams competing in nationally televised games in London, Berlin and Tokyo. Also, a
new season subscription service named "NFL Sunday Ticket" was launched
for satellite television dish owners; in the early 2000s, the league renewed its
multiyear agreement with Westwood One/CBS Radio Sports to continue as
the exclusive network radio outlet of the NFL.

Another feature of the merger was that in the long run it contributed to
an increase in the market value of all NFL franchises, particularly those that
had transferred from the AFL in 1970. In fact, five were valued at more than
$1 billion each in 2008 (see Appendix G). From most to least in value were,
accordingly, the top-ranked Patriots at $1.324 billion to the tenth-ranked
Oakland Raiders at $861 million. Of the remaining 29 NFL clubs, the only

franchises worth more than the Patriots were the Dallas Cowboys at $1.612 billion and Washington Redskins at $1.538 billion. The lone team worth less than the Raiders was the Minnesota Vikings at $839 million. With respect to other financial data of the ten former AFL teams as of 2008, the Patriots had the highest revenue and operating income among the group while the Bengals and Raiders tied and finished with the lowest in revenue, as did the Bills and Chiefs in operating income.

The special business effects and other results of the NFL-AAFC and NFL-AFL mergers were the final topics analyzed in this chapter. Since these two alliances increased the number of franchises and furthermore contributed to the league's realignment, they were important factors in the short- and long-run development, prosperity, and success of the NFL. To conclude, next is a summary of Chapter 1 followed by the notes.

Summary

This chapter examines when, where, and why the organization and strategy of the NFL changed since originally becoming an establishment in 1920, named then as the American Professional Football Association (APFA). The formation and history of all the APFA's and NFL's expansion franchises are discussed and their performances as teams during their existence without or within divisions and/or conferences. Furthermore, Chapter 1 provides facts and other detailed information about the NFL's mergers with the All-American Football Conference in 1950 and American Football League in 1970.

To list the NFL expansion teams and determine their locations, and to measure the success of them and those from other professional football leagues, there are a few tables of historical data in this chapter and the appendices. As such, this qualitative and quantitative information includes APFA and NFL team nicknames and also their home-based metropolitan areas, total number and specific years of football seasons, win-loss percentages, regular season results and postseason appearances, and their number of division titles, conference championships, and Super Bowl victories.

In short, readers realize from Chapter 1 how expansion teams in the APFA and NFL became organized, competed for one or more regular seasons, and then disbanded or continued to perform in different years of the mid- to late 1920s to early 2000s. Moreover, readers understand that the business, operation, and popularity of these enterprises denotes to what extent they prospered or failed as sports enterprises while located within their home-site market areas.

2

Team Territories
and Relocations

As with the other American-based professional sports leagues, each owner or syndicate of owners of a football franchise decides where to establish the organization's headquarters and play the team's pre-season and regular season home games. During the late 1800s and early 1900s, amateur, semiprofessional, and professional football emerged in urban and rural areas of regions within the Midwest and Northeast United States. As a result, a majority of the professional football teams in leagues organized and scheduled games in places, within a distinct region, from New Jersey in the east to Illinois in the west, and from Michigan, New York, and Wisconsin in the north to Ohio in the south.[1]

For many years, the regiona center of the sport consisted of urban areas throughout western Pennsylvania and eastern Ohio. There, football leagues consisted of athletic clubs and associations as well as other types of teams that used a mixture of amateur, semiprofessional, and professional players. Before the APFA formed and its teams played their first schedule of regular season games in 1920, some populations in different cities already contained hundreds or even thousands of football fans who enjoyed the sport because of its action, competitiveness, roughness, and most importantly, for its overall entertainment value.

Based on the sport's history but more specifically on its demographic and spatial growth and the geographical allocation of home sites, this chapter primarily focuses on two aspects of professional football. The first is a consideration of the attributes — including any significant differences or similarities — among urban places (later metropolitan areas) that had hosted one APFA-NFL team or more from the 1920s to 1950s inclusive, and then in the 1960s to early 2000s. In other words, the home territories of teams are identified and then compared relative to their locations, sizes, and other characteristics.

The second major topic covered in this chapter is the relocation of several APFA-NFL clubs between 1920 and 2008. More specifically, I discuss the time and circumstances of their relocation, and their performances before and after they relocated. A table contains descriptive statistics and other information that measures these teams' performances. In short, Chapter 2 is essentially about when, where, and why a number of APFA-NFL franchises became established in traditional and new sports markets of America and how well they performed prior to and subsequent to their movement.

APFA-NFL Team Territories

Table 2.1 quantifies the distribution of a football league's teams in various years among metropolitan areas of various sizes. In part, the table denotes the number and proportion of clubs in the APFA-NFL that existed at home within the smallest-to-largest areas. Spaced in ten-year increments, it also indicates changes in the population sizes of places that had hosted NFL teams in years within 1920 to 2000 inclusive.

TABLE 2.1 APFA-NFL RANK OF TEAMS'
HOME AREAS, SELECTED YEARS

		Rank		
Year	*Very Small–Small*	*Midsized*	*Large–Very Large*	*Total*
1920	5 (36)	5 (36)	4 (28)	14
1930	2 (18)	3 (27)	6 (55)	11
1940	1 (10)	3 (30)	6 (60)	10
1950	1 (8)	5 (38)	7 (54)	13
1960	1 (8)	7 (54)	5 (38)	13
1970	8 (30)	9 (35)	9 (35)	26
1980	5 (18)	13 (46)	10 (36)	28
1990	6 (21)	10 (36)	12 (43)	28
2000	9 (29)	12 (39)	10 (32)	31

Note: These three ranks reflect the home population of each NFL franchise's urban or metropolitan area. Total is the number of teams in the league during these different years. The numbers in parentheses are percentages of the total for that year. In 1920, for example, 36 percent of the 14 teams were based in very small-to-small or midsized metropolitan areas, and four or 28 percent of the total had played their home games within large-very large metropolitan areas.

Source: *The World Almanac and Book of Facts.*

Consequently, Table 2.1 reflects the decisions of franchise owners to operate sports enterprises by locating their football clubs in areas of specific sizes in order to perform in the league's regular seasons and perhaps postseasons for the short and/or long run. As such, in the following two subsections of this chapter I identify a number of former and current APFA-NFL teams and then compare the quality of their territories as home sites for regular season games.[2]

1920s–1950s

Between the early 1920s and mid–1930s, the number of clubs in the professional league varied from 21 in 1921 to nine in 1935 and 1936. While several new teams joined the NFL and played for one or more years, others eventually went bankrupt and disbanded, merged, or simply stopped competing. The NFL franchises that failed in the 1920s and early 1930s were located in both within metropolitan and rural areas, with a wide range of populations. These included, for example, such very small-to-small places as Evansville, Hammond, and Muncie in Indiana, such midsized places as Canton, Columbus, and Dayton in Ohio, and such large places as Brooklyn, Rochester, and Staten Island in New York.

Thus before the mid–1930s, the local population and its size were not significant factors as to whether or not an NFL team would survive as a business and become popular among local fans. In fact, after the Spartans relocated from Portsmouth to Detroit in 1934 and the Cincinnati Celts folded, the Green Bay Packers were the only club from a small market remaining in the league for several decades.

From the early-to-mid 1930s to the late 1950s, the number and proportion of NFL teams based in midsized areas became more abundant. Meanwhile, these number of teams/markets located in other tended to decline or remain about the same. As a result, from years in the 1930s to 1950s, the number of franchises within midsized markets nearly equaled those in large to–very large markets and far outnumbered those in very small-to-small markets. Indeed the midsized areas of Baltimore, Cleveland, Pittsburgh, San Francisco, and Washington hosted successful clubs in 1950 when the league consisted of six teams playing in the American Conference and another seven in the National Conference. After the Dallas Texans failed in 1952, however, the NFL remained composed of clubs in the same 12 cities until the early 1960s.

In sum, the league decreased from 14 franchises in 1920 to a dozen in 1959. The Green Bay Packers were the only team located in a very small city in 1959 while big places like Chicago hosted the Bears and Cardinals, New

York contained the Giants, and Los Angeles was home to the Rams. Four decades earlier, the smallest urban places with clubs in the league included Canton, Decatur, Rock Island and Hammond. In contrast, the largest places with one or more clubs were Chicago, Cleveland, and Detroit.

Therefore, during its first 40 years in operation, the NFL had expanded by several teams in the 1920s and 1930s, but only by one each in the 1940s and 1950s. Furthermore, the number and proportion of franchises in very small-small cities had significantly declined and were replaced by those located in either midsized or large-very large markets. This suggests that gradually NFL teams settled to play at home in some of America's most populated places and were thereby better able to compete, mature, and thrive as business enterprises.

1960s–2000s

During this 49-year period of football's regular seasons, some new NFL franchises entered into different metropolitan areas while others shifted among them. As reflected in Table 2.1, domestic markets of various sizes became more popular in different years as home sites of teams but not as proportions of the total number of them. That is, midsized and large-very large areas shrank proportionally from 54 and 38 percent in 1960 to, respectively, 39 and 32 percent in 2000. Meanwhile, very small-small areas that hosted NFL teams increased from one in 1960 to nine in 2000 or from 8 to 29 percent.

The most dramatic and profound change of market sizes within the league occurred in 1970 when ten teams from the former AFL joined the NFL's American Conference. Relative to each other and 13 franchises in the National Conference, populations of areas were comparatively small to support the American Conference's Bengals in Cincinnati, Bills in Buffalo, Broncos in Denver, Chargers in San Diego, Chiefs in Kansas City, and Dolphins in Miami. In contrast, midsized or large-very large areas were of sufficient size to host and sustain the conference's Browns in Cleveland, Colts in Baltimore, Jets in New York, Oilers in Houston, Patriots in Boston, Raiders in Oakland, and Steelers in Pittsburgh. In the NFL's National Conference, the Packers in Green Bay and Saints in New Orleans played their home games in relatively small places while the other 11 clubs in the conference competed at home within midsized or large-very large markets.

Interestingly, the locations of the 32 NFL franchises ranked nearly equal proportionately, with each about 33 percent of the total throughout the early 1970s. Thus, the NFL-AFL merger in 1970 caused these clubs to play their home and away games before football fans from areas whose populations were similarly distributed. With respect to Super Bowls in 1970–79, Pittsburgh won four of these championships, Dallas and Miami two each, and Baltimore and Oakland each won one. In short, teams from midsized areas that had played in the AFL during the 1960s excelled and won more Super Bowls than those located at home within small or large markets.

After 1980, very small-to-small metropolitan areas became relatively more popular as the home sites of NFL clubs and thus the totals increased in number from five to nine and in proportion from 18 to 29 percent. Charlotte, Indianapolis, Jacksonville, and Nashville had football stadiums and achieved enough population growth and prosperity to host new expansion or relocating teams. Meanwhile, midsized and large areas hosted proportionately fewer NFL teams after 1980. This shift indicated that cities in the South had developed into attractive and lucrative sports markets for professional football clubs between the 1980s and 2000s.

Thus far, I have discussed some changes and specific trends in NFL franchises' home territories, including their populations and sports during two distinct periods. Based on the distribution of data in Table 2.1, the number of clubs within each of three types of areas increased between the 1920s and 2000s. However, there were proportionately fewer professional football teams located in very small-small areas in the 1930s–2000s than in the 1920s. This occurred, in part, because some metropolitan areas in the U.S. realized above-average growth after World War II and their populations expanded at a faster rate than did the others. As such, they eventually became midsized areas with respect to the number of residents and households. Consequently, in 2000, less than 30 percent of NFL teams played their home games in stadiums within very small-small territories. Indeed, the smallest was — and continues to be in 2009 — the Packers at Lambeau Field in Green Bay, Wisconsin.

According to economic studies, population is one factor that affects the demand for and revenue potential of a professional sports team in a given area. Population size alone does not determine whether a specific area is inferior, average, or superior in quality as a home for an NFL franchise. In the next major section of this chapter, I list and discuss the movements of various APFA-NFL franchises and denote some important differences between their pre-move and post-move locations. Furthermore, some general statistics reveal the success of these clubs before and after their relocations.[3]

To support my analysis, I constructed Table 2.2 to provide information about professional sports teams prior and subsequent relocation. I selected seasons and area populations as important characteristics of relocations because they reflect these teams' histories, and in part, which areas were dominant and more demographically attractive than others as home territories for NFL franchises.

APFA-NFL Team Relocations

Decatur Staleys–Chicago Staleys

In 1919, the A.E. Staley Company in Illinois formed and sponsored an APFA team named the Decatur Staleys. Football player George Halas served as the club's first coach and Edward "Dutch" Sternaman as its manager.

TABLE 2.2 APFA-NFL CHARACTERISTICS
OF TEAM RELOCATIONS, 1920–2008

	Team Relocations	Seasons		Area Populations	
Year	Before→After	Before	After	Before	After
1921	Decatur Staleys→Chicago Staleys	1	88	43	2,700
1929	Duluth Eskimos→Orange Tornadoes	5	1	101	35
1929	Pottsville Maroons→Boston Bulldogs	4	1	24	781
1930	Dayton Triangles→Brooklyn Dodgers	8	15	200	6,900
1930	Orange Tornadoes→Newark Tornadoes	1	1	35	442
1934	Portsmouth Spartans→Detroit Lions	4	75	41	1,600
1937	Boston Redskins→Washington Redskins	5	72	775	660
1946	Cleveland Rams→Los Angeles Rams	8	49	1,400	4,300
1949	Boston Yanks→New York Bulldogs	5	1	2,400	12,800
1960	Chicago Cardinals→St. Louis Cardinals	38	28	6,200	2,100
1982	Oakland Raiders→Los Angeles Raiders	12	13	5,300	11,500
1984	Baltimore Colts→Indianapolis Colts	32	25	2,300	1,200
1988	St. Louis Cardinals→Phoenix Cardinals	28	21	2,400	2,100
1995	Los Angeles Rams→St. Louis Rams	49	14	15,400	2,500
1995	Los Angeles Raiders→Oakland Raiders	13	14	15,400	6,600
1996	Cleveland Browns→Baltimore Ravens	46	13	2,900	7,100
1997	Houston Oilers→Tennessee Oilers	27	1	4,400	1,100
1998	Tennessee Oilers→Tennessee Oilers	1	11	1,100	1,200

Note: APFA is the American Professional Football Association. NFL is the National Football League. These teams included those that played their home games in football stadiums within an area but also whose nicknames changed, such as the Chicago Staleys/Bears, Duluth Kelleys/Eskimos and Orange/Newark Tornadoes. Year is when a team moved and played its first season at the new site. Team Relocations Before and After are self-explanatory. Seasons are teams' number of NFL seasons before and after they had relocated. Area Populations are the home-site metropolitan populations in thousands of each team prior to and after it had moved. Before the 1940s, population reports existed for places in the United States but not for metropolitan areas. The Tennessee Oilers moved from Memphis to Nashville after the 1997 NFL season. In 1999, the Tennessee Oilers acquired a new nickname, Tennessee Titans.

Source: 2008 NFL Record & Fact Book and The World Almanac and Book of Facts; Pay Dirt, 488–494.

Because of these men's leadership, the Staleys finished with a win-loss-tie record of 10–1–2 and second to the Akron Pros in the APFA's 1920 season. Despite the team's success, its attendance was mediocre at home games, which were played at Staley Field in Decatur.

Therefore, in 1921, Halas and Sternaman purchased the franchise from the company and assumed complete control of its operation. Disappointed by the turnout of fans to games in 1920, Halas and Sternaman moved the Staleys from Decatur to northeast Illinois where it shared Wrigley Field with major league baseball's Chicago Cubs. In turn, former owner A.E. Staley paid Halas a sum of $5,000 to keep the club's nickname as Staleys while in Chicago for one year.

While playing all of its 11 games in Chicago during 1921, the Staleys won nine and finished first in the APFA. Because of these victories, the club's average attendance increased to 6,000 that season. Twelve thousand fans watched the Staleys defeat the league's second-place Buffalo All-Americans, 10–7, while a similar crowd saw the All-Americans win, 7–6, in a game on Thanksgiving Day. Although the All-Americans finished 9–1–2 in 1921, APFA president Joe Carr declared the Staleys to be the league's champion that season. Evidently, large-market Chicago was far superior to Decatur as a home territory for the Staleys, which developed into a popular and successful football team coached by the great George Halas. An aside, Halas renamed his team the Bears in 1922 to reflect these animals being parents of cubs and to acknowledge the city's current professional baseball club, the Chicago Cubs.

Duluth Eskimos → *Orange Tornadoes*

After joining the NFL in 1923, the Duluth Kelleys played three consecutive seasons and finished no higher than fourth in the league. One year after changing its nickname to Eskimos and then sold for $1 to Ole Haugsrud, the team played each of its games on the road, losing eight and winning only one. Despite earning estimated profits of $4,000 in 1926 and another $1,000 in 1927, the franchise suspended operations for the 1928 NFL season. Thus during 1923–27, the Kelleys/Eskimos teams won 41 percent of their total games and averaged almost 4,100 spectators at each home game. One of football's all-time greatest players, Ernie Nevers, played for the Eskimos, which then was the "Iron Men of the North." A former All-American in football at Stanford University, Nevers was outstanding and a very popular athlete, especially when he played in the Eskimos' 29 exhibition and league games held during 1926.

In 1929, Ole Haugsrud received a commitment from the NFL. The league granted Haugsrud the right to bid first on any new NFL franchise to be located within the state of Minnesota. Because of that deal, he sold his franchise for $2,000 to Edwin Simandl, who then moved the club to New Jersey and renamed it the Orange Tornadoes. Years later, Haugsrud exercised his right to bid when the NFL expanded in 1960 and placed a new team in the Twin Cities. Thus, Haugsrud acquired 10 percent of the league's Minnesota Vikings and became a minority owner of that franchise. Given the previous facts, Duluth was a tiny city that did not adequately support Kelleys/Eskimos teams throughout the early-to-mid 1920s, and after the team suspended operations in 1928, caused the franchise to relocate from Minnesota to New Jersey.

Pottsville Maroons → Boston Bulldogs

Located in the very small town of Pottsville, Pennsylvania, for four years, the Maroons won approximately 56 percent of their regular season games and attracted about 4,400 fans to each of them. The franchise struggled, however, due to money problems, rumors of strikes by its players, and the unfortunate loss of a league championship and its franchise in 1925 after playing in an unauthorized exhibition game in Philadelphia. Nevertheless, to keep the Maroons from transferring into the American Football League, the NFL readmitted the team in 1926. Nevertheless, the Maroons finished third in 1926, eighth in 1927, and eighth again at 2–8 in 1928.

For the 1928 season, however, owner Dr. John G. Striegel had relinquished control of the Maroons by loaning the team to a group of three players. Although attendance averaged about 6,000 per game that year, the club lost 80 percent of its games and any hope of a comeback appeared futile among the Maroons coaches, players, and hometown fans. In 1929, Striegel sold his franchise to a New England–based syndicate headed by George Kenneally. Within a few weeks, this ownership group decided to move the club from Pottsville to eastern Massachusetts and rename it the Boston Bulldogs.

Despite a ban in 1925 and having its championship revoked by the NFL, the Pottsville area still admires and respects the Maroons. Within the city, some businesses and schools have displayed pictures of the team and others are nicknamed Maroons. At an NFL meeting in 2003, the league's franchise owners had considered to reexamine the circumstances of the Maroons' forfeit of a league title in 1925. That effort failed, however, and the Chicago Cardinals remain as the official champion of the NFL's sixth regular season.

Dayton Triangles → Brooklyn Dodgers

Organized and sponsored by the Dayton Engineering Laboratories Company (Delco) of Ohio, the Triangles played eight seasons in the league.

After finishing sixth in 1920 at 5–2–2, the club's performances tended to decline such that during 1925–1929, all its games were played in stadiums away from home. Nonetheless, while competing earlier for four seasons at Triangle Park in Dayton, the team averaged about 4,300 spectators per game. In 1929, the Triangles ended 0–6 and then went broke. As a result of the Triangles' demise, a New York–based group led by business official John Dwyer purchased the franchise for an unknown price and moved it from Dayton to Brooklyn, New York. The team's name changed to Brooklyn Dodgers.

More specifically, this relocation occurred because of the Triangles poor performances in the league and Delco's refusal to invest more money into its franchise. Furthermore, playing road games for five regular seasons caused the club's gate receipts and revenues to be small, and its profits to be negative. Thus, Delco's decision to sell the team was the franchise's best option after the 1929 NFL season.

Orange Tornadoes → Newark Tornadoes

After it had suspended operations in 1928, the Duluth Eskimos moved to New Jersey in 1929 and played home games in the East Orange Oval Stadium while nicknamed the Orange Tornadoes. For that NFL season, the club won three (25 percent) of its total games and finished eighth in the league. Since home attendances averaged less than 7,000 per game, owner Edwin Simandl decided that Orange's population of 35,000 was unenthusiastic and too small in size to adequately support his team. Therefore, in 1930, Simandl moved this franchise to Newark, which was a much larger city than Orange within New Jersey.

Subsequent to winning one (9 percent) regular-season game, the Newark Tornadoes cancelled its remaining schedule because of financial problems and the lack of support from football fans in the area. In 1931, the franchise returned to the NFL and then was offered for sale as a business. As a result, the Tornadoes disbanded when there were no bids received for it prior to the league's 1931 season. In short, the majority of sports fans in the Orange and Newark areas failed to attend the Tornadoes home games and become emotionally involved with it as a professional football club. After almost two years in operation, this franchise stopped competing and went out of business.

Portsmouth Spartans → Detroit Lions

The Spartans of Portsmouth, Ohio, formed in 1929 and hired players from defunct amateur, professional, and semiprofessional football teams within a tri-state area. Having been successful in games against other independent teams that year, the Spartans entered the NFL in 1930. During 1930–1933, the various Spartan teams were somewhat competitive since they had finished eighth, second, third, and second in the NFL's Western Division. In 1932, Portsmouth played the Chicago Bears in an unscheduled championship game and lost, 9–0. This was the league's first playoff game, and it generated such interest for fans that the NFL established an Eastern Division and a Western Division in 1933.

Despite win-loss-tie records of 11–3–0, 6–2–4, and 6–5–0 in 1931–1933, the Spartans failed to attract enough people to its games in tiny Portsmouth. As a result of playing at home within a very small area along with financial problems from the Great Depression, the franchise generated amounts of revenues that were too low for it to operate. With the team unable to survive for another year in the league, radio executive George Richardson purchased the Spartans in 1934 for $15,000 (plus $6,500 to pay outstanding debts) and then moved his team to a large city in southeast Michigan. While there, Richardson renamed his club the Detroit Lions as a gesture of goodwill to professional baseball's Detroit Tigers and, like a lion in the jungle, he predicted the team would be a monarch within the NFL.

Boston Redskins → Washington Redskins

While located in the Boston area, the Braves (renamed Boston Redskins in 1933) finished second, third, or fourth in each regular season during 1932–35 before placing first at 7–5–0 in the league's Eastern Division in 1936. The club, however, struggled to convince fans in eastern Massachusetts to attend its home games at Braves Field and later in Fenway Park. Boston was foremost a baseball town that primarily supported the American League Red Sox and National League Braves. To illustrate, despite winning five games and scoring 103 points, the Redskins incurred a loss of $46,000 in 1933. Subsequently, George Marshall and his partners acquired control of the franchise from current owners Vincent Bendix and Jay O'Brien. Given the team's low attendances at home games, small fan base, and financial problems, Marshall's group moved the franchise from Boston to Washington, D.C., in 1937. Within weeks, they changed the team's name to Washington Redskins.

In brief, the Boston Braves/Redskins had one outstanding regular season in the franchise's five years of operating within the NFL. After it sold in 1933, the club's average attendance at home games exceeded 10,000, but this result did not meet the expectations of Marshall's ownership syndicate. In fact, less than 8,000 fans attended each of the team's four home games in 1936. Since the Boston Redskins preferred to play their home games in a football stadium and not share a baseball ballpark with the Red Sox, the Washington, D.C., area had the potential of being more hospitable than Boston and a more profitable place for Marshall to locate his team. Even so, it would be several years before the Redskins occupied a single-purpose football facility in the nation's capital.

Cleveland Rams → Los Angeles Rams

After finishing second in the American Football League, the Cleveland Rams entered the NFL in 1937 as an expansion team. Although the Rams placed no higher than third in seven regular seasons, the club improved and won a league championship in 1945 by defeating the Washington Redskins, 15–14. During its history, however, the franchise had an unpredictable fan base and variable attendances at its home games and thus played before much smaller crowds than the AAFC Cleveland Browns. After experiencing financial losses of $82,000 during 1941–45, owner Dan Reeves and his syndicate decided to transfer their franchise from Cleveland to eastern California in 1946. The team was renamed Los Angeles Rams, and Reeves' group signed a lease with the city to play its home games in the Los Angeles Memorial Coliseum. This agreement, in turn, existed for more than two decades.

Los Angeles contained a moderately successful AAFC team named the Los Angeles Dons throughout the mid-to-late 1940s. Nevertheless, the area was relatively large, had an expanding economy, and was attractive as a sports market on the West Coast. In contrast, Cleveland was located in northern Ohio where the area's industrial sector, blue-collar jobs, and population growth were nearing a peak. Meanwhile, the AAFC Browns and MLB Indians were dominate sports teams in Cleveland and received the support of fans and corporate sponsors within the city.

Even though the Rams drew at least 75,000 to its four home games in 1945, that volume of spectators did not prevent the franchise from losing more than $50,000. Therefore, because of these differences in demographic and economic conditions between the two sports markets, and a profitable long-term lease for the Rams, Los Angeles was located in an ideal area to host an NFL team in 1946 and years thereafter.

Boston Yanks → New York Bulldogs

During its five regular seasons within the NFL, the Boston Yanks never finished in first or second place of the Eastern Division. Although the team played its home games at Fenway Park, attendance averaged more than 19,000 per season. The Yanks, however, merged with the Brooklyn Tigers in early 1945. A few months later, the NFL cancelled Brooklyn's franchise and its players transferred to the Yanks. Undoubtedly, this event caused confusion among football fans and contributed to the Yanks' fifth-place finish in the league's Eastern Division in 1946 and 1948. Because of these problems, owner Ted Collins decided to relocate his franchise to another area in the East. When attendance significantly declined in 1948, Collins moved the Yanks from Boston to New York. Renamed the New York Bulldogs, the club played its home game at the Polo Grounds, which also hosted the Eastern Division's New York Giants.

Based on its merger with the Tigers in 1945 and a history of losing most games, the Yanks never became a popular team while located in Boston. The tension between Ted Collins and Brooklyn owner Dan Topping apparently interfered with the Yanks' ability to play well and compete for a championship. Furthermore, other distractions affected the Yanks, such as low attendances, financial difficulties, and performing at home in Fenway Park or within the Manning Bowl in Lynn, Massachusetts. Consequently, it was no surprise to NFL officials when Collins moved his club from Boston to New York in 1949.

Chicago Cardinals → St. Louis Cardinals

While based in Chicago, the NFL Cardinals had some unusual experiences and a number of events happen during 1920–59. The club was sold and resold more than once, lost 29 consecutive regular season games between 1942 and 1945 inclusive, and won its last NFL championship in 1947. Then, in the 1950s, the club won a total of only 33 regular season games while its rival and the more popular Chicago Bears finished first or second in the league's Western Division in 1950, 1954–56, 1958, and 1959.

After Cardinals owner Charles Bidwill died in 1947 and his widow, Violet, married Walter Wolfner two years later, football fans in the Chicago area seemingly lost their enthusiasm for and interest in various Cardinals teams. As a result, the Cardinals' attendances at Comiskey Park declined in the late 1950s except when playing the Bears, who, as predicted, won most of their hard-fought games. These problems, in part, caused the Cardinals' revenues from operations to decrease and remain low throughout the 1950s.

During 1957–1959, the Cardinals won seven and lost 28 regular season games in the NFL. As a novelty, and to attract more fans in 1959, the club abandoned Comiskey Park and played four of its games at the Bears' Soldier Field and also competed in another two games at a neutral site in Minneapolis, Minnesota. When that strategy failed to excite Cardinals fans in the Chicago area, the NFL authorized the Wolfners to move their franchise to St. Louis, Missouri, and thus block the entry of a team into that area from the emerging American Football League (AFL). Interestingly, the MLB Cardinals did not object to an NFL team invading its territory since the city had been home to one or more professional baseball franchises for several decades. Therefore, St. Louis was a city honored to host a new football club that was nicknamed the Cardinals.

Oakland Raiders → Los Angeles Raiders

After joining the NFL in 1970 from the AFL, the Oakland Raiders became a very competitive and locally popular team in the league's American Conference for 12 years. In eight playoff appearances, for example, the club won six Western Division titles and also a conference championship and Super Bowl in 1976 and 1980. Although it shared the San Francisco–Oakland market with other professional sports teams, the Raiders' attendances at Oakland-Alameda County Stadium usually exceeded 50,000 per game.

During the early-to-mid 1970s, former AFL commissioner and Raiders managing general partner Al Davis took control of this franchise from other co-owners. To increase the market value of his investment in a relatively large sports area, Davis proposed to move the Raiders from Oakland to Los Angeles in 1980. However, the NFL won a court injunction that blocked this proposal. In response to the injunction, Davis joined the Los Angeles Coliseum Commission to file an antitrust suit against the league. When a jury in a federal district court ruled in favor of Davis and the commission, he transferred the Raiders to Southern California in 1982 and revised the club's name to Los Angeles Raiders.

Davis was a colorful, controversial, and innovative business executive in the sport. While owning the Raiders, for example, he hired the league's first Latino head coach, Tom Flores, in 1979 and ten years later employed the NFL's second African American head coach, former Raiders player and current Hall of Famer Art Shell. Furthermore, Davis appointed Amy Trask to serve as president of the Raiders, which was one of the highest executive positions held by any woman in professional football. Although Davis caused trouble for the NFL commissioner and created tension among other franchise owners and city officials, his teams in the 1970s and early 1980s were respected by their fans for being aggressive, ruthless, and tough to defeat, especially at home in Oakland and later while based in Los Angeles.

Baltimore Colts → Indianapolis Colts

Since 1953, Colts teams had played their regular season home games in Baltimore's Memorial Stadium. During those years, the club won one Super Bowl, three NFL and five conference championships and several division titles. After the Colts experienced a series of dismal performances in the late 1970s and early 1980s, owner Robert Irsay realized the franchise needed more revenues to be successful and effectively compete against such rivals in the

American Conference's Eastern Division as the Miami Dolphins and New England Patriots. Because attendances at Colts games in Memorial Stadium varied across seasons from a low of 20,000 to a high of 50,000, the most advantageous and necessary solution to increase the club's revenues, according to Irsay, was the construction of a new stadium in the Baltimore area.

After disputes and some intense negotiations with public officials from Baltimore and the municipality, Irsay concluded it would be years before the city approved and built a new stadium for the Colts in eastern Maryland. Indianapolis, meanwhile, started construction on a new football facility to entice an existing or new NFL team to locate there. Given these circumstances, Irsay moved the Colts from Baltimore to Indianapolis in late March of 1984. This relocation occurred at nighttime when vans were loaded with equipment and other assets of the Colts and then driven from Baltimore to Indiana's capital city. For his covert, way of moving the club, Irsay was condemned by the media in Baltimore and hated by thousands of football fans within the area. In Indianapolis, however, he became a hero in the community.

St. Louis Cardinals → Phoenix Cardinals

During its 28 years in St. Louis, the Cardinals appeared in three NFL playoffs and won Eastern Division titles in 1974 and 1975 but no National Conference championships. Besides those events, franchise owner Violet Wolfner died in 1962 and ten years later, her son, Bill Bidwill, became the team's majority owner. Because of many close games against rivals during some regular seasons of the 1970s, St. Louis sportswriters and football fans named the club as "Cardiac Cardinals."

Despite a series of disappointing drafts of college football stars and some unfortunate movements of its coaches and players to other teams, the Cardinals won a majority of regular season games in 1982–84. Nevertheless, the attendances at Busch Memorial Stadium in St. Louis averaged about 40,000 per game. Owner Bill Bidwill declared that the Cardinals needed more revenues to compete against such division rivals as the Dallas Cowboys and New York Giants. Consequently, he challenged city officials to provide funds and resources for the construction of a new football stadium in the St. Louis area. While these discussions stalled, the Cardinals finished fifth in the Eastern Division in 1985–86 and then third in 1987. Meanwhile, the team's average attendances at home plummeted to about 35,000 per game in each of these seasons.

Frustrated from not concluding a deal with the city for a new stadium and the club's poor performances in the NFL after 1984, Bill Bidwill sensed better business opportunities existed elsewhere for his franchise. Therefore, in March 1988, he received approval from the league to move his team to a diverse, expanding, and prosperous metropolitan area in the Southwest. That decision, in turn, led to the relocation of the Cardinals from St. Louis to Phoenix, Arizona. Renamed the Phoenix Cardinals in 1988, the club played its home games for eight years in Arizona State University's Sun Devil Stadium. Then in 2006, the team opened a new regular season to playing home games in the new University of Phoenix Stadium.

Los Angeles Rams ➜ *St. Louis Rams*

After relocating from Cleveland in 1946, the Rams performed at home for 49 years in Los Angeles. While there, the club qualified for 20 NFL playoffs and won ten division and four conference titles and a league championship in 1951. During its multi-year history, the franchise experienced some changes in ownership. Furthermore, football experts respected the Rams organization for such innovations as training and assigning scouts to evaluate college players, drafting African American athletes, and implementing realistic business marketing practices, managerial strategies, and public relations.

After owner Carroll Rosenbloom died in 1979, his widow, Georgia, and their children inherited the Rams. One year later, she purchased all minority shares to become the club's sole owner. Also in 1980, the team moved its home games from the Los Angeles Memorial Coliseum to Anaheim Stadium. While in the National Conference's Western Division, however, the Rams finished third or fourth from 1990 to 1994, and during these regular seasons, its attendances at home steadily declined from 60,000 to 42,000 per game. Meanwhile, Georgia married Hollywood composer and celebrity Dominic Frontierre.

When the Frontierres failed to receive rights from Anaheim public officials to develop plots of land near the football stadium, they convinced other NFL owners to allow them to transfer the Rams out of Anaheim. Although the Baltimore area was originally preferred as a new site to host the team, the league permitted the Rams to relocate to St. Louis after the Frontierres agreed to share their revenues from the sale of permanent seat licenses with other NFL franchise owners. As a result, in 1995 the St. Louis Rams began to play home games in the Trans World Dome, now known as the Edward Jones Dome. In short, it was a series of poor performances and falling attendances in games, disputes with the City of Anaheim about the use of land, and the economic benefits from a new stadium in Missouri that caused the Rams to move from Anaheim to St. Louis.

Los Angeles Raiders ➤ *Oakland Raiders*

After moving from Oakland to Los Angeles in 1982, the Raiders appeared in seven NFL playoffs through the 1994 season. As such, the club won three Western Division titles and one conference championship and a Super Bowl XVIII in 1983. However, during the early 1990s, Raiders owner Al Davis became pessimistic because his team's attendances fell at home games played in the Los Angeles Memorial Stadium.

Therefore, in 1995, Davis moved the Raiders from Los Angeles to Oakland and sued the NFL for not supporting his efforts to build a new football stadium in Inglewood's Hollywood Park. In 2001, a jury in a California court rejected Davis' claim about the league's role in acquiring a new stadium and his so-called rights of owning the professional football market within the Los Angeles area. This verdict, however, was overturned later by a state appeals court due to a biased juror and the misconduct of another one. However, in 2007, the California Supreme Court ruled for the NFL and dropped Davis' case.

To recap, Al Davis was belligerent, cocky, and an independent maverick who refused to accept some rules of the league, especially the NFL's decision and lack of participation in helping him secure a new stadium for his team in Inglewood, California. Since the Raiders' attendances and performances in Los Angeles had deteriorated during the early 1990s and because he was familiar with the consumer market in the Bay Area, Davis received official approval from the NFL in July 1995 to relocate the Raiders from Los Angeles to the Oakland-Alameda County Stadium in northern California. Unfortunately, his court case in the mid–1990s was costly for him and the league. It also damaged the image, reputation, and success of professional football among sports fans on the West Coast.

Cleveland Browns ➤ *Baltimore Ravens*

Since 1946, the Cleveland area hosted the Browns while the club played four regular seasons within the AAFC and then another 46 in the NFL. Throughout these many years, the club won several division and a few conference titles, four championships in both the AAFC and NFL, but no Super Bowls between the late 1960s and 2008. During the early 1990s, the Browns attendances at home averaged about 70,000 per game even though the club usually placed third or fourth in the American Conference's Central Division. Therefore, to discourage Browns owner Art Modell from moving his franchise to another area within the U.S., Cleveland voters approved the allocation of $175 million in public money to refurbish the city's Municipal

Stadium. Even so, Modell announced in November 1995 that he had signed an agreement to relocate the Browns to Baltimore one year later.

Art Modell's decision caused the filing of more than 100 lawsuits by local sports fans and various groups, organized protests against Modell by football diehards in Cleveland and other NFL cities, and the termination of contracts by some of the Browns' advertisers, partners, and sponsors. This controversy, in turn, continued until the NFL and representatives from the City of Cleveland reached a settlement in February 1996. The agreement specified that, first, the Browns' archives, heritage, and history including the franchise's name, awards, trophies, uniform design, and colors and historical records would remain in Cleveland and, second, that the Cleveland area would be awarded a new expansion team to begin playing in the league's 1999 regular season. Based on these and other conditions in the settlement, Modell received approval from the NFL during March 1996 to move his franchise from Cleveland to eastern Maryland and rename it the Baltimore Ravens.

Thus, in 1995–96, three NFL clubs relocated from their home sites to other metropolitan areas. This number of movements had not occurred in consecutive years since 1929–30, when four of the league's teams changed their locations. Each of the deals in the mid–1990s involved franchise owners' problems with their supposedly inferior stadiums and the potential of more revenues earned in another stadium within a different market area. As of 2009, the Rams, Raiders, and Ravens seem to be as or more affluent, prosperous, and valuable in, respectively, St. Louis, Oakland, and Baltimore than they were before in Los Angeles, Los Angeles, and Cleveland.

Houston Oilers → Tennessee Oilers

During the franchise's 37 years in the NFL, the Houston Oilers appeared in ten playoffs and won only two titles in the American Conference's Central Division. Nevertheless, despite some success in regular seasons of the late 1980s-to-early 1990s, the club's average attendance at the Astrodome steadily declined from 61,000 in 1992 to 31,000 in 1996. Years earlier, however, the city spent more than $65 million to renovate the Astrodome by adding Astroturf, 65 luxury boxes, and 10,000 seats. This investment of taxpayer dollars occurred, in part, because Oilers franchise owner Bud Adams had threatened to move his team to another city. Therefore, when Adams lobbied public officials repeatedly for a new stadium in Houston, Mayor Bob Lanier rejected his request for funds. Although football fans, government officials, and many businesses located within southwest Texas wanted the Oilers to remain in Houston, they refused to provide money for a new Oilers stadium.

As a result of these circumstances in Houston, Adams began to market his club to various communities in other markets. Among the different officials at these places, Adams and Nashville mayor Phil Bredesen discussed plans to move the Oilers franchise to Tennessee. When Adams received a commitment from Bredesen that Nashville would contribute at least $140 million toward the construction of a new football stadium and also guaranteed $70 million in ticket sales for Oilers games, Adams announced in late 1995 the relocation of his team from Houston to Memphis and then from Memphis to Nashville. More specifically, the newly named Tennessee Oilers would play one year of its home games in Memphis' Liberty Bowl and then move in 1998 from Memphis to Nashville and compete there in future NFL regular seasons.

Tennessee Oilers → Tennessee Oilers/Titans

With respect to the 1997 NFL season, the Oilers team played its home games in Memphis before extremely small crowds at the Liberty Bowl. Even so, the club finished 8–8 and third in the conference's Central Division, following the Pittsburgh Steelers and Jacksonville Jaguars. To fulfill the franchise's commitment as originally planned, the Oilers then moved in 1998 from Memphis to Nashville, where the team played its home games in Vanderbilt Stadium, which was located on the Vanderbilt University campus. Again, the Oilers finished its regular season at 8–8 and second in the division but ahead of the Steelers, Ravens, and Bengals. Therefore, in the two years after relocating from Houston, the club had won exactly 50 percent of its total games.

During late 1998 and early 1999, Bud Adams appointed an advisory committee in Nashville to rename the Oilers in such a way that it reflected leadership, power, strength, and other heroic qualities. After the committee evaluated numerous potential titles, the group recommended Tennessee Titans to Adams as a name for his team. The word "Titans" satisfied Adams' requirements as an appropriate nickname and also highlighted Nashville's reputation as "Athens of the South" because of the city's schools and their focus on undergraduate and graduate education, the classical architecture of Nashville's downtown buildings, and the city's full-scale replica of the Parthenon. Thus, from 1997 to 1999, the franchise's movements from Houston to Memphis and then to Nashville and the renaming of the team in 1997 to Tennessee Oilers and in 1999 to Tennessee Titans had been successfully completed.

To review, the previous paragraph concludes a section of this chapter that discussed the relocation of one APFA and several NFL teams. As such, the section included some dates, facts, and other historical information about when, where, and why these franchises had transferred their operations from one territory to another within the U.S. and then existed in the league for one or more years. To continue analyzing this topic, the next section of

Chapter 2 describes how successful these clubs were after they had moved. I highlight the changes in attendances and winning percentages of teams before and after their relocation to reveal some prominent improvements, if any, of these professional football franchises' business environment and fan base, and additionally, their organizational and strategic development.

APFA-NFL Team Performances

The differences, if any, in teams' attendances at their home games before and after they relocated and also whether each had won a lower or higher proportion of regular season and postseason games and championships at a postmove site are rough measures of their competitiveness, popularity, and perhaps success as businesses. To reveal these results, I created Table 2.3. Based on

TABLE 2.3 APFA-NFL CHARACTERISTICS OF TEAM PERFORMANCES, 1920–2008

	Team Relocations	*Attendance*		*Win-Loss*	
Year	*Before → After*	*Before*	*After*	*Before*	*After*
1921	Decatur Staleys→Chicago Staleys/Bears	2.0	8.4	90	80
1929	Duluth Kelleys/Eskimos→Orange Tornadoes	4.1	6.5	41	37
1929	Pottsville Maroons→Boston Bulldogs	3.5	3.5	56	50
1930	Dayton Triangles→Brooklyn Dodgers	4.0	15.3	6	38
1930	Orange Tornadoes→Newark Tornadoes	6.5	5.2	37	9
1934	Portsmouth Spartans→Detroit Lions	6.7	18.5	63	68
1937	Boston Braves/Redskins→Washington Redskins	13.0	26.5	45	71
1946	Cleveland Rams→Los Angeles Rams	14.2	35.9	48	63
1949	Boston Yanks→New York Bulldogs	19.2	8.0	26	9
1960	Chicago Cardinals→St. Louis Cardinals	26.0	22.4	30	54
1982	Oakland Raiders→Los Angeles Raiders	50.0	56.7	60	71
1984	Baltimore Colts→Indianapolis Colts	35.0	57.5	27	38
1988	St. Louis Cardinals→Phoenix/Arizona Card.	38.1	45.3	43	31
1995	Los Angeles Rams→St. Louis Rams	50.2	63.1	28	43
1995	Los Angeles Raiders→Oakland Raiders	54.2	49.4	58	43
1996	Cleveland BrownsvBaltimore Ravens	69.2	63.3	45	45
1997	Houston Oilers→Tennessee Oilers	45.9	28.1	48	50
1998	Tennessee Oilers→Tennessee Oilers/Titans	28.1	68.0	50	65

Note: APFA is the American Professional Football Association. NFL is the National Football League. Year is when a team moved and played its first season at the new site. Team Relocations Before and After are each self-explanatory. Attendance (at home stadiums in thousands) and Win-Loss (in percent) are each averages per season up to — but not exceeding — five years before and then following the movement of a team. For example, the average attendance per game of the Staleys in Decatur was 2,000 in 1920 and the team won 90 percent of its games that season. The home attendance at the Staleys/Bears games in Chicago averaged 8,400 during 1921–25 and the team won 80 of games played during five seasons. Card. is an abbreviation for Cardinals. After the 1997 NFL season, the Tennessee Oilers moved from Memphis to Nashville. In 1999, the team's nickname changed from Oilers to Titans while located in Nashville.

Source: 2008 NFL Record & Fact Book; "Sports Business Data" The Pro Football Encyclopedia: The Complete and Definitive Record of Professional Football.

values depicted in the table and other information within the literature, these are experiences of NFL clubs that transferred from one area to another and thus performed below or above expectations of their fans.[4]

Chicago Staleys/Bears

After finishing second to the Akron Pros in the APFA, the Staleys moved from Decatur to Chicago in 1921. During each of the next five years, the club won fewer games per season than it did while in Decatur but played before a greater number of spectators at Wrigley Field and then in Soldier Field than at Staley Field. Because of such former coaches as George Halas, Mike Ditka and Lovie Smith, and such prominent players as Gale Sayers, Walter Payton and Sid Luckman, the Bears appeared in numerous playoffs and won a total of 17 division and four conference titles, eight NFL championships, and a Super Bowl in 1985. Through the years, team owners like Halas, Dutch Sternaman, and Virginia and Michael McCaskey invested in the franchise and therefore improved its operation, productivity, and net worth as a business enterprise.

Since the mid-to-late 1980s, however, the various Bears teams have won only one conference championship. Although the franchise continues to become richer from a financial perspective while based in the Chicago area, it has failed to play in any recent Super Bowls. Even so, the Bears have been one of the NFL's most lucrative and respected organizations. Indeed, for many years in the future, the franchise will realize more gate receipts at home games played in Soldier Field and thereby increase its future cash flows, operating income, and market value.

Orange Tornadoes

The Duluth Kelleys/Eskimos failed to win more than six games in any of its five years within the league. Thus, in 1927, the club played nine games away from Duluth and won only one. Consequently, the Eskimos moved from

Minnesota to New Jersey in 1929 and became the Orange Tornadoes. While based in the small town of Orange for one season, the club's performance moderately declined while its attendances increased by more than 50 percent. The team won three (25 percent) of its games that season and finished eighth in the league before approximately 6,500 fans at each home game.

Even so, owners of the franchise in Orange experienced financial difficulties. Because of these problems, the Tornadoes left the Orange area in 1930 and relocated to Newark, which was then a midsized city in New Jersey. In short, a Tornadoes team was somewhat more popular for one season in Orange than the Eskimos in Duluth and less competitive. However, because it could not operate as a business more than one year at its new site, the Tornadoes transferred to a larger area in 1930 to play another season.

Boston Bulldogs

After the somewhat successful Pottsville Maroons moved from Pennsylvania to Massachusetts in 1929, the team changed its name to the Boston Bulldogs. While located in Boston, the Bulldogs home attendances remained at 3,500 per game, similar to the Maroons in previous years. During its first season, however, the Bulldogs played only two games in Pottsville and defeated the Buffalo Bisons and Orange Tornadoes. Because of poor attendances at home in Boston and losing 50 percent of its games, the Bulldogs folded in late 1929 or early 1930.

In hindsight, the relocation to Boston from Pottsville was probably a mistake and an extremely bad decision by the franchise's owners. In fact, the Maroons drew almost 6,000 to each of its home games in 1928. Given this and other information, the incentive of playing games within a larger metropolitan area and potentially earning more money from gate receipts, in part, caused this move to occur but ultimately fail from a business perspective. Nonetheless, another NFL club did not move to Pottsville and play there after the Maroons had departed from the area. In short, the city's population may have been too small to support a team in professional football for more than a few years.

Brooklyn Dodgers

While based for eight years in Dayton, the Triangles played three of its final five years as a travelling team. Therefore, the club won few of its games and had poor attendances at home in Triangle Park. After relocating from Dayton to New York in 1930 and changing its nickname to the Brooklyn Dodgers, the franchise improved to win more games and became a more productive business enterprise. The club's attendances, which had averaged 4,000 per game in Dayton, soared to 15,000 during the 1930–1934 seasons despite a great slowdown in the economy of the New York area. Although they never won an NFL championship, the Dodgers finished second in the NFL's Eastern Division in 1933, 1935, and 1940–1941.

Following some sales and repurchases of the team during the 1930s, the Dodgers name was changed to Brooklyn Tigers in 1944; one year later, the club merged with the Boston Yanks. When the Yanks co-owner Dan Topping announced sometime in 1945–1946 the transfer of his team from the NFL to the AAFC, the Brooklyn franchise cancelled itself. In short, the relocation of the Triangles from Dayton to Brooklyn after the 1929 NFL season caused the league to be increasingly competitive in the short run but more financially stable with the Dodgers organization rather than with the Triangles.

Newark Tornadoes

As indicated in Table 2.3, the Tornadoes had smaller attendances at its home games in Newark than in Orange and played much worse as an NFL team. In part, the stock market crash and economic depression in America contributed to the failure of this franchise in Newark. Besides these factors, the Tornado teams had four different head coaches in two years. Moreover, it lacked any talented football players who could consistently defeat such East Coast rivals as the New York Giants, Providence Steam Roller, and Staten Island Stapletons.

After a 34–7 loss to the New York Giants in October 1930, the Newark Tornadoes folded and its owner returned the franchise to the NFL. When the team became available for sale by the league, there were no bids from investors. Therefore, in late 1930, the club suspended its operations for one year. Shortly thereafter, the Tornadoes simply folded and ceased to exist as a football organization. As a group, the Duluth Kelleys/Eskimos, Orange Tornadoes, and Newark Tornadoes were inferior teams that lacked leadership and the financial capital to sustain their business operations within the NFL. Unfortunately, the two movements of this football franchise did not provide opportunities for its long-term success or even to survive, especially against opponents that were located in the big cities and those in small places like Canton, Ohio, Green Bay, Wisconsin, and Pottsville, Pennsylvania.

Detroit Lions

Since moving from tiny Portsmouth, Ohio, to the southeast Michigan area in 1934, the Detroit Lions have appeared in 14 playoffs and won seven division and four conference titles, and four NFL championships. The club's most successful head coaches included Raymond Parker, George Wilson and Wayne Fontes, while its best players have been quarterback Bobby Layne, running back Barry Sanders, and receiver Herman Moore. Besides the contributions of these coaches and athletes, one or more members of the Ford family have owned the franchise since the early 1960s.

Because of various human relations problems and other financial issues, the Lions won its last conference title in 1957. In fact, during the 2006–2008 seasons, the team finished respectively at 3–13, 7–9, and 0–16 in the North Division. To challenge the Bears, Packers and Vikings, and win its home games at Ford Field, the team's coaches and players must be more productive in all aspects of the sport. Certainly, the Lions will improve if owner William Clay Ford invests more money in college scouting programs, players' salaries, and coaching contracts. Otherwise, the Lions will continue to struggle each year against league rivals.

Although the Lions have not excelled since the 1950s, the relocation of the Spartans from Portsmouth to Detroit in the mid–1930s expanded the business of the NFL. The league's attendances per game increased as did the revenues of the Lions and of visiting teams from other NFL cities. In 2009 and thereafter, however, the Lions will not likely win a majority of their regular-season games. But as a football enterprise, the franchise has sufficient gate receipts, operating income, and market value based on the opening of a new stadium in 2002 and because of the league's multibillion-dollar television contract and generous revenue-sharing policy. In other words, it is not likely that the Lions will relocate from Detroit despite the team's embarrassing win-loss record in recent years.

Washington Redskins

This team has performed significantly better in Washington than it did during the 1930s in Boston. Such sports entrepreneurs as George Marshall, Edward Williams, and Dan Snyder invested millions of dollars into various Redskins teams while they owned all or part of the franchise. As a result, since 1937 the Redskins have won 11 division and five conference titles, two NFL championships, and three Super Bowls. Some prominent leaders of the club were head coaches George Allen, Joe Gibbs and Norv Turner, who joined such great players as quarterback Sammy Baugh, running back John Riggins, and receiver Art Monk.

In 2008, the Redskins ranked first in market value at $1.53 billion among 32 NFL franchises. Furthermore, the team's gross revenues have recently exceeded $325 million, and while playing games in FedEx Field, the club has broken the league's single-season attendance record for eight consecutive years. In addition to being a popular attraction to sports fans in the Washington area, the Redskins are a powerful business because of amenities from its stadium, owner Snyder's investments in coaches and players, and the revenues received from local and national television broadcast contracts.

For the Redskins to be more successful in home and away games, Jim Zorn and his assistant coaches must lead the team to victories and especially defeat East Division rivals that include the Cowboys, Eagles, and Giants. Given the abundant revenues generated from FedEx Field and Snyder's immense wealth, the Redskins are a threat to make the playoffs each season despite competition from its NFL opponents. Thus, I predict that Washington will win another conference championship before 2012 and earn its fourth Super Bowl title.

Los Angeles Rams

After playing for eight years in Cleveland, the Rams moved to Los Angeles in 1946. While there, the team won 11 division and four conference titles, an NFL championship in 1951 and Super Bowl XXXIV in 1999. The Rams most effective coaches were George Allen, Chuck Knox and Hamp Pool, and such players as passer Norm Van Brocklin, runner Eric Dickerson, and receiver Tom Fears were among the stars on the field. For many of its home games, the team played 34 years before large audiences in the Los Angeles Memorial Coliseum and another 15 in Anaheim Stadium.

From 1982 to 1994 inclusive, the Rams shared the professional football market in Southern California with the Los Angeles Raiders and San Diego Chargers. In some way, this number of teams in that region may have contributed to the Rams poor performances after the 1970s. The club won a division title in 1985 despite appearing in six playoffs. Another reason that the club did not win championships in the mid-to-late 1980s and early 1990s was the decisions made by Georgia Frontierre, who had become the franchise's sole owner in 1980. For example, she hired head coach John Robinson. Although he was a great leader of the football program at the University of Southern California, Robinson failed to coach the Rams to a conference championship.

As the Rams' performances declined during the early 1990s, the team's attendances at Anaheim Stadium were below those of the cross-town Raiders. Consequently, after leaving Cleveland in 1946 and playing in the Los Angeles area for 49 NFL regular seasons, the Rams had business problems during the early 1990s that caused the franchise to seek another home. Given these results, however, it was profitable for the Rams to relocate from northern

Ohio to California in the mid–1940s and then perform there for many years as a member of the league's National Conference.

New York Bulldogs

When owner Ted Collins moved his team from Boston to New York, the club's home-game attendances decreased from 12,000 in 1948 to 8,000 while playing at the Polo Grounds in 1949. Furthermore, even though Collins' Boston Yanks won only three games in 1948, one year later his New York Bulldogs team earned but one victory and finished fifth in the league's Eastern Division. Apparently disappointed by the Bulldogs' poor attendance and inferior performance in 1949, Collins relinquished his franchise to the NFL and then purchased New York's AAFC team from co-owners Dan Topping and Del Webb as part of the AAFC-NFL merger agreement.

Even though home attendances of the Yanks had decreased from 25,000 per game in 1945 to 12,000 per game in 1948, the relocation of the club from Boston to New York was not justified. Since the NFL Giants played at home in New York as did two MLB teams and the NBA Knickerbockers, the Bulldogs had a small opportunity of surviving more than one season in America's most populated city. Alternatively, Collins should have advertised and promoted his football team throughout the Boston area for a few years since baseball's Braves left there in 1953 for Milwaukee. As a result, perhaps some sports fans in Boston might have switched their support to the NFL Yanks. Anyway, it would be 12 years before another professional football team played its games at home in Boston.

St. Louis Cardinals

After moving from Chicago to midsized St. Louis in 1960, the Cardinals continued to struggle in the league's regular season games. In 28 years, the club appeared in three conference playoffs and won two division titles. During these seasons, the Cardinals most effective head coaches were Charley Winner and Don Coryell while some good performances in games came from quarterback Jim Hart, running back Ottis Anderson, and field goal kicker Jim Bakken. While playing at home in Busch Memorial Stadium, the NFL Cardinals attracted relatively small crowds because St. Louis in the twentieth century was primarily a baseball town whose sports fans tended not to be interested in games of professional football teams, especially of those who were inferior.

Since football's Cardinals earned relatively small gate receipts at home games and performed below expectations while in the Eastern Division of the

National Conference, owner Bill Bidwill tried to convince city and Missouri government officials to build his club a new football stadium with public money. When that effort failed, Bidwill received permission from the NFL to move the Cardinals from St. Louis to Phoenix, Arizona, in 1988. Given the franchise's financial problems, Bidwill's Cardinals took advantage of an opportunity to move from a stagnant industrial city in the Midwest to an expanding metropolitan area with warm temperatures in Arizona. In other words, the Cardinals had more potential to generate cash flows and earn revenues and profits by relocating from St. Louis to a fast-growing region in the Southwest.

Los Angeles Raiders

When he won an antitrust case against the NFL, owner Al Davis moved his franchise from Oakland to Los Angeles in 1982. For 13 regular seasons, the Raiders played their home games in the city's Memorial Coliseum. While based there, the club appeared in seven playoffs and won three division titles and one conference championship, and Super Bowl XVIII in 1983. To achieve these results, the Raiders head coaches included Tom Flores and Art Shell, and featured such excellent athletes as rusher Marcus Allen, receiver Tim Brown, and kicker Chris Bahr. In 1992, Davis and Shell received recognition for their contributions to the game and sport and were inducted into the Pro Football Hall of Fame.

Despite good attendances of his team's home games during the late 1980s and very early 1990s and their winning seasons in 1990–91 and 1993–94, Davis sued the NFL again because of the league's resistance to help him campaign for a new stadium at Hollywood Park in Inglewood, California. This distraction, in part, caused the Raiders' attendances in the Coliseum to decline from approximately 63,000 in 1991 to 51,000 in 1994. Three months after approving the move of the Rams from Los Angeles to St. Louis in 1995, the NFL authorized the Raiders to leave Southern California and return to the Bay Area. Thus, the Raiders shifted from America's second-largest television market to share an area where the San Francisco 49ers were located. In the end, this relocation occurred because of Davis' conflict with the league and his problem with hosting games in a large but dilapidated and obsolete stadium in Los Angeles.

Indianapolis Colts

Since moving from eastern Maryland to Indianapolis in 1984, the Colts have appeared in more playoffs and won more division titles — but fewer conference championships — than the franchise did while it was located in Baltimore. Yet playing in sports' greatest event, however, Colts teams won Super Bowl V in 1970 and Super Bowl XLI in 2006. Prior to 1984, the Colts most successful head coaches were Webb Ewbank, Don Shula and Don McCafferty, and after that year the team's best coaches included Jim Mora and Tony Dungy. Meanwhile, the Colts have featured such great players in the 1990s and/or 2000s as quarterback Peyton Manning, running back Edgerrin James, receiver Marvin Harrison, and kicker Mike Vanderjagt. As officials, Robert Irsay's son, James, now owns the team while former Carolina Panthers executive Bill Polian serves as its president.

Because Lucas Oil Stadium opened in downtown Indianapolis for the 2008 NFL regular season, the Colts will become increasingly popular and more prosperous as a business enterprise in professional football. Besides more gate receipts from its home games, the franchise's operating income and market value will likely rise in 2009 and each year thereafter. Recently, Dungy and Harrison retired while James transferred to another NFL team. However, if Manning, running back Joseph Addai, and kicker Adam Vinatieri remain healthy in regular seasons, the Colts should continue to be competitive and qualify for the playoffs as a member of the American Conference's South Division.

After reviewing the Colts history, it was a shrewd decision and a profitable strategy for Robert Irsay to move his team in 1984. The club's attendances in Baltimore averaged approximately 35,000 per game between 1979 and 1983. During the late 1980s, its average attendance soared to 55,000 or more while in Indianapolis. When Peyton Manning joined the team in the late 1990s, he developed into an outstanding leader, and that maturity resulted in seven consecutive playoff appearances, five back-to-back division titles, and a conference championship and Super Bowl. For the next few years, Colts teams will challenge their rivals during regular seasons and thus compete to win the conference's South Division.

Phoenix/Arizona Cardinals

Because of declining attendances at its home games and lack of fan support in St. Louis, and due to owner Bill Bidwill's frustration with the city about financing the construction of a new football stadium, the Cardinals transferred from eastern Missouri to southern Arizona in 1988. Since that year the club has appeared in two playoffs, and in 2008, won a division title and National Conference championship. After seven head coaches lost a majority of their regular season games, the Cardinals hired Ken Whisenhunt in 2007. As a result, the team finished 8–8 that year and then exceeded fans' expectations in 2008 by playing in Super Bowl XLIII against the Pittsburgh Steelers. This success occurred primarily because of veteran quarterback Kurt Warner, running back Edgerrin James, and wide receivers Larry Fitzgerald and Anquan Boldin.

At its home games in the 65,000-seat University of Phoenix Stadium, the Cardinals have played before capacity crowds. Given the team's results in 2008 and Warner's decision to sign another contract, the Cardinals will earn additional revenue from gate receipts and increase its operating income and market value as an enterprise in the NFL. Soon after 2009, however, Warner may retire from the sport. If so, Bidwill must decide whether to keep his team competitive in the conference's West Division by investing more money in head and assistant coaches and players. If he does not commit and spend enough to adequately replace Warner and other free agents, the Cardinals will be mediocre again and lose a large number of its division games to the 49ers, Rams, and/or Seahawks.

St. Louis Rams

Subsequent to its relocation from Los Angeles to St. Louis in 1995, the Rams' attendances at its home games increased on average from approximately 50,000 at Anaheim Stadium in Southern California to more than 63,000 at the Trans World Dome in eastern Missouri. Furthermore, the club's win-loss–tie record improved in St. Louis. For example, the Rams after 1995 appeared in six playoffs and won three division titles and two conference championships, and Super Bowl XXXIV in 1999. To accomplish these victories, there were contributions from head coaches Dick Vermeil and Mike Martz, and from such players as quarterback Kurt Warner, halfback Marshall Faulk, and receiver Isaac Bruce.

After Kurt Warner decided to play quarterback for the Cardinals, the Rams did not perform up to expectations. The club won its last division title in 2003 and one year later qualified as a wild card. Nevertheless, in 2004–2007, the Rams' best finish was second in the West Division at 8–8 in 2006. As such, for the Rams to win more home and away games, it is the responsibility of head coach Scott Linehan and his assistants to provide leadership and inspire passer Marc Bulger, runner Steven Jackson, and other players on the team.

From a business perspective, this franchise in St. Louis has not been very successful in recent years. The problem may be because of wrong management decisions made by co-owners Dale "Chip" Rosenblum, Lucia Rodriguez and Stan Kroenke, of problems in football operations caused by Jay Zygmunt and Samir Suleiman, and of player personnel issues created by Tony Softii and Lawrence McCutcheon. With more effective decision-making from these and other directors, executives and/or vice presidents, and higher productivity from coaches and players, the Rams will be competent each season and therefore win important games in its division against the 49ers, Cardinals, and Seahawks.

Oakland Raiders

On average, the Raiders played before smaller crowds at their stadium in Oakland, but also won fewer games there than they did during the regular seasons while located in Los Angeles. In fact, since 1995, the club has appeared in three playoffs, won three division titles, and in 2002, excelled to win a conference championship. Jon Gruden and Bill Callahan were productive head coaches of Raiders teams while some excellent performers in games included those of passer Rich Gannon, runner Napoleon Kaufman, and receiver Tim Brown. Unfortunately, these athletes had retired or were traded to other clubs before 2009.

During 2003–2008 the Raiders finished third or fourth in the American Conference's West Division. In contrast, the Broncos, Chargers, and Chiefs dominated that division. According to some football experts, Raiders owner Al Davis is content or simply not motivated enough to invest more money and/or resources into his franchise. Because of generous revenue-sharing and a salary cap in the NFL, Davis is satisfied to accept the Raiders' share of the league's national television contracts and to control his team's expenses by not bidding very often for expensive free agents and not over-compensating any college players that he selects in the draft. Based on the club's recent performances, the Raiders will struggle each season against its rivals within the conference's West Division.

Baltimore Ravens

Since the franchise moved from Cleveland to Baltimore in 1996, the Ravens have played six years in the American Conference's Central Division, and as of 2008, another seven in the North Division. During some of these 13 regular seasons and postseasons, the club appeared in five playoffs and won two division titles, one conference championship, and Super Bowl XXXV in 2000. The team's most effective head coach has been Brian Billick, whose prominent players included quarterback Kyle Boller, wide receiver Derrick Mason, and linebacker Ray Lewis. Moreover, there is an impressive list of club officials, extending from owner Steve Bisciotti to various vice presidents and directors. For sure, the Ravens are a well-structured organization.

At 71,000-seat M&T Bank Stadium in Baltimore, the Ravens' attendances each year average more than 67,000 per game. Thus, the franchise is popular among football fans in the area despite the NFL Redskins being located about 40 miles south in Washington, D.C. That difference in distance, however, has not deterred the Ravens from being very competitive in its division each season against the Steelers, Bengals and Browns. Because Ravens teams tend to excel on defense, new head coach John Harbaugh will likely focus his efforts on scoring more points on offense. If that occurs, this franchise will increase its gate receipts and other revenues, and likely become more prosperous and valuable as a business enterprise in the sport.

Tennessee Oilers

After existing for ten years in the AFL and another 26 in the NFL, the Oilers moved from Houston to Tennessee in 1997 and played its home games for one regular season in Memphis' Liberty Bowl Memorial Stadium. As a result of relocating from Houston, the Oilers' attendances at home games fell by approximately 3,000, from an average of 31,000 in 1996 to 28,000 in 1997. Moreover, the club finished at 8–8 in the 1997 season, three games behind the Steelers and Jaguars in the American Conference's Central Division. Undoubtedly, the Oilers failed to establish a large fan base while located in Memphis. Indeed, the NFL rejected the city when the Memphis Hound Dogs and Mid-South Grizzlies attempted to became a member of the league prior to the late 1990s. In addition, various newspapers reported in early 1996 that the NFL had approved the movement of the Oilers from Memphis to Nashville to play in the league's 1998 season.

Because Oilers owner Bud Adams had permission from the NFL to abandon Memphis after the league's 1997 regular season concluded, he openly highlighted his intentions for the club and discussed his strategy in interviews with the media. Thus, a majority of local sports fans who attended NFL games in Memphis rooted for opposing teams rather than supporting the Oilers. When the 1997 season ended, Adams completed his plans and moved the Oilers franchise from Memphis to Nashville.

Tennessee Oilers/Titans

One year after playing its home games in Vanderbilt Stadium, the club was renamed the Tennessee Titans and opened its 1999 NFL regular season in Nashville's Adelphia Coliseum. Besides these two changes, the team's performances immediately improved while it played as a member of the conference's Central Division from 1996–2001 and since then within the South

Division. Through 2008, the Titans' results consisted of six appearances in the playoffs, winning three division titles and one conference championship. The transformation in this franchise's performances occurred, in part, because of head coach Jeff Fisher and the inputs of such players as quarterbacks Vince Young and Kerry Collins, running backs Eddie George and LenDale White, and field goal kickers Al Del Greco and Rob Bironas.

If Coach Fisher and his staff continue to excel and owner Bud Adams Jr. invests more resources into the development of his franchise, the Titans will challenge the division's Colts, Jaguars, and Texans in each regular season. Based on economic growth in the Nashville area and the club's popularity in the region, the Titans will likely play before capacity crowds at its natural grass, open-air, state-of-the-art stadium, which was renamed LP Field in 2006. If that result occurs in 2009 and in years thereafter, the increasing gate receipts, operating income, and market value of the team should benefit it as a business and reward such stakeholders as Adams and his staff, coaches and players.

To review this section of Chapter 2, 18 NFL teams relocated between 1920 and 2008. As a group, they moved from small and midsized urban places or metropolitan areas to those with larger populations. Furthermore, the majority of clubs, on average, had more fans attend home games in stadiums at their post-move sites, and they had higher win-loss percentages after relocating than before at their pre-move sites. More specifically, NFL franchises with the most impressive results at their post-move locations included the Brooklyn Dodgers, Washington Redskins, and Los Angeles Rams. Meanwhile, three teams whose performances significantly declined after relocating were the Newark Tornadoes, New York Bulldogs, and Oakland Raiders.

It has been more than 87 years since the Staleys left Decatur for Chicago and about 13 since the Tennessee Oilers moved from Memphis to Nashville. To determine whether any current NFL teams may or may not relocate from their territories in the future, the next section briefly discusses some important aspects and implications of this issue.

Future Team Relocations

Based on the research of books and readings in the literature, there are several reasons that may cause a professional sports franchise to move from a city within a small, midsized, or large metropolitan area to another place. In comparing a team's current site to each of its potential locations, these factors include such variables as the differences in economic growth, total population and population growth, differences in income per capita or per household, and the number of other professional teams in the local and prospective markets. Other considerations may be any changes in a franchise's ownership, financial problems of a franchise's current owner or group of owners (syndicate), and the amount and availability of public money to invest in and construct a new stadium for a team or to renovate an existing football stadium.[5]

Given these and other reasons, the following are some facts, insights, and topics to consider about future movements of franchises in the NFL. First, the Minnesota Vikings, New Orleans Saints, and Oakland Raiders are three teams most likely to request permission from the league to relocate somewhere else after the 2009 regular season. Each of them plays in substandard stadiums that existed more than 25 years ago (see Appendix E). The attendances of the Vikings in the Twin Cities and Raiders in the Bay Area rank below average within the league while the Saints performed their home games in other places when the Louisiana Superdome was in disrepair after Hurricane Katrina seriously damaged it. Because of their stadium lease, fan base, and/or commitment to the local community, it is unlikely the other 29 NFL clubs will move in the next ten years.

Second, although the Bills, Jaguars, and Packers each play at home in areas with the smallest populations of the 32 franchises, they will not move anytime soon from, respectively, Buffalo, Jacksonville, and Green Bay. Furthermore, and as indicated in Appendix E, home stadiums of the Bears, Jaguars, and Packers rank as the oldest of all NFL clubs. Even so, the Bears are entrenched in Chicago's Soldier Field and the Packers in Green Bay's Lambeau Field. Meanwhile, the Jaguars established themselves as an expansion team in 1995. Therefore, the Jaguars franchise needs more time to penetrate the sports market in northeast Florida before its owner decides to ask the league to approve its movement from Jacksonville into another area.

Third, the league's revenue-sharing agreement, salary cap, and other amenities essentially protect the NFL teams located in small and midsized markets from folding their operations or seeking another home. Besides the Bills, Jaguars and Packers, other NFL clubs with area populations of less than two million include the Carolina Panthers, Indianapolis Colts, Kansas City Chiefs, New Orleans Saints, and Tennessee Titans. Other than the Saints, these four clubs generate enough revenues each year from their stadiums and television broadcasts of games to exist for a decade or more within their current cities.

Fourth, a large majority of the former sites of NFL franchises are not attractive as future locations of existing or new professional football teams. As listed in Tables 2.2 and 2.3, these places in alphabetical order include Dayton, Decatur, Duluth, Memphis, Newark, Orange, Portsmouth, and Pottsville. Except for Boston and Los Angeles, the other places in these tables contained NFL clubs in 2009. Since the New England Patriots play at home in Foxboro, Massachusetts, Boston is not a viable relocation site for a team. Alternatively, Los Angeles is large, prosperous, and populated enough to host at least one NFL franchise and, perhaps, two. If for some reason such teams as the Raiders, Saints, and/or Vikings experience extreme financial problems, the owners of these franchises may request the league to approve their decision to move into Los Angeles or to another city. In part, this request depends on the growth of their local economies, number and support of football fans within the areas, and/or the replacement or renovation of their hometown stadiums.

Fifth, there are very few occupied or unoccupied areas in the U.S. of sufficient size and wealth to host the thirty-third, thirty-fourth, and thirty-fifth NFL teams. Besides putting a third franchise in New York, another in Chicago and perhaps one in the city of Boston, the five most populated metropolitan areas in America without teams are Los Angeles-Long Beach-Santa Ana, Riverside-San Bernardino-Ontario, Portland-Vancouver-Beaverton, Sacramento-Arden-Arcade-Roseville, and San Jose-Sunnyvale-Santa Clara. Following these five places in population rank are San Antonio, Orlando, and Columbus. States of the latter three areas, however, were overcrowded with NFL clubs in 2009 since Texas hosted the Cowboys and Texans, Florida contained the Buccaneers, Dolphins and Jaguars, and Ohio hosted the Bengals and Browns.

Sixth, a few provinces/territories within Canada may be potential sites for existing NFL clubs that wish to relocate. The most populated of these areas in 2004 were Ontario at 12.6 million, Quebec at 7.6 million, British Columbia at 4.2 million, Alberta at 3.3 million, and Manitoba at 1.2 million. The Canadian Football League (CFL), meanwhile, has teams in some cities of these provinces. In fact, four CFL clubs play as members of the West Division and another four as competitors within the East Division. The population of 5.3 million in Toronto, 3.6 million in Montreal, 2.2 million in Vancouver, and more than 1.1 million each in Edmonton and Calgary support, respectively, the Argonauts, Alouetts, BC Lions, Eskimos, and Stampeders. Since these five cities as well as Hamilton, Saskatchewan, and Winnipeg are occupied with CFL clubs while Ottawa will host an expansion team in 2010, an NFL franchise might propose to invade other territories in Canada, such as Halifax, London, Quebec City, and/or Windsor.

Seventh, there were CFL teams located in a few American cities because of the league's expansion during the 1990s. Although these clubs played only one or two regular seasons in the CFL, they performed at home in Baltimore, Birmingham, Las Vegas, Memphis, Sacramento, San Antonio, and Shreveport. Except for Baltimore, the other six U.S. cities contain no professional teams in the NFL or MLB. As a strategy, the NFL may form a minor league and place professional football clubs in these and other locations to determine their feasibility and potential as future sites.

Eighth, the most popular team sports in Mexico are baseball and outdoor soccer. Nevertheless, the country has four cities with more than 1.5 in population. These include Mexico City with 19.5 million, Guadalajara with 4.1 million, Monterrey with 3.6 million, and Puebla with 1.8 million. The probability of any NFL teams moving to one or more of these places before 2015 is equal to or about zero percent. However, other than provinces in Canada, such metropolitan areas in Mexico may welcome teams in a developmental football league that clubs in the NFL subsidize.

In short, these are a few facts, implications, and topics regarding the potential movements of NFL teams from domestic areas into other U.S. sports markets and/or foreign territories. From a business perspective, I identified and discussed them in this chapter to reveal how complicated and risky relocation decisions are, and will be, for the league and its member franchises.

Summary

Chapter 2 focused on when, where, and why 18 NFL franchises had moved their operations between 1920 and 2008, and whether any relocations of the current 32 teams will or will not occur in the future. Data and other information are contained in the chapter's three tables. In total, the tables provided some descriptive statistics about the distribution of NFL teams' home areas in various years; these clubs' number of regular seasons and also their area populations before and after they had relocated; and the average home attendances and win-loss percentages at their pre-move and post-move sites.

Basically the data denoted that the proportion of NFL franchises located in very small–small areas had declined in 2000 when compared to 1920, while those located in midsized and large–very large areas each increased in number and proportion during this period. Furthermore, eight (44 percent) of the teams that had moved played relatively more regular seasons at their post-move sites, ten (55 percent) of them transferred to more populated markets, 11 (61 percent) of the group had higher attendances at their home stadiums after they moved, and ten (55 percent) of the 18 won a larger proportion of their regular season games at the post-move sites but not necessarily more division titles, conference and NFL championships, and/or Super Bowls.

The final section in this chapter discussed some important facts, implications, and insights regarding the future movements, if any, of existing NFL franchises. The section highlighted which of the league's teams may or may not move, what are the most and least attractive metropolitan areas in the United States as places for the professional football clubs that seek new homes, and how major provinces/territories in Canada and cities in Mexico rank as potential sports sites for NFL franchises. In sum, Chapter 2 analyzes relocation as a prior, current, and future business strategy of the league and its member teams and their owners.

3

Franchise Organizations and Operations

History

Since the early 1900s, it has become increasingly complex to successfully acquire, and operate a franchise as a business enterprise in the National Football League. Indeed, the primary goals of such early teams in the league as the Canton Bulldogs, Hammond Pros, and Rochester Jeffersons had been simply to locate a stadium or another facility within their cities in which the team could play, recruit a number of local athletes, and collect enough money from admissions and any concessions to finish the regular season. These goals were very difficult to accomplish for franchise owners as well as league officials, especially during the league's early decades, because professional football had not yet established itself as a popular team sport within the United States.[1]

While the sport emerged and then matured throughout the twentieth and the early twenty-first centuries, however, NFL franchises had to deal with exceedingly more difficult, costly, and sensitive types of circumstances. Many of the matters involved reforms that the league adopted, which resulted from the conduct and decisions of some team owners, coaches and players, and occurred because of policies made by businesses, political groups, and other organizations within the U.S. Consequently, the professional football evolved into more of a regional and eventually national activity.

More specifically, between 1920 and 2008 inclusive, policies implemented by the NFL affected the short-run development of professional football and also improved the long-run economic environment of franchises that played within the league. By decade, a few of these actions are described below.

During the 1920s, for example, the Chicago Bears owner formulated a rule whereby the league's teams were prohibited from signing any players whose college class had not graduated. Second, the NFL president Joe Carr secured the league's future by eliminating some financially weak clubs and finding quality players and reassigning them to a limited number of success-ful teams. In the 1930s, the NFL developed such innovations as placing inbounds lines and hash marks on the field, installing posts at the two goal lines, and legalizing the forward pass on offense. Furthermore, the league approved Philadelphia Eagles owner Bert Bell's proposal to hold an annual draft of college players, with teams selecting these athletes in reverse order of their finish in the previous regular season.

In the 1940s, the NFL adopted the free substitution of players, man-dated the wearing of helmets by players, permitted the use of a flexible but artificial tee on kickoffs, established a regular season schedule of ten games, and announced a merger with the All-American Football Conference. Mean-while, in the 1950s, many NFL franchises signed contracts with television broadcasting companies, including teams like the Los Angeles Rams, which had all of its home and away games televised. Second, the DuMont Network paid $25,000 for the rights to the league's championship game, and in 1955 the National Broadcasting Corporation (NBC) paid the NFL a rights fee of approximately $100,000. for the rights to televise the championship.

The 1960s and 1970s were important decades for the development, growth, and increasing popularity of the NFL for a large majority of its mem-ber franchises. In addition to an expansion of the number of franchises in the league during the 1960s, a judge ruled against the American Football League (AFL) in an antitrust suit that charged the NFL with monopoly and conspir-acy regarding player signings, television rights, and other economic matters. Furthermore, the NFL purchased Ed Sabol's Blair Motion Pictures and renamed the company NFL Films in 1965. Four years later, the league announced an agreement with the American Broadcasting Corporation (ABC) to televise a new series of games titled *Monday Night Football*. In the 1970s, the NFL signed a number of lucrative business contracts with television net-works, joined the National District Attorneys Association to oppose legalized gambling on any professional team sports, ratified a five-year collective bar-gaining agreement with the NFL Players Association (NFLPA), and adopted a four-game preseason and 16-game regular season.

During the 1980s, the league's franchise owners agreed to play a series of preseason football games in Western Europe. Moreover, the NFL experi-enced two players strikes, established a special payment program to benefit former players, and won an antitrust case against the United States Football League. Then in the 1990s, the NFL expanded its American Bowl series of preseason games to the cities of Berlin and Montreal and formed a new divi-sion in New York titled NFL Enterprises, which was responsible for home video programs and special domestic and international television programming. In addition, the league passed a rule whereby club owners could own professional teams in other sports located in their home market, that was without an NFL franchise.

Between 2000 and 2008, other events affected the professional football business in America. First, the NFL clubs agreed to pool visiting teams' shares of gate receipts from all preseason and regular season games and then equally divide these amounts earnings their franchises. Second, the league and DirecTV announced a five-year extension of the NFL Sunday Ticket subscription television package for fans. Third, the NFL and NFLPA jointly created USA Football, which has become a national advocacy organization that represents and supports all levels of amateur football in the nation.

Fourth, the league strengthened its steroids program when it adopted testosterone testing and then tripled the random tests of players during the league's offseason, added to the banned substances list, and revised a policy to further test players for designer drugs. Fifth, the NFL's Retired Players Association, Alumni Association, Charities, and its Pro Football Hall of Fame joined with the NFLPA to organize an alliance that coordinates medical support services to improve the health of former players.

Because of these and other actions implemented and enforced by the league since the 1920s, current franchise owners are more aware of and educated about the NFL's policies and better understand their roles as members of this elite group. Whether they fail or succeed as and owners of a professional sports business still depends, in part, on how well they manage their organizations.

In the next two sections of this chapter, I discuss in detail the organizational structures, officials, and offices within NFL franchises of the American and National Football Conferences that existed in 2008. These sections, in turn, reveal the business and prominent decision makers of these franchises and their responsibilities as executives and senior managers and supervisors.

Franchise Organizations

Throughout the years of the twentieth century, economic and social conditions within the United States and other nations changed and forced businesses in major industries of the private sector to modernize, reform, and restructure themselves as organizations. In professional team sports, for example, franchises in the NFL responded according to these conditions and then periodically had to readjust internally in order to survive and meet the demands of their communities, fans, local governments, team partners, players, sponsors, and other stakeholders. As a result, before the early 2000s,

TABLE 3.1 NATIONAL FOOTBALL LEAGUE TYPES OF FRANCHISE OFFICIALS, BY TEAM, 2008

| | | *Types of Officials* | | | |
Team	President	Executive/ Senior VP	VP	Director	Total
American Football Conference					
Baltimore Ravens	1	2	11	18	32
Buffalo Bills	1	4	8	6	19
Cincinnati Bengals	1	2	3	11	17
Cleveland Browns	0	3	5	18	26
Denver Broncos	1	2	5	3	11
Houston Texans	1	2	5	21	29
Indianapolis Colts	1	3	7	7	18
Jacksonville Jaguars	0	3	2	8	13
Kansas City Chiefs	1	2	2	15	20
Miami Dolphins	1	4	1	12	18
New England Patriots	1	0	8	8	17
New York Jets	1	3	2	15	21
Oakland Raiders	NR	NR	NR	NR	NR
Pittsburgh Steelers	1	0	2	4	7
San Diego Chargers	1	6	1	14	22
Tennessee Titans	1	3	4	15	23
National Football Conference					
Arizona Cardinals	1	1	6	11	19
Atlanta Falcons	1	1	5	15	22
Carolina Panthers	2	0	0	14	16
Chicago Bears	1	0	1	28	30
Dallas Cowboys	1	1	2	14	18
Detroit Lions	1	4	0	7	12
Green Bay Packers	1	1	3	20	25
Minnesota Vikings	1	0	6	14	21
New Orleans Saints	1	3	5	11	20
New York Giants	1	2	7	19	29
Philadelphia Eagles	1	3	4	14	22
St. Louis Rams	2	2	6	2	12
San Francisco 49ers	0	1	4	15	20
Seattle Seahawks	1	3	5	8	17
Tampa Bay Buccaneers	1	3	0	16	20
Washington Redskins	0	4	1	8	13

Note: To clarify, columns two through five include the number of various types of top-level managerial positions within these football organizations. To avoid the double counting of officials, these lists are not the total number of personnel who had occupied each position. VP is Vice President. The slash (/) indicates that column three consisted of two positions, Executive Vice President and Senior Vice President. The totals beneath Director include only one executive, senior, associate, or assistant director. Some teams' presidents also served as chairman of the board, chief executive officer, chief operating officer, and/or general manager. In 2008, the Carolina Panthers had two president positions, one titled Panthers Football LLC and the other named Panthers Stadium LLC. The St. Louis Rams had a President and a position titled President, Football Operations/General Manager. The Oakland Raiders did not report (NR) such club officials as President, Vice President, and Director in 2008.

Source: *2008 NFL Record & Fact Book*.

a typical franchise in the league had similar types of officials in offices that strove to maximize profit or market value.

As reported in the *2008 NFL Record & Fact Book*, there were different combinations of officials in jobs of each of the 32 clubs. To be specific, Table 3.1 provides a distribution of five officials who had held the most important offices within each of these professional football organizations in 2008. As denoted in various columns of the table, there were some major and minor differences between them.[2]

Listed in column two of the table, four (12 percent) of the teams did not have an individual assigned with the title of president in 2008. Ranked below each of these four franchise owners, the Browns had a vice chairman, the Jaguars a chairman/chief executive officer, the 49ers a chief executive officer, and the Redskins a chief operating officer. Thus, these men performed as executives at the top level of their respective organizations and made decisions similar to the presidents in the other 28.

In contrast, two (6 percent) of the clubs sported two presidents. That is, reporting to the Panthers founder/owner Jerry Richardson were his sons, Marc and Jon, as the president of Panthers Football LLC and president of Panthers Stadium LLC. Meanwhile, the executives that reported to the Rams owner/chairman Dale "Chip" Rosenbloom were president John Shaw and President of Football Operations/General Manager Jay Zygmunt. Apparently, the Panthers and Rams separated responsibilities of the highest office of their businesses and therefore assigned two qualified individuals to preside over and operate the franchise.

For business and personal reasons, the Oakland Raiders listed its top official in the *2008 NFL Record & Fact Book* to be chief executive officer Amy Trask. As an executive, she likely reported to owner Al Davis. In 2008, Trask was one of the highest-ranking woman officials among the 32 NFL franchises. Moreover, there were other women within the hierarchy of the Raiders organization that year. Indeed, they had managed such departments as Multi-

Cultural Initiatives and Youth Initiatives and the team's cheerleading squad, nicknamed the Raiderettes. Therefore, as a veteran franchise owner, Davis has ethnically diversified his pool of executives so they could be successful in applying their experiences and talents in these three important and useful functions of the club.

In column three of Table 3.1, there are five NFL teams listed without officials assigned in the position of executive/senior vice president. Within each of these organizations, the role of executive/senior vice president was fulfilled, in part, by Patriots president Jonathan Kraft, Steelers president Arthur J. Rooney II, Panthers presidents Mark and Jon Richardson, Bears president and chief executive officer Ted Phillips, and for the Vikings, co-owner/president Mark Wilf and co-owner/vice chairman Leonard Wilf.

At the other extreme of this distribution, the Chargers employed six executive/senior vice presidents in 2008. Four of these officials also served as the general manager, chief operating officer, football operations officer or financial officer, while the other two officials had no specific subtitle. Thus, San Diego president and chief executive officer Dean Spanos had six subordinates to supervise, which was a relatively wide span of control for any person with authority in an organization. Evidently, Chargers owner Alex Spanos trusted that Dean was skilled enough to perform his assignments and efficiently operate the Chargers' business despite the large number of executives that reported to him.

Besides these six clubs, there were five (15 percent) of the total with one executive/senior vice president and another 20 (62 percent) with two, three, or four of them. In other words, the majority of NFL franchises in 2008 had more than one but less than five officials who ranked below an owner and also the president, chairman, chief executive officer, and/or vice chairman on their organization charts. As mentioned before for the president, the Oakland Raiders did not assign any of its officials with a title that consisted of executive/senior vice president.

As denoted in column four of Table 3.1, 28 NFL franchises had at least one vice president as an official in their office. Consequently, other than the Raiders, Panthers, Lions and Buccaneers, more than 87 percent of the teams had a position in their organization titled vice president. Those that had the most of these officials included the Ravens with 11, and the Bills and Patriots with eight each. Alternatively, only one vice president worked to complete assignments for the Dolphins, Chargers, Bears, and Redskins.

Since the average number of junior vice presidents was four, 14 (43 percent) of the franchises had more than average while the same proportion employed fewer than four of them. As in other types of organizations within the private sector, these vice presidents tended to report to executive/senior vice presidents. Nevertheless, for those five clubs without the latter officials, their vice presidents, if any, must have received assignments from the franchise's president or another official at the highest level.

As expected, there was more of a deviation in the distribution of vice presidents among the various NFL teams in 2008 than the differences in the number of presidents and in the quantity of executive/senior vice presidents. These various distributions occurred, in part, because of how professional football organizations were structured and existed to perform as business enterprises. Such factors as budgets, historical traditions, owner preferences, and types of tasks to be completed by officials determined whether the hierarchy of one or more of the 32 franchises in 2008 was relatively flat or steep, and shaped from top to bottom like a pyramid or inverted. Interestingly, however, a few teams had unique organizational structures in which there were more presidents than executive/senior vice presidents, but fewer vice presidents than executive/senior vice presidents.

Another type of official in a typical NFL franchise is a director whose subordinates may or may not include assistants and associates. As indicated in column five of Table 3.1, ten (33 percent) of these franchises had fewer than ten directors, 18 (58 percent) employed between ten and 20 directors, and three (nine percent) of them used 20 or more directors. While the average number of directors was 13 per team, the distribution of these officials across teams varied between a high of 28 for the Bears and a low of two for the Rams.

In being the most common officials within NFL franchises, directors are low-level managers or supervisors who likely report to vice presidents or executive/senior vice presidents. Besides the Bears, the Texans, Packers, and Giants also employed a relatively large number of directors, whereas the Rams, Broncos and Steelers each had fewer than five. After I compared the distributions of two types of officials listed in Table 3.1, there were approximately three directors assigned to a franchise for each of their vice presidents. This suggests that several of the 32 clubs had too many or too few directors on their staff and thus under- or over-utilized them in performing different office tasks.

Based on the distributions of these four types of officials, only ten (32 percent) of the NFL franchises in 2008 had an organizational structure whereby the number of officials incrementally increased from the president to director. These included, for example, such clubs as the Bengals and Titans in the league's American Conference, and Saints and Eagles in its National Conference. Thus, more than two-thirds of the various franchises in Table 3.1 should consider restructuring their organizations to establish a more efficient and uniform allocation of officials, from the president or chief executive at the top level in the office to director at the lowest managerial position.

To be sure, the totals in column six of the table are interesting numbers to analyze and understand. It appears, for example, that in 2008 the Ravens, with a total of 32, the Bears with 30, and then the Texans and Giants, each with 29, had an excessive number of these officials. In contrast, the Steelers with seven officials, the Broncos with 11, and the Lions and Rams each with 12 employed an insufficient number to be effective and complete their organization's tasks. In other words, the four former clubs may have used less technology but more personnel to perform various office jobs or they had simply too many executive assignments; the latter four clubs delegated responsibilities for accounting, human resources, marketing, and operations to employees who were also assistants or associates to vice presidents and directors. As competitors within their conferences, a historical difference among teams in these two groups was that the Ravens, Giants, and Steelers were much more successful in their regular season performances during 2008 than the Bears, Texans, Lions, and Rams.

Another interesting issue to analyze is the distribution of these four officials within some franchises. Unsurprisingly most teams with 20 or more officials assigned at least 85 percent of them to act as junior vice presidents and/or directors, but so did a few clubs with a dozen or fewer officials. In contrast, franchises with more than 12 but fewer than 20 had significantly different proportions of them. To illustrate, four (22 percent) of the Colts' officials consisted of a president and executive/senior vice presidents versus two (11 percent) for the Cowboys and one (about six percent) for the Patriots.

Thus the groups of teams with the most and least numbers of officials tended to be more alike and consistent between each other in types than the franchises at or near the average number of officials. In short, a majority of decision makers in NFL franchises had different careers, experiences, and jobs while being successful executives in industries besides sports. Consequently, as members of a professional football league, they each established and operated their organizations objectively in order to be efficient and profitable.

Team Owners

Since the league originally formed in 1920, individuals or different types of groups have primarily owned its teams. Prior to 1960, however, at least two NFL franchises in financial distress temporarily returned to the league and then dissolved, merged, and/or resold. This occurred in 1952, for example, when owner Ted Collins returned his New York Yankees team to the league. Yet later a group of Dallas executives purchased this franchise for $300,000 from the NFL and eventually moved it to Texas. One year earlier, however, owner Abraham Watner had returned his Baltimore Colts franchise and player contracts to the league for $50,000 because he had lost more than $100,000 while operating it during the 1950 regular season. Therefore, because of selling 15,000 tickets for games in the 1953 season, a group of Baltimore businesspersons successfully reorganized the Colts. Thus, the NFL awarded these entrepreneurs the draft rights and players from the defunct Dallas Texans.[3]

Besides reorganization of the New York Yankees and Baltimore Colts, the league also assumed total control of the Frankford Yellow Jackets and Newark Tornadoes in 1931. Subsequently, the league sold the assets and other rights of the former club in 1933 to Bert Bell and Lud Wray, who then renamed their team the Philadelphia Eagles. Meanwhile, the latter franchise was suspended for one season after which the NFL sold it for approximately $7,500 in 1932 to a new syndicate of owners. That group, in turn, moved the team to eastern Massachusetts and changed its name to the Boston Braves.

For an overview of the NFL's 32 franchise owners as of 2008, I selected a few characteristics that reveal some basic facts about the group and financial information with respect to their teams (see Appendix F). First, families or their personal estates or trusts have owned the Chicago Bears for 89 years (through 2008) and Kansas City Chiefs since 1960. Of the remaining 30 clubs in the league, 29 were the property of either a person and/or his or her syndicate, while a corporation has owned the Green Bay Packers since 1923.

Second, three of the most experienced owners within this group of 32 include the Pittsburgh Steelers' Dan Rooney, the Buffalo Bills' Ralph Wilson, and the Oakland Raiders' Al Davis. The league had charged Rooney $2,500 for the rights to acquire his expansion team in 1933 while Wilson paid $25,000 and Davis $180,000 to buy their clubs prior to the merger of the NFL and American Football League (AFL) in 1969–1970.

Third, four men became majority owners of an NFL franchise during years of the 2000s. Their investments in, respectively, the Falcons, Ravens, Vikings, and Jets have provided each of them with significant financial returns as denoted in Appendix F. In fact, these clubs have appreciated from their year of purchase by totals of 60 percent for Atlanta owner Arthur Blank, 77 percent for Baltimore owner Steve Bisciotti, 40 percent for Minnesota's Zygi Wilf, and 84 percent for Johnson's Jets. Fourth, the 49ers' Denise DeBartolo York shared ownership of this San Francisco-based club in 2008 with her husband, John York, and limited partners Rick and Carla Morabito and Franklin Mieuli. As such, different members of the Morabito family have been involved with the franchise since 1946, with Mieuli beginning in the mid–1960s.

Fifth, the amounts spent by this group of owners to purchase their clubs from the league ranged from a minimum of $100 for the Bears in 1920 to a maximum of $750 million for the Redskins in 1999. The other lowest and highest prices paid for teams were, respectively, $2,500 for the Steelers (then named Pittsburgh Pirates) in 1933 and $700 million for the Texans in 1999. Furthermore, the owners of original teams in the AFL had each paid a fee of $25,000 to join the league in 1959–1960.

Sixth, 19 (approximately 60 percent) of NFL clubs in 2008 had market values that exceeded $1 billion. Indeed, these amounts had greatly appreciated in recent years, especially for the league's teams that had performed at home games or will play them in new stadiums. For franchises with the lowest values, such as the Vikings, Raiders, 49ers, and Jaguars, they lag behind the others, in part, because their stadiums are obsolete and thus do not earn enough revenues for them to appreciate any more than an average return.

According to one sportswriter, the Green Bay Packers are the best-managed NFL franchise from an organizational perspective. From the 1920s, it has existed as a nonprofit corporation that now consists of 112,015 shareholders, many of whom own only one share. Because of revenue sharing, a salary cap, and the club's performances in regular season and postseason games since the early 1990s, the Packers have accumulated a contingency fund of $127 million. Besides, a seven-member executive committee chosen from a 45-member board elected by the shareholders makes most of the team's important business decisions.

While the Packers' board selects the franchise's chief executive officer, the executive committee approves major expenses and meets each month to review football operations and financial matters. Both of these groups serve pro bono, that is, for the good of the public or local community. In 2003, the *Sports Business Journal* declared the Packers to be the world's most efficiently operated sports franchise. After executive Bob Harlan retired from the franchise, Mark Murphy replaced him to become the club's current president and chief executive officer.

Based upon research into the history of NFL teams, the Carolina Panthers' Jerry Richardson and his syndicate is a model of ownership. Born in Spring Hope, North Carolina, Richardson played football as a halfback and fullback at Wofford College in South Carolina. Then after graduating in 1958, he performed as an end in 22 games for the Baltimore Colts in 1959–60. After selling his numerous Hardees fast-food restaurants for a huge profit, he organized a group of Carolina businesspersons during the late 1980s and early 1990s and successfully led them to bid for and then awarded by the NFL an expansion franchise to be located in the Charlotte area.

Rather than request public money from the city, county, and/or state government, Richardson's organization used the proceeds from the sale of Permanent Seat Licenses to construct the team's 73,500-seat stadium that opened in 1996. As the club's majority owner since the mid–1990s, he has been well respected as a person by Panthers coaches and players and those from other NFL clubs because of his commitment to the sport and close relationships with businesses, fans, the media, and others in the local community and throughout the Carolinas. After Richardson had a heart transplant at a Charlotte hospital, others also praised him for his dedication, ethics and leadership, and his beliefs in community affairs, family, and the Panthers organization.

Since most but not all of them have retired from the sport, several NFL team owners — who may also have coached and/or played in the league — were inducted into the Pro Football Hall of Fame in Canton, Ohio, prior to 2008. These prominent individuals include the following men and one or more of their franchises: Bert Bell of the Philadelphia Eagles and Pittsburgh Steelers; John Conzelman of the Detroit Panthers; Al Davis of the Los Angeles and Oakland Raiders; George Halas of the Decatur/Chicago Staleys and Chicago Bears; Lamar Hunt of the Dallas Texans and Kansas City Chiefs; Wellington Mara of the New York Giants; George Preston Marshall of the Boston Braves/Redskins and Washington Redskins; Dan Reeves of the Cleveland/Los Angeles Rams; and, Art and Dan Rooney of the Pittsburgh Pirates/Steelers.

Coaching Staffs

To be sure, a vital task for any NFL franchise owner is to recruit, hire, and compensate a head coach who will be successful in games and then allow him to choose a group of assistants and other personnel as a staff. To report the coaching organization of 16 teams in the American and National Conference, I developed a table that shows differences and similarities in the staffs of these 32 professional football clubs with respect to the league's 2008 regular season (see Appendix G).

Besides one head coach, the highest and lowest number of other coaches among the staff of teams in each category of Appendix G were as follows: on defense, eight and three; on offense, ten and four; on special teams, two and one; and in the other category — which includes assistant and associate head coaches, coaches for strength and conditioning, and special and staff assistants — seven and zero. For these clubs, the Vikings had a total coaching staff of 24 in 2008 while the Steelers employed the lowest number with only 13 on their staff.

To highlight the coaching groups of a few NFL teams, the Texans had the most coaches on defense and the Patriots the fewest; the Browns and Vikings each used the most coaches on offense, and the Patriots the least with four; and the Raiders allocated the largest number of coaches for other assignments while the Texans and Steelers had the smallest number of them. Thus, on average, each team hired one head coach plus approximately five-to-six on defense, seven on offense, one-to-two on special teams, and two-to-three for other duties. The average of the 32 teams, therefore, was between 17 and 18 coaches on their staff.

Some NFL clubs had a unique distribution of their coaching staffs. For example, such teams as the Patriots and Steelers excelled with fewer than 11 total defensive and offensive coaches while the Texans and Vikings each used 17. As such, the former clubs play competitively and win championships because they assign their most productive coaches to train players at different skilled positions, such as the line to block, tackle, and otherwise protect or rush quarterbacks, in the secondary to defend against passes and also tackle opposing runners, and in the backfield to run for yards and first downs and to score touchdowns. Furthermore, the Texans and Steelers did not assign any coaching staff to roles in strength and conditioning, being an associate or assistant head coach, or working in quality control. Evidently, these two teams' coaches on defense, offense, and special teams had also performed these other jobs in addition to their primary duties.

In short it was remarkable that some NFL clubs, which appeared to be understaffed, won titles in the league's 2008 postseason while other teams with more than the average number of coaches failed to succeed in their respective divisions. Indeed, the former franchises included the Cardinals, Panthers and Titans, while three of the latter were the Broncos, Lions and 49ers. Consequently it is which — and not how many — coaches that owners decide to recruit and hire that determine an NFL team's success during the majority of the league's regular seasons and postseasons. This suggests, in turn, that the best decisions in selecting their coaching staffs in 2008 were made by such owners as the Dolphins' Wayne Huizenga, the Patriots' Robert Kraft and the Steelers' Dan Rooney, and the worst by proprietors like the Rams' Dale Rosenbloom, the Seahawks' Paul Allen, and the Detroit Lions' William Clay Ford.

To acknowledge their important and memorable contributions to the sport, the Pro Football Hall of Fame contains a number of former NFL coaches. After reviewing them as a group, I selected ten of these coaches and determined their most memorable team. They are mentioned here and listed in alphabetical order by last name as follows: George Allen of the Washington Redskins, Paul Brown of the Cleveland Browns, Bud Grant of the Minnesota Vikings, Tom Landry of the Dallas Cowboys, Vince Lombardi of the Green Bay Packers, John Madden of the Oakland Raiders, Earle Neal of the Philadelphia Eagles, Steve Owen of the New York Giants, Don Shula of the Miami Dolphins, and Bill Walsh of the San Francisco 49ers.

The previous paragraphs conclude my discussion of how the NFL franchises had existed in 2008 as organizations with their different combinations and types of officers. Furthermore, they provided some information with respect to their owner or owners and the teams' head coaches and coaching staffs.

Based on those topics and to further discuss the business aspects of the sport, in the next section I focus on and examine the specific offices within 32 football franchises and what tasks the offices included, how they ranked in priority to accomplish their organization's mission, and why they differed with respect to three different types of officials. Because of this analysis, the readers of *Football Fortunes* will appreciate why operating an NFL franchise as a commercial enterprise is a complex, dynamic, and rewarding challenge for their owners and especially for officials and other members within their departments.

Franchise Operations

Most small businesses in America have limited assets, budgets, bank credit lines and resources, and insufficient inflows of cash and revenue. Furthermore, their owners lack the knowledge, experience, and training necessary for full information about their markets. Thus, these entrepreneurs likely outsource to other companies some or all of their internal tasks, such as preparing and analyzing financial statements, generating sales projections, establishing marketing plans, interpreting contracts, and recruiting new employees.

In contrast to small firms, however, the majority of midsized partnerships and most of the large and very large corporations located in the U.S. have money deposits, personnel, and resources to perform these and other specialized tasks within their own organization. Yet in a number of enterprises within the private sector, some of this work is neglected each year and therefore causes short- and long-run problems with clients, competitors, and customers relative to their products and/or services.

During the early-to-mid twentieth century, NFL franchise owners and their executives did not need to be highly educated and knowledgeable about topics in finance, operations management, or modern business methods. Thus, with guidance from a respective team owner and his or her chief executive officer, chairman and/or vice chairman, such staff were told how to dedicate a majority of their efforts concentrating on a few basic but time-consuming tasks.

But as the sport of professional football developed and gradually expanded into cities across America and NFL teams became increasingly competitive, this progress required that different and more sophisticated and specialized business standards be assigned and completed by personnel who worked in offices of clubs within the league. As a result, the in-house activities of franchises changed from being cheap and simple to expensive and complex.

In other words, the owners and officials of NFL teams continued to focus on winning games but also had to become more efficient and profitable in their off-the-field business operations. In turn, those franchises that had organized an outstanding staff prospered and perhaps earned increasing amounts of revenue, and thus maximized their value in dollars as business enterprises.

Since the 1950s–1960s, such actions as the national broadcast of NFL games on television, the construction and utilization of multimillion-dollar football stadiums within metropolitan areas, the increasing inflation of coaches and players salaries, and the involvement of professional athletes in community affairs had, in total, required faster and more precise decision-making by the owners and officials of franchises. Moreover, such actions forced them to invest more resources in computers, software and support systems, and to satisfy a need for accurate and timely services from offices of all NFL teams. In fact, these were events and opportunities that not only changed the composition and organizational structure of NFL franchises throughout the twentieth century, they also influenced the financial, marketing, and operating aspects of these relatively small but popular sports enterprises.

In the literature on sports, there is very little data and other information about jobs, types of officials, and internal work schedules of personnel and staff within NFL teams. Nevertheless, the *2008 NFL Record & Fact Book* reported some specific titles of offices and names of officials for each of the franchises in the league. Although this publication does not describe these positions in any detail, it indicates to some extent what are and are not important responsibilities that existed in 2008 for operating pro football franchises from a commercial perspective.

Therefore, based on information reported in the 2008 edition of the *NFL Record & Fact Book*, I created Table 3.2. Essentially, it lists the primary and some secondary offices of 32 NFL clubs and three types of officials who may or may not have been employed within each of these offices. Consequently, the following paragraphs highlight some office titles and numbers of officials presented in the table that reveal any relationships about the distributions of them among various franchises in the league. As a result, readers of *Football Fortunes* will learn how these NFL organizations decided to operate and successfully accomplish their internal workloads and likewise be efficient while competing in regular season and postseason games against their rivals in the American and/or National Conferences.[4]

Offices and Officials

Entered in column one of Table 3.2, there are 24 different categories of offices for 32 NFL franchises as of 2008. As such, these offices appear from first to twenty-fourth in the column based on the total number of officials who were assigned within each of them. Furthermore, columns two-to-four of the table include, respectively, 49 executive/senior vice presidents (approximately two per office), 97 vice presidents (four per office), and 278 directors (11 per office).

Column five, meanwhile, contains 424 total officials employed in the 24 categories of offices (17 per office) in 2008. However, because they occupy few employees, any offices of teams with five officials or fewer are not included in column one of Table 3.2. Even so, the second part of this section discusses

TABLE 3.2 NFL FRANCHISES SELECTED
OFFICES, BY TYPES OF OFFICIALS, 2008

	Types of Officials			
Offices	Executive/ Sr. VP	VP	Director	Total
Football Administration/Operations	11	9	24	44
Player Development/Personnel/Programs/Relations	1	8	25	34
Community/Public Relations	1	7	23	31
Marketing/Marketing Services/Sales	5	14	12	31
Video Director/Operations	0	0	29	29
Ticket Operations/Sales	1	5	20	26
Pro Personnel/Scouting	1	2	19	22
College Scouting	0	1	18	19
Stadium/Facilities Operations	1	5	13	19
Information Technology/Systems	0	4	14	18
Security Operations/Systems	0	2	15	17
Media Relations/Products	1	3	12	16
Corporate/Football Communications	0	8	6	14
Business Affairs/Development/Operations	6	2	5	13
Chief Financial Officer/Treasurer	7	6	0	13
Broadcast Administration/Operations	0	2	9	11
Finance Administration/Controller	2	6	3	11
Corporate Development/Sales	0	5	5	10
Legal/General Counsel	4	5	1	10
Human Resources	0	1	8	9
General Manager	8	0	0	8
Premium Seating/Services/Suites	0	1	6	7
Cheerleaders	0	0	6	6
Event Entertainment/Services	0	1	5	6

Note: VP represents Vice President. In column one, the slash (/) indicates that these offices of franchises had different but nearly identical titles because they performed essentially the same tasks. Team A, for example, may have assigned officials to complete tasks in Football Administration while Team B had one or more of them in Football Operations. Executive Vice President and Senior Vice President are each included as officials in the totals of teams in column two. To avoid double or triple counting, each office of a team includes as an official only one director or type of director, such as an assistant, executive, or senior. That is, if Team C had an assistant and executive director, only one of them counted in column four. Although offices with five officials or fewer are not included in Table 3.2, they are briefly discussed later in a subsection of this chapter.

Source: *2008 NFL Record & Fact Book*, 35–230.

these other offices and their minor but perhaps useful roles within one or more NFL franchises.

Football Administration/Operations

Besides a franchise's owner — and if they exist in the enterprise — its president, chairman and/or vice chairman, this is the most populated office of teams. In fact, about 50 percent of the officials who occupy it ranked as an executive, senior, or junior vice president. In 2008, such clubs as the Broncos, Packers, and 49ers had more than two individuals in positions within football administration/operations.

Generally, any decisions that involve the football program of a franchise require the approval of and/or review by officials from this office. Thus, all NFL clubs appoint someone who is responsible for the team's administration and/or operations. These persons in 2008 included, for example, the Ravens' Pat Moriarty and the Bills' Jim Overdorf in the American Conference, and the Falcons' Nick Polk and the Panthers' Brandon Beane of the National Conference.

Player Development/Personnel/Programs/Relations

Because this office had at least four different titles but similar activities among the 32 franchises in 2008, I consolidated them into one. Primarily headed by some type of director, this office was responsible for any matters that affected the development of football players and their relationships with an NFL franchise. For example, any contractual commitments required by the league's Collective Bargaining Agreement and this document's impact and influence with respect to the behavior, conduct, and employment of teams' athletes may be issues monitored by officials within this office.

Some clubs like the Chiefs, Vikings, and Saints each had a vice president and director assigned to make decisions that concerned player development/personnel/programs/relations. As examples of specific officials assigned to this office within the American Conference in 2008, there was Eric Ball of the Bengals and Jerry Butler of the Browns, while in the National Conference two officials were the Cardinals' Anthony Edwards and the Bears' Isaiah Harris.

Community/Public Relations

Most of the coaches and players on NFL teams expect to engage in some type of charitable activities, events meetings, and/or programs within their local communities. Thus, the officials in this office, who tend to be directors, are responsible to assist coaches and players by scheduling them for public appearances, making sure they meet their commitments, encouraging them to interact with others at an activity site, and recording their actions for publication in the franchise's newsletters to fans and/or in reports to the media and community.

In recent years, these relationships have become increasingly important for the personnel on teams. That is, they should be available and willing to participate in such programs within poor, middle class, and wealthy neighborhoods of their team's cities and counties. Four officials who served in this office during 2008 were, in the American Conference, the Colts' Craig Kelley and the Chiefs' Brenda Sniezek, and in the National Conference, the Cowboys' Rich Dalrymple and the Lions' Tim Pendell.

Marketing/Marketing Services/Sales

As denoted in Table 3.2, there were a total of 19 vice presidents and 12 directors from franchises assigned to this office in 2008. Tied for third with 31 officials, marketing is a vital task of any business enterprise, especially for franchises within the NFL. Members of this office dealt with advertisements, promotional campaigns, and the sales of any products and/or services related to their NFL teams.

More specifically, this office's vice presidents and directors made decisions about the marketing of merchandise at retailers in the local area, ads in their stadium during home games, and promotions on the Internet, radio stations and television networks, and in magazines, newspapers, and trade journals. Some prominent people in marketing for three American Conference clubs during 2008 were Patriots vice president Jennifer Ferron, Steelers director Tony Quatrini, and Chargers chief marketing officer Ken Derrett.

Video Director/Operations

Twenty-nine (approximately 91 percent) NFL franchises had one or more officials assigned to this office in 2008. The Oakland Raiders employed three people in video operations; however, they were not designated as club officials in that year. The Broncos and Rams did not indicate the office of video director within their respective organizations. Interestingly, there were no vice presidents that worked in this office and only a few assistant, executive, or senior directors.

Simply put, any video tasks of the league's teams in 2008 were performed by a person with the title of director and his or her staff. Undoubtedly, this franchise official had to coordinate with such offices as football operations, community relations, and marketing to schedule videos and other projects that needed filmed. Two of these directors within teams of the National Conference during that year included the Packers' Bob Eckberg and the Vikings' Bob Marcus.

Ticket Operations/Sales

Any of the major and minor activities that involved ticket sales and other tasks at NFL preseason and regular season games, and if necessary at postseason games were planned and accomplished within this office by vice presidents and/or directors and their staffs. In 2008, the Bills were the only NFL franchise with an official assigned as a senior vice president in ticket operations. Furthermore, the Texans allocated two officials to ticketing jobs. For some reason, however, six NFL franchises had no vice president or director employed in the office of ticket operations/sales.

Besides selling ordinary tickets, this office was also involved with the prices of tickets for those teams' fans and groups that may have purchased permanent seat licenses, premium seats, and/or corporate suites. An especially important objective of the ticketing staff is to sell out each of its club's home games in order to maximize revenue from seats at the stadium. Two vice presidents from franchises in each of the league's conferences were the Ravens' Baker Koppelman and the Texans' John Schriever, and the Rams' Michael Naughton and the Saints' Mike Stanfield.

Pro Personnel/Scouting. A number of staff members within this office study the work ethics and measure performances and skills of key players who perform in various positions on other NFL teams in order to determine how these athletes might contribute to their respective club. Most officials in this office were directors in 2008 because they frequently reported their findings to a vice president of football operations and/or the head coach.

In contrast, the Cowboys had an executive vice president/director assigned to player personnel in that year while the Bills employed two vice presidents, one in pro personnel and the other in scouting. Meanwhile, 19 other NFL clubs appointed directors to manage this office. The directors of three successful franchises that contained this office before 2009 were the Buccaneers' Mark Dominik, the Colts' Clyde Powers, and the Giants' David Gettleman. For some reason, ten of the league's teams did not have an office with this title.

College Scouting

To prepare for the draft each year and, furthermore, to maintain a historical record of athletes who had successfully played football in American colleges and universities, the Bills had a vice president who supervised the task of scouting players in school while directors headed this office in 18 other franchises. As a result, 13 NFL teams performed college scouting duties in 2008 in which vice presidents or directors had not been assigned as officials within this office. Perhaps the job of scouting students were accomplished for these teams within another office, such as football administration, player personnel, or by the team's head coach and his staff.

Some important directors within franchises who had performed as administrators of college scouts or had scouted players themselves in 2008 included the Jets' Jay Mandolesi, the Titans' Mike Ackerely, and the 49ers' David McCloughan. Besides that group, a few scouting directors were provided assistants that year. Among the 32 franchises, there was no executive/senior vice president assigned to this office.

Stadium/Facilities Operations

In 2008, six (approximately 19 percent) NFL franchises used vice presidents while 13 (40 percent) assigned directors to jobs in this increasingly important office. In fact, the dedication and performance of these officials determined, in part, the amounts of revenues their teams earned from playing in stadiums at home games.

Because franchises equally share 75 percent or more of the league's revenues, each team has an incentive to generate additional cash from its hometown facilities and especially the local stadium. Indeed, such clubs as the Cowboys, Panthers, and Redskins have become wealthier and more popular because of income from concessions, sales of merchandise at their facilities, and advertisements, promotions and sponsorships at, respectively, former Texas Stadium in Irving, Bank of America Stadium in Charlotte and FedEx Field in Landover. For sure, vice presidents of three teams' hometown football buildings in 2008 included the Ravens' Roy Sommerhof at M & T Bank Stadium in Baltimore, the Bills' Joe Frandina at Ralph Wilson Stadium in Orchard Park, and the Patriots' Jim Nolan at Gillette Stadium in Foxborough.

Information Technology/Systems. Eighteen (56 percent) NFL franchises in 2008 had assigned a vice president and/or director as an official to this office. As a group, these officials were responsible for establishing the different types of computer hardware and software programs used by teams' staff, and they designed, implemented, and upgraded the information system and database files of their respective club. In turn, these systems involved the entry, processing, and storage of accounting, financial, human resources, marketing, and operations data and statistics for other offices within each franchise.

Because of business and technical complications with respect to information technology, the 14 NFL teams that did not establish this specific office in 2008 must have assigned such tasks internally to other departments or divisions, or they had outsourced the work to specialists in local companies. For sure, each NFL team has a need for information about all aspects of its operations. A few directors who performed in this office from three teams included the Bengals' Michael Kayes, the Jets' Tom Murphy, and the Titans' Russ Hudson.

Security Operations/Systems

Because of electronic messages and other types of communications such as threats from various individuals and/or extremist groups before, during and after games, NFL coaches and players and perhaps their families need protection to ensure that they are relatively safe from being stalked or physically hurt in any way. This office, therefore, recommends and invests in, installs, and/or monitors security systems for franchises, especially at stadiums when regular season games take place on weekends and Monday nights.

Based on these matters, 17 (53 percent) of the league's clubs had appointed a vice president or director to supervise this office in 2008. While the Browns and Cardinals employed the former type of official, such teams as the Chargers, Eagles, and 49ers had designated a director to be responsible for the tasks of this internal office. Alternatively, the other 15 teams contracted with local businesses to provide security personnel, operations, and/or systems.

Media Relations/Products

Sports franchises depend on advertising, marketing, and sales to promote their games and other events on television networks, radio stations, and the Internet, and to report them in magazines, newspapers, and similar publications. Therefore, 16 (50 percent) teams in the league had an official assigned to this office during 2008. As such, the tasks of these men and/or women officials have included, in part, scheduling interviews for their coaches and players, informing the media of any current news and/or future events that involved their club, and preparing press releases and other statements to be read by team executives during conferences and interviews. So as a group, media relations personnel act as the liaison between an NFL franchise and various local, national, and international media.

During 2008 some media relations experts who represented teams were the Dolphins' senior vice president Harvey Greene, Giants vice president Dan Lynch, and Eagles director Derrick Boyko. Yet, because some franchises had limited budgets and staff or maybe they owned a communication department or division, no office that contained officials in Media Relations/Products had existed in 2008 for such popular clubs as the Colts, Cowboys, and Packers.

Corporate/Football Communications

For business, economic, and/or personal reasons, less than 50 percent of the NFL franchises during 2008 had an office of Corporate or Football Communications that included any type of official. Instead, the staff in media or public relations, for example, may have performed the communication tasks of these 18 clubs. Regarding the 14 teams in which this office existed that year, some jobs of officials likely included the research and publication of corporate information and statistics about the performances of football players, and the actions and strategies of each team's head coach and his assistants.

That year, the Browns and Saints each had a vice president and director assigned to this office while another 12 NFL clubs utilized a vice president or director. To be more specific about three of these clubs, there were such officials in communications as the Bengals' Jack Brennan, the Falcons' Reggie Roberts, and the Redskins' Zack Boino. In short, only 43 percent of the 32 NFL franchises used communication officials in their operations during 2008 while the other 57 percent of them survived without such an office titled corporate or football communications.

Business Affairs/Development/Operations

As expected, the officials within this office participated in many of their franchise's decisions, plans, and strategies that involved different aspects of business. These affairs included specific transactions with respect to team events, facilities, merchandise, personnel, products, services, and/or technology. From a business perspective, the staff within this office had opportunities to contribute advice, recommendations, and/or suggestions to their respective team owner and his or her executives about a number of commercial issues and problems.

Because the internal activities of NFL clubs — except for the publicly owned Packers — are not required by government authorities to be disclosed, the business affairs, developments, and operations of franchises become news after they happen or when leaked as rumors to the media. For example, reports published weeks later indicated that Dolphins owner Malcolm Glazer had officially purchased England's Manchester United soccer team. In 2008, three men who served as vice presidents of clubs with this office were the Cardinals' Ron Minegar, the Jaguars' Tim Connolly, and the Rams' Jim McCallum.

Chief Financial Officer/Treasurer

With finance being a demanding, difficult, and stressful topic for officials in most businesses of the private sector, this office only existed within 13 NFL franchises during 2008. As a position of authority, the office in that year was administered by an executive/senior or general vice president. In other words, an official or other staff within this office influenced important decisions regarding the amount and allocation of bank reserves and credit, use of funds for franchise investments and operations, the preparation of financial reports and statements, and payment of fees and taxes.

To perform such tasks in the other 19 teams without a chief financial officer or treasurer, members of their financial administration office or a controller likely performed any assignments that related to accounting, finance, and treasury. Otherwise, these clubs may have delegated this type of work to an outside consultant or business firm. Of the seven NFL franchises that had an executive or senior vice president who managed this office during 2008, three of them and their officials were the Eagles' Don Smolenski, the Saints' Dennis Lauscha, and the Seahawks' Martha Fuller.

Broadcast Administration/Operations

As denoted in Table 3.2, this office within NFL franchises consisted of a staff and 11 officials, that is, a total of two vice presidents and nine directors. Although less popular with fewer officials than the previous offices discussed in this section, the tasks to be performed here involved the oversight and administration of teams' business connections and operations with television networks, radio stations, and other types of broadcasters. This work included such activities as how, when, and where to broadcast games each year, determining the location and population of television and radio football markets, and allocating funds to these activities in order to attract the largest sports audience.

Because technological advances create potentially new and better methods and ways to broadcast games and other events, especially internationally and online, more clubs will establish a broadcast administration/operations office in 2009 and thereafter. The two highest-ranked officials of NFL franchises that occupied this office during 2008 were the Ravens' vice president Larry Rosen and the Jets' vice president Bob Parente. Indeed, the Ravens had another official who served as a director of broadcasting administration.

Finance Administration/Controller

This office appeared in eight (25 percent) NFL franchises in 2008. In fact, the Browns had assigned both a vice president and director to positions in finance while the Texans employed three individuals as business officials. These included a senior vice president as treasurer and two junior vice presidents, one who performed as controller and the other as an official in financial administration.

Therefore, as a group, 14 (43 percent) franchises had an office with such officials as a controller, executive/senior vice president, and/or financial administrator. Meanwhile, in offices of the other 18 teams, a manager, supervisor, or simply a department or division head led the staffs in accounting and finance. During 2008, the three directors who served within this office were the Browns' Gregory Rush, the Chiefs' Dale Young, and the Bears' Jake Jones.

Corporate Development/Sales

Only about one-third of the NFL franchises had a vice president or director as officials in corporate development or sales during 2008. In that year, apparently there were not enough tasks or work assignments for the other 22 clubs to establish this office and employ officials within it. Nevertheless, the owners of ten NFL teams decided this office had the expertise and potential to improve their revenues by creating new relationships with big businesses and/or by assigning some staff to sell more of the franchise's products and services.

This office, in turn, may also have assisted or supported other departments within franchises, such as business affairs, corporate communications, customer relations, marketing, and operations. Anyway, three officials assigned to corporate sales in 2008 were the Bengals' Vince Cicero, the Jets' Mark Ricco, and the Ravens' Mark Burdett.

Legal/General Counsel

For some reason a staff of legal officials or general counselors did not exist as a group within the majority of franchises in 2008. Thus, most teams contracted with consultants and other agencies to handle their legal matters rather than hire and pay lawyers as full- or part-time employees. Even so, the type of work that involved these professionals for teams consisted of defending lawsuits filed by businesses, fans, partners and/or sponsors, negotiating contracts with agents of players, developing and interpreting the contracts of coaches and office personnel, and supporting the legal interests and rights of their franchises in courts.

In addition to these responsibilities, an internal staff of legal experts may also assist and counsel other offices in franchises with their commitments, obligations, and problems. Four officials within this office of teams in the National Conference during 2008 were the Packers' Jason Wied, the Vikings' Kevin Warren, the Saints' Vicky Neumeyer, and the Seahawks' Lance Lopes.

Human Resources

Since the 1980s–1990s, the assignments and other tasks accomplished by this office have become increasingly important to the conduct, ethics, and image of NFL franchises. Indeed, the staff in this office keeps busy dealing with such sensitive issues as discrimination, employee benefits, promotions and salaries, hiring and termination policies, and any legal matters in employment. Interestingly, there was no executive/senior vice president assigned to this office by teams in 2008.

Instead, that year the Patriots had a general vice president while eight other clubs employed directors to perform within human resources. A few of these directors were the Falcons' Karen Walters, the Panthers' Jackie Jeffries, and the 49ers' Annette Snyder. Thus, women and especially minorities served in key positions within this office because they had a college education and also the necessary experience and training to be successful as officials of their NFL clubs. In contrast, 23 franchises in the league had managers and supervisors in other offices that had established and enforced personnel policies, practices, and rules.

General Manager

This office existed in eight (25 percent) NFL teams during 2008. Appointed to serve as executive or senior vice presidents, these officials likely reported to the owner and/or president of their respective franchise. Some of them monitored the projects of junior vice presidents or directors who served in such offices as business affairs, community and public relations, corporate sales, finance, football administration or operations, and marketing. Indeed, many general managers had the managerial authority, power, and responsibility to become directly involved with any issue vital to the business, development, and success of a team.

Surprisingly, 24 NFL clubs had no official with the title of general manager in 2008. Besides the Ravens' Ozzie Newsome, other general managers of clubs in the American Conference during 2008 included the Browns' Phil Savage, the Chargers' A.J. Smith, and the Titans' Mike Reinfeldt. Meanwhile, for teams in the National Conference, various general managers participated within organizations like the Lions, Packers, Saints and Giants.

Premium Seating/Services/Suites

The types of officials within this office frequently have been directors. As such, they oversee any business matters that affect the number, location, and value of premium seats, services, and suites at their respective stadiums. More specifically, their responsibilities may include such duties as the arrangement, condition, and cost of these seats, different combinations of premium services offered to fans before, during, and after home games, and the amenities of suites.

During 2008, only seven (approximately 22 percent) NFL franchises had a vice president or director who was an employee of this office. Otherwise, some officials in stadium/facilities operations may also have the responsibility for assigning and managing premium seats or that the top officials in this office were managers and supervisors and not vice presidents or directors. The Colts' Greg Hylton was the only vice president of this office within either conference of the league while directors completed similar tasks for six other franchises, such as the Texans, Titans, and Seahawks.

Cheerleaders

Within the NFL, only six (18 percent) franchises had directors assigned as officials of their cheerleading squad in 2008. These directors were, in part, responsible for the conduct, performance, and selection of men and/or women who participated in this entertainment activity during games. Besides performing on the sidelines before fans at various periods of home games, these entertainers also attended numerous charitable, goodwill, and social functions within the metropolitan area of their team.

The Panthers' TopCats, for example, visit during NFL regular seasons several businesses, hospitals, and schools in the Charlotte area of North Carolina, where they entertain kids and adults by participating in activities while promoting the team and its image, coaches, and players. For the names of each director of this office in 2008, there was the Dolphins' Emily Snow, the Patriots' Tracy Sormanti, and the Titans' Stacie Kinder of the AFC, and the Cardinals' Heather Karberg, the Cowboys' Kelli Finglass, and the Panthers' Riley Fields of the NFC.

Event Entertainment/Services

As denoted in Table 3.2, this and the previous office tied for twenty-third in rank with respect to the total number of officials within each of them in 2008. In fact, only six franchises allocated a junior vice president or director to event entertainment or services. As such, this office coordinated, evaluated, and scheduled the various pre-game, halftime, and post-game events of these six teams during the NFL's preseason, regular season, and postseason. For some events, a team's cheerleaders participated as did some groups and individuals from local businesses, churches, and schools.

To entertain hometown fans who attended games at teams' stadiums, some events involved athletes, kids, young adults, and/or others from the local community. Any events that honor former NFL coaches and players, men and women who serve or served in the military, and leaders of social organizations are popular among football fans at NFL games. While six clubs had officials within this office, another 26 planned events without establishing this office for them. During 2008, the Giants' vice president Don Sperling was an executive producer of entertainment while the Bears, Dolphins, Eagles, Falcons, and Texans had directors with staffs to create and implement event services.

In short, Table 3.2 lists 24 classifications of offices for NFL franchises in 2008 and furthermore provides a numerical distribution of three types of officials within these departments. The top and bottom offices on the list relative to the number of officials assigned within them was, respectively, football administration or operations with 44 officials, while with six each were cheerleaders and event entertainment or services.

During that year, however, some other offices existed within the business organization of the league's 32 teams. Indeed, these appeared on various pages in the *2008 NFL Record & Fact Book*. Therefore, in the following section, I identify and discuss some of these offices based on their number of vice presidents and directors and because of their unusual types of activities. This analysis, in turn, reveals somewhat different operations of offices than those described before and exposes the unique sets of tasks and specialized jobs completed by personnel in franchises besides that performed by owners and their teams' coaches and players.

Minor Offices and Officials

For various reasons, several offices of NFL franchises contained only four officials or fewer in 2008. Ranked from most to least common next are the numbers of officials in different offices that existed during that year. These included four each in new media, sponsorship sales and youth development/ programs, three each in equipment services and medical services/athletic trainer, and two each in charities, customer relations, development, government relations, Internet and publications, merchandise, national/regional partnerships/sales, production and entertainment, rehabilitation, and strategic planning.

Finally, there was one official each in advertising and branding, alumni relations, fields and grounds/head groundskeeper, marketing and broadcasting, records and archives, research and development, sales and public affairs, scoreboard, and sports medicine. A few of these offices are interesting and worthwhile to highlight from a business, cultural, and/or sports perspective.

Youth Development/Programs

Four NFL franchises had one director assigned to this office in 2008. As a result, their staff designed, allocated resources, and implemented education, health, and/or sports activities and programs to benefit mostly disadvantaged and underprivileged kids and teenagers who lived in communities of the local area. Undoubtedly, these events were fun for the participants but also of value to them in other ways. Besides the challenge of competition while having fun playing games in various individual and team sports, the programs' leaders also offered advice, guidance, and information to youth, such as how to maintain good health, attend and perform well in school, avoid the use of illegal drugs, behave and listen to their parents, and establish goals to be successful in the future as adults.

Because they developed and provided these and other programs to children of all ages, these four NFL teams received economic and social benefits and perhaps promotion in publications of the media. For their contribution as directors within this office, there were the Browns' Ed Suggs, the Dolphins' Twan Russell, the Giants' Beth Roche, and the Eagles' Sarah Martinez-Helfman.

Medical Services/Athletic Trainer

Surprisingly, only three NFL franchises had established and operated this office during 2008. Regarding its purpose, the staffs within these teams' offices provided players with medical services and athletic training to prevent them from being injured or help them recover quickly from previous injuries, and also to keep players physically fit and well prepared to vigorously compete in games. Apparently, the other 29 clubs did not have a vice president or director assigned to this office and/or they had outsourced these services and this type of training to a business or other organization within the community.

For sure, the athletes on all NFL teams require medical care. Thus, some assistance is available to them while their team practices and before, during, and after games. Likewise, players may receive athletic training from some of the staff associated with their club. In 2008, specific officials in this office were the Ravens' vice president Bill Tessendorf, the Jets' director John Mellody, and the Giants' vice president Ronnie Barnes.

Government Relations

Officials within this office administer any major or minor laws, policies, and principles that involve government agencies and/or external affairs. Such matters as city and national ordinances, regulations, and taxes affect franchises and the financial performances of their teams in different ways. Thus, at least two NFL clubs had officials in the office of government relations and/or external affairs. These two vice presidents were the Bills' Bill Munson and the Browns' Diane Downing. For the other 30 NFL clubs, this work had been neglected, performed within the offices of legal counsel or public relations, and/or outsourced to firms that specialize in government matters.

Strategic Planning

The staff in this office is responsible for coordinating, organizing, and developing intermediate business objectives and any long-range plans for NFL franchises. These efforts, in part, include plans for the future construction, location, and cost of a modern stadium, significant ads, marketing campaigns, and promotions funded and implemented in 2015 and thereafter, expansion of broadcasting and media opportunities, more community and public relations activities, and such business affairs as five-year budgets of financial requirements, payroll expenditures for coaches and players, and discovering new sources of revenue. Only two NFL clubs established this office and operated it in 2008. The officials who supervised strategic planning that year and improved its contribution as an office were the Bills' vice president Mary Owen and the 49ers' co-owner and vice president Jed York.

Alumni Relations

A Cleveland Browns director named Dino Lucarelli had supervised this office in 2008. Because this city's original NFL franchise had moved to Baltimore in 1995 and an expansion club entered there in 1999, thousands of diehard football fans in northern Ohio remember the history of the club and especially its championship seasons during the late 1940s and early-to-mid 1950s. Such veteran players as quarterback Otto Graham, running back Jim Brown, and field goal kicker Lou Groza are former alumni. Thus, this is the only office of a team that specifically maintains relations with athletes who formerly played for the previous or current Cleveland Browns and with those men who had coached and managed one or more of its teams.

The previous five paragraphs conclude a discussion of other operations assigned to officials within some NFL franchises during 2008. To be sure, this information indicated the offices that various teams had established to complete tasks deemed important to their business, development, and prosperity as football enterprises. Because of financial constraints and other reasons, however, the majority of NFL clubs did not adopt these offices or implement such activities or programs as parts of their organization.

Financial Information

From an economic perspective, NFL franchises operate as private businesses in order to maximize their profits or market values in the short and long run. Thus each year the league's 32 team owners try to earn the largest amount of dollar difference between total revenues and total costs when they make decisions with respect to investments in their sports enterprises. So while motivated to win titles and championships in the league with their respective coaches and a roster of players, these clubs struggle to keep ticket prices and other costs affordable for those who attend games, including individual fans, families, and other groups of people of all ages.

Several factors affect revenues and thus the potential profits of NFL franchises. Besides the price and volume of tickets sold at home and away games, revenues will also be affected by the number of broadcast and media contracts, and by the growth, inflation, and population of the local economy, disposable income of households within their metropolitan area, cash inflows from selling food, merchandise, and other items at the local stadium before, during and after games, weather conditions, and, of course, team performances. In other words, a club's revenues occur from various sources and vary each game and regular season based on these and other factors.

Meanwhile, a franchise's costs are primarily fixed because these amounts tend to be budgeted and thus closely reflect the salaries of coaches, players and office staff, the travel expenses incurred by a team to and from away games, any expenditure for advertising, marketing campaigns and promotions, payment of taxes, and money spent for other operations associated with the sport. Therefore, in a winning season, an NFL team will likely earn a profit and an above-average financial return on the owner's investment. Alternatively, if it loses a majority of games and finishes at or near the bottom of a division, a club may break even or even realize an accounting loss.

Some detailed financial statistics are available in the literature about the total cost for families to attend any NFL game, including the average price of teams' tickets, and furthermore, about the revenue, operating income, and value of each franchise in the league. From surveys, the former types of data have been collected for almost 20 years by a Northbrook, Illinois, company named the Team Marketing Report, who reports these numbers on its website. Meanwhile, *Forbes* magazine has published the latter three statistics since the late 1990s to early 2000s.[5]

To that end, I prepared four tables that indicate these amounts for various years. They are, respectively, Tables 3.3 and 3.4 in this chapter and Appendix H and I. Based on the contents within each of these tables, I reveal various results about the financial history of the NFL and operations of the league's teams from the early 1990s to 2008 inclusive.

As denoted in Table 3.3, the Fan Cost Indexes (FCIs) and Average Ticket Prices (ATPs) of teams within each of four professional leagues have significantly increased since 1991. For this group, the NFL's FCIs and ATPs were the highest almost every year while those of teams in Major League Baseball (MLB) ranked as the lowest. Furthermore, relative to the increases in FCIs between 1991 and 2008, the NFL's rose by a total of $245 (162 percent), which

TABLE 3.3 FOUR PROFESSIONAL SPORTS LEAGUES FAN COST
INDEX AND AVERAGE TICKET PRICE, SELECTED YEARS

League	Year									
	1991	1993	1995	1997	1999	2001	2003	2005	2007	2008
Fan Cost Index										
MLB	76	90	97	105	121	145	148	164	176	191
NBA	141	168	192	214	266	277	261	267	281	291
NFL	151	173	206	221	258	303	301	329	367	396
NHL	NA	NA	203	228	267	274	256	247	282	288
Average	122	143	174	192	228	249	241	251	276	291
Average Ticket Price										
MLB	8	9	10	11	14	18	18	21	22	25
NBA	22	27	31	36	48	50	44	45	48	49
NFL	25	28	33	38	45	53	53	58	67	72
NHL	NA	NA	34	40	45	49	44	41	48	49
Average	18	21	27	31	38	42	39	41	46	48

Note: These sports leagues are Major League Baseball (MLB), National Basketball Association (NBA), National Football League (NFL), and National Hockey League (NHL). NA means the data is not available. To my knowledge, Team Marketing Report has not reported the Fan Cost Indexes and Average Ticket Prices of teams for the league or clubs in Major League Soccer.

Source: "Fan Cost Index" at http://www.teammarketing.com and "Sports Business Data" at http://www.rodneyfort.com.

was more inflationary than MLB's $115 (151 percent) and the NBAs $150 (106 percent), and from 1995 to 2008, the NHL's $85 (42 percent).

In other words, a family of four who attended the eight regular season home games of their hometown NFL team in 2008 spent a total of $3,168. Alternatively, for tickets that season at home, a four-person family paid $15,471 for 81 games in MLB, $11,931 for games in the NBA, and $11,808 for games in the NHL. From this perspective, a season ticket to NFL games is a bargain, especially for families with children who prefer football games to those played in these other team sports in the United States.

Similar but not identical relationships in costs also existed among the ATPs of teams in these regular seasons. That is, between 1991 and 2008, the NFL's ATPs increased by $47 (188 percent), while MLB's rose by $17 (212 percent), the NBA's leaped by $27 (122 percent), and from 1995 to 2008, the NHL's expanded by $15 (44 percent). Indeed, the largest changes in ticket prices within MLB occurred during the late 1990s because of numerous home runs hit by St. Louis Cardinals slugger Mark McGwire and the Chicago Cubs Sammy Sosa, and again in 2003–2005 and 2007–2008 when tight pennant races occurred in the American and National leagues while small-market clubs became increasingly competitive within their divisions.

Another comparison in ATPs of these leagues is the differences in 1991 versus 2008. For example, it cost $17 per ticket more to watch an NFL game in 1991 than one MLB game that year. Eighteen years later, however, the difference in amounts per game between the two leagues was $47. Therefore, from the early 1990s through 2008, NFL teams' regular season games were relatively more expensive than those offered by the other sports leagues.

To be more specific about fan costs and ticket prices, Table 3.4 shows the FCIs of each NFL team for ten years while Appendix H reports their ATPs. Based on the information contained within these two tables, the following are some important facts, comments, statistics, and/or viewpoints about the FCIs and ATPs of these particular groups of NFL franchises.

First, the three teams with the lowest and highest FCIs in 1991 were completely different from those in 2008 (see Table 3.4). For some reason, clubs with relatively low FCIs in 1991, such as the Chargers, Lions, and Chiefs, had changed in costs and replaced eighteen years later by such teams as, respectively, the Bills, Jaguars, and Browns. Likewise, the 49ers, Cowboys, and Redskins had the three highest FCIs in 1991 but in comparison, so did the Patriots, Bears, and Giants in 2008. As such, these differences in costs denote a significant shift In FCIs among some NFL teams that provided games for family entertainment during this 18-year history and the expansion of the league.

Second, while the league's average FCI increased by 162 percent from 1991 to 2008, the average had marginally declined between 2001 and 2003. This was in large part due to deflation of the U.S. stock markets, disruption of business because of terrorist incidents in New York, Pennsylvania and Washington, and the nation's economic recession, which in turn caused the slight drop in the NFL's FCI from $303 in 2001 to $301 in 2003. While it cost considerably more for a family of four to attend a home game of the Bears, Eagles and Lions in 2003, for example, the reverse was true for each of the eight home games played by the Broncos, Dolphins, and Titans. This information about FCIs seems to suggest from a business perspective that these and other NFL franchises responded much differently to events that happened during the early 2000s than perhaps to those that had occurred in previous years.

Third, there were 11 NFL teams whose FCIs had considerably increased between 1991 and 2008. Apparently, their indexes did not decline or remain the same despite different regular season performances, slowdowns in the nation's growth rate, and/or recessions within their local economic conditions. In comparison, the other franchises in the league experienced at least one decrease or no change in their FCIs within a three-year period. The

TABLE 3.4 NATIONAL FOOTBALL LEAGUE TEAMS FAN COST INDEX, SELECTED YEARS

Fan Cost Index

Team	1991	1993	1995	1997	1999	2001	2003	2005	2007	2008
Bears	171	187	213	223	230	273	367	384	468	484
Bengals	143	143	176	190	211	298	254	317	364	387
Bills	158	173	194	195	235	267	251	229	274	298
Broncos	146	164	188	213	271	426	317	348	378	400
Browns	132	165	201	NA	261	280	268	297	303	323
Buccaneers	140	155	180	202	329	355	296	363	406	483
Cardinals	167	164	180	207	230	230	229	289	322	356
Chargers	124	167	209	235	280	304	265	312	400	436
Chiefs	127	170	192	216	239	285	328	360	382	422
Colts	138	164	173	207	239	298	273	330	373	435
Cowboys	184	195	213	243	276	298	292	344	416	435
Dolphins	149	175	205	236	244	316	260	282	363	368
Eagles	176	203	238	248	228	271	341	349	371	383
Falcons	143	167	185	188	226	228	232	299	341	356
49ers	197	207	235	257	286	293	342	347	341	376
Giants	151	172	213	241	267	322	349	388	427	480
Jaguars	NA	NA	229	222	307	337	325	234	271	302
Jets	143	157	169	201	249	327	346	387	425	476
Lions	125	162	181	203	218	248	305	317	326	383
Oilers	138	172	177	NA	NA	NA	NA	NA	NA	NA
Packers	128	157	168	205	235	299	317	317	357	354
Panthers	NA	NA	225	249	304	331	244	292	299	330
Patriots	171	180	204	230	236	284	405	477	482	596
Raiders	157	193	287	275	294	298	331	331	349	359
Rams	139	174	198	195	206	280	306	336	386	387
Ravens	NA	NA	NA	230	261	292	315	351	411	425
Redskins	181	196	200	275	391	442	372	389	441	441
Saints	136	161	192	197	229	291	253	279	298	335
Seahawks	154	164	171	195	209	258	264	286	322	364
Steelers	165	158	178	196	226	334	302	322	354	384
Texans	NA	NA	NA	NA	NA	NA	307	336	359	376
Titans	NA	NA	NA	230	300	332	264	285	330	347
Vikings	142	184	194	236	260	296	325	361	377	386
Average	151	173	206	221	258	303	301	329	367	396

Note: The NA in various columns means "not applicable" since an NFL team with that nickname did not exist in the league during the year. The Oilers, however, played home games in Houston in 1970–1996, and then in Memphis, Tennessee, during 1997 and in Nashville, Tennessee, in 1998–2008. Because Oilers in column one is the Houston Oilers, the FCI of $230 appears for the Titans in 1997, although the team's nickname that year and in 1998 was Tennessee Oilers.

Source: "Fan Cost Index" at http://www.teammarketing.com and "Sports Business Data" at http://www.rodneyfort.com.

former clubs included, for instance, the Bills, Broncos and Buccaneers during 2001–2003, while among the latter were the Bengals in 1991–1993, Cardinals in 1999–2001, and Packers in 2003–2005.

Fourth, it was usually more expensive on average for families to attend the local games of NFL teams that performed within large markets than to see games of those who had played at home in midsized or small markets. During most years of the 1990s and early 2000s, the FCIs of the Bears, Eagles, and Giants exceeded the indexes of the Browns, Dolphins, and Saints. Thus, because of the strong demand for NFL games played at home in Chicago, Philadelphia and New York, it was more costly for families to attend them in these and other big cities having huge populations and households with above-average incomes in comparison to games played in stadiums within midsized and small places. In fact, the majority of clubs that had FCIs greater than the average of $396 in 2008 were either located at home in large-to-very large areas and/or had a successful season in 2007.

Fifth, according to the values in Appendix H, the ATPs of the various NFL clubs had increased by a total of $47 (188 percent) between 1991 and 2008. In fact, it cost more money each of these seasons for spectators to attend the home games of the Chiefs, Giants, Lions, and Vikings. Nevertheless, for the remaining teams, their average prices occasionally decreased or remained constant across three regular seasons. Evidently, these two groups of NFL franchises had implemented different pricing strategies to attract customers to attend their home games.

Sixth, similar to the volatility of FCIs in Table 3.4, there were some interesting patterns in the ticket prices of specific NFL teams. For example, the cost of tickets charged by the Buccaneers, Chargers, and Chiefs were among the lowest in 1991 but also the highest in 2008. Meanwhile, the ATPs of the Cardinals, Eagles, and 49ers fell from being high during the early 1990s into the mid-to-low range in 2007–2008. In short, it was the various performances of these teams, changes in their owners' policies, unique local economic conditions, and/or the construction of new stadiums that in part caused these differences to occur in ATPs.

Seventh, the ATPs of some clubs far exceeded the league's total growth rate in prices of 188 percent. These ATPs included, for example, the Patriots' 303 percent, Colts' 268 percent, and the Giants' 266 percent. For sure, such inflation in ticket prices within these years indicates the market power of NFL clubs that were successful, played at home in midsized or large market areas, and/or became very popular among local sports fans. In fact, the Bills were the only club whose ATP did not double from 1991 to 2008 even though its teams had appeared in four consecutive Super Bowls during the early 1990s.

Eighth, another unique pattern in ATPs existed within these 18 regular seasons of the NFL. That is, the Raiders' average price for tickets to home games remained at $51 for four two-year periods, the Rams' at $33 per game for three two-year periods, and several other clubs for two consecutive regular seasons. In contrast, the ATPs of many clubs decreased in 2003 but stayed consistent in 1995, 2007, and 2008. There was a strong upward trend in ATPs throughout the 1990s and most of the early 2000s because the NFL gradually became America's most popular team sport while the league's franchises dominated sports games in their respective markets from September to February of these years.

Ninth, the U.S. economic recession in 2008–2009, lack of wage inflation in the economy, and overpricing of tickets by a number of franchises will freeze or perhaps reduce the costs of admission to some NFL games, at least in the short run. This may especially affect teams whose prices increased by large margins in 2008, such as those of the Buccaneers, Colts, and Patriots. Alternatively, the ticket prices to games of the Dolphins, Rams, Ravens, Redskins, and several others will moderately increase since they had small or no change in these amounts from 2007 to 2008.

Tenth, Table 3.4 and Appendix H depict what changes occurred, respectively, in the FCIs and ATPs of NFL teams in ten previous years. As such, these numbers indicate trends in average costs and ticket prices that may or may not continue in 2010 and thereafter. Unexpected events could happen, however, such as a players' strike that tarnished the reputation of MLB in 1994–1995 and an owners' lockout within the NHL in 2004, and/or an increase in economic costs from new antitrust legislation imposed on the league by Congress.

If one or more of these events occur, then the business risks of operating an NFL franchise will change for owners of teams and thus make it more difficult for them to pass along their cost and/or price increases to individuals and groups who attend games and those who purchase subscriptions or pay fees to watch them online. Furthermore, the opportunity of using public money for the construction of stadiums may end for current NFL clubs that need taxpayers to finance the principal and interest of debt on their facilities. Consequently, it is extremely important for the league to communicate and establish honest and open relations with the NFLPA and other stake-holders to ensure their franchises' success in the future.

In several of its editions since the late 1990s, *Forbes* magazine has published some interesting financial information about the numerous franchises in professional team sports. This data included such statistics as the annual revenue, operating income, and estimated market value of all NFL teams. In Appendix I, I report these amounts for each of the league's clubs as of 1999 and 2008. As a result, the table denotes the distributions of three financial statistics and how much each of them had differed among the various NFL franchises within two specific years and also between them for a recent ten-year period while two recessions punished the U.S. economy.

To indicate the financial performances of NFL teams, columns two and three of Appendix I reveal that the average revenue of 30 clubs — excluding the Cleveland Browns and Houston Texans — increased by approximately $116 million (109 percent) during 1999–2008. Furthermore, the average operating income (pretax profit) and estimated market value of them rose in amounts and percentages by, respectively, $6 million (27 percent) and $655 million (170 percent). Consequently, the average value of these franchises appreciated the most because of their market power and popularity and the ability to generate considerably more revenue from operations even though there was only a 2.7 percent per year increase in their average operating income.

Regarding the statistics in Appendix I, the Cowboys at $162 million, Red-skins at $152 million, and Buccaneers at $129 million had the three highest dollars of revenue in 1999, while in 2008, the Vikings at $195 million, 49ers at $201 million, and the Cardinals, Falcons, and Colts each at $203 million earned the least amounts. Moreover, the revenues of such mediocre clubs as the Bengals, Lions, and Titans each expanded from less than $100 million in 1999 to greater than $200 million in 2008. That year, the Redskins at $327 million, Patriots at $282 million, and Cowboys at $269 million dominated the group in revenue. In short, all NFL teams realized more revenues during 1999–2008, especially from the league's lucrative television contracts and other sources, like higher gate receipts at home and away games, inflows from own-ers, partners and sponsors, and their cash sales of merchandise.

The next financial statistic evaluated here is operating income. Some interesting changes in teams' operating income from 1999 to 2008 were the relatively large decline in amounts for such franchises as the Ravens, Cow-boys and Chiefs, and the huge increases for the Patriots, Giants, and Eagles. These various changes in amounts may have occurred because of differences in the teams' performances and game attendances, charging lower or higher ticket prices and fees, and collecting payments from advertisers, sponsors, and local and regional television and radio outlets. Furthermore, column four in the table denotes the vast differences in operating income in 1999 between the Cowboys at $57 million and Titans at $4 million, and column five in 2008 between the Redskins at $58 million and 49ers at $4 million. In addition, such clubs as the Bengals, Broncos, and Chargers more than doubled their operating income in ten years while amounts of the Lions, 49ers, and Seahawks each fell to less than $10 million in 2008. Therefore, various business, economic, and team-specific reasons caused most NFL franchises to experience relatively moderate-to-large changes in their operating incomes from 1999 through 2008.

Columns six and seven in Appendix I list the estimated market values in U.S. dollars of, respectively, 30 NFL franchises in 1999 and 32 of them in 2008. It reveals, for example, how much these teams had appreciated during ten years in operation. In fact, their average growth in value was $655 million (170 percent). In 1999, for example, the highest-valued teams were the Cowboys at $663 million, Redskins at $607 million, and Buccaneers at $502 million. The lowest-ranked clubs, meanwhile, were the Lions, Raiders, and Cardinals, each below $302 million. Ten years later, the Cowboys and Redskins placed first and second in value with each worth more than $1.5 billion, followed by the Patriots at $1.3 billion. In contrast, the values of 13 clubs finished below $1 billion in 2008, such as the Vikings at $839 million, Raiders at $861 million, and 49ers at $865 million.

In retrospect, Appendix I reflects the immense financial strength of NFL franchises and their prosperity, success, and wealth as sports enterprises that officially operate in regular season games from August or September of one year through January of the next year. Every team in the league more than doubled in value during the last decade while their total revenues expanded by an average of 109 percent. Although the operating income of nine (29 percent) of them had decreased from 1999 through 2008, the stock market and housing crises and two economic recessions that occurred during the early 2000s in the U.S. did not diminish the quality of their business models in marketing professional football to fans within America while broadcasting games into other countries of the world.[6]

Summary

Chapter 3 discusses NFL franchises and how they operate and perform as business enterprises. Tables within the chapter and Appendix denote these teams' numbers and types of officials and their various offices, and indicate the average amounts of dollars families with children spent in 1999 and 2008 to attend regular season games, including payments for tickets. Furthermore, this chapter reveals coaching staffs of clubs and the distribution of them on defense, offense and special teams, and for other coaching tasks.

In 2008, the league's franchises had different combinations of officials — from president to director — who were assigned to major and minor offices in order to complete tasks and support their respective organization. Two of the most common offices of franchises with officials were football administration/ operations and community/public relations. There were several offices, however, with only one official of a team, such as alumni relations, scoreboard, and sports medicine. In short, this information discloses the internal offices of these franchises and which operations they performed to accomplish their mission.

Since the early 1990s, the average cost for families to attend NFL games increased by 162 percent while ticket prices rose by 188 percent. These amounts varied among franchises because of such demographic, economic, and sports factors as the construction and cost of new football stadiums, income and wealth of local households, and inflation in the economy. Other factors were the population and population growth of metropolitan areas, team's performances during the league's regular seasons and postseasons, and decisions by team owners to maximize profits and their return on investments in football facilities, officials and staff, and professional coaches and players. Thus, Chapter 3 provides statistics and other detailed information about the commercial activities, popularity, and prosperity of NFL franchises in recent years.

4

Football Stadiums and Markets

Introduction

Similar to the arenas, ballparks, and other midsized and large structures where teams in other professional sports play, National Football League clubs have played games in a wide variety of facilities since the league formed in 1920. Most NFL teams conducted their events before the late 1930s — to-early 1940s in places named simply as fields or parks. The former facilities and their capacities included, for example, 25,000-seat Redland Field for the Cincinnati Celts in 1921, 30,000-seat Navin Field for the Detroit Panthers in 1925–26, and 40,000-seat Braves Field for the Boston Bulldogs in 1929.[1]

Some of football's parks, meanwhile, had also hosted the games of Major League Baseball (MLB) franchises. Three facilities that were home sites teams in both MLB and the NFL were respectively, the 32,000-seat National Park for the two leagues' Washington Senators in 1921, 34,000-seat Sportsman Park for the St. Louis Cardinals and St. Louis Gunners in 1934, and 38,000-seat Cubs Park for the Chicago Cubs and Chicago Tigers in 1920.

Throughout the 1940s–1950s and in subsequent years, many NFL teams became increasingly popular within their local communities. Thus, after this organization merged with the All-American Football Conference (AAFC) in late 1949 and then 20 years later with the American Football League (AFL), such competitive and successful clubs as the Chicago Bears, Green Bay Packers, and San Francisco 49ers had played a majority of their home games on grass surfaces in relatively large stadiums. Consequently, during the early 1970s to 2000s, practically all NFL franchise owners decided to abandon their dilapidated, low-valued, and unattractive football buildings. They replaced them with new and bigger stadiums containing amenities that generated additional revenue for their organization.

In time, these entrepreneurs realized that local politicians in various communities were willing to allocate and spend public money for the construction, maintenance, and operation of modern football stadiums. These investments, in turn, provided more funds for each franchise to acquire experienced and talented coaches and skilled players in order to compete for and win division and conference titles and league championships.

Besides problems associated with the age, condition, and value of their outdated football venues, other factors caused the demand for new or renovated sports stadiums to increase in America, beginning in the early 1970s. First, various franchise owners in the NFL decided to follow business strategies applied by some of those proprietors in MLB and the National Basketball Association (NBA) and National Hockey League (NHL). Due to economics and their market power, many team owners and syndicates in the former league threatened to move their teams to another location if a city, county, or state government did not help finance and build a modern and more profitable facility for them. As a result, more than 25 new NFL stadiums were built in the United States between 1970 and 2009.

Second, after the late 1960s, each professional sports league eventually negotiated and signed lucrative contracts with companies to have their teams' games broadcast on local and national television networks and radio stations. Thus, this exposure and growth encouraged nearly all NFL clubs to modernize or upgrade their facilities, which they would then show them off in promotions during preseason, regular-season, and postseason games.

Third, as the sport of professional football developed and became more popular, its commercial aspects became increasingly important for NFL franchise owners, who were cognizant of the potential revenues to be earned through the facilities before, during, and after home games. These inflows included income collected from advertisers, partners and sponsors, and likewise from concessions, parking, ticket receipts, and the sales of different types of merchandise.

Fourth, extravagant and modern stadiums and team facilities appeal to players. Most players, as one would expect, prefer to compete before enthusiastic and large crowds. Good facilities attract good players. The Dallas Cowboys and New York Giants excelled as a result in the 1970s, the Minnesota Vikings and Miami Dolphins in the 1980s, the Los Angeles and St. Louis Rams in the 1990s, and Pittsburgh Steelers and New England Patriots in the early 2000s. When such clubs played well enough to win division and conference titles, their revenues soared due to the money spent by large number of fans who attended regular season and postseason games.

Fifth, some city newspapers and other local media in America tend to hype a glamorous and luxurious — rather than an obsolete and poor — stadium. Many sportswriters, for example, criticize NFL franchise owners for being too frugal, lackadaisical, and uninterested in the success of their club and welfare of fans. These criticisms are less intense, however, if that owner or syndicate invested in the improvement of the ambience, appearance, and infrastructure of a stadium. Indeed, such sports entrepreneurs as the Panthers' Jerry Richardson, the Redskins' Daniel Snyder, and the Patriots' Robert Kraft earned the goodwill of fans, businesses, and other organizations within their communities because of the millions of dollars they invested in, respectively, the Bank of America Stadium in Charlotte, North Carolina, FedEx Field in Landover, Maryland, and Gillette Stadium in Foxborough, Massachusetts.

In short, NFL franchise owners are smart if they concentrate on what satisfies consumers within the marketplace and thereby provide an enjoyable experience for fans attending any games at their team's stadium. Taxpayers have financed the construction and renovation of most venues of current NFL clubs, and as spectators, they may or may not be season ticket holders that rent luxury suites or purchase club and premium seats. Fans expect not only exciting games but also amenities, quality products, and convenient services in a stadium while watching a game. If franchise owners and team officials neglect to meet the needs of fans, the home attendances for their club can decline and so may the organization's operating income, revenue, and market value.

In the literature on sports, two books are excellent sources for research into the topic of stadiums. Published in 2001 by Millbrook Press, *Football Stadiums: Sports Palaces* focuses on the HOK Sports Facilities group and various aspects of this company's stadiums, such as design, economics, history, planning, and replacement. The author, Thomas Owens, organized the book to include chapters on the CFL and, moreover, on such important stadium matters as the roles of accounting and finance, lobbyists, stock sales, competition between cities, and the concept of preserving the past while creating a future.[2]

The second title is *The New Cathedrals: Politics and Media in the History of Stadium Construction*. Authored in 2006 by Pennsylvania State University communications professor Robert C. Trumpbour, this book analyzes historical relationships between building stadiums and cultural attitudes that involved civic leadership, media coverage, and sporting institutions. According to Trumpbour, such distinct periods in stadium construction occurred in concert with evolving attitudes towards such construction among politicians, the public and the media.[3]

In other words, a number of media organizations, civic leaders, commercial entities, and political institutions each had influenced the construction of athletic facilities and consequently, their cultural and economic impacts on urban centers.

In the next sections of this chapter I examine some important business, demographic, and sport-specific features of NFL stadiums, and furthermore the performances of teams that played their home games within them. This analysis, in part, reveals information about the, development and popularity of these stadiums and success of their occupants. Also explored is the subject of naming rights of NFL stadiums and why such rights as these matter to franchises, especially from business and economic perspectives.

Football Stadiums

To compare a few characteristics of NFL stadiums, I researched the literature and organized the five columns in Table 4.1. These columns provide some qualitative and quantitative information about stadiums of the 32 NFL teams listed in column one. For example, most of these facilities were nicknamed to represent a business (Qualcomm) while others used different first-name titles, such as that of an animal (Dolphin), a city (Cleveland), a founder-owner (Ralph Wilson), a politician (Hubert H. Humphrey), a state (Georgia), and a team (Giants).

Interestingly, these and the other nicknames identify with and represent specific franchises even though some venues are privately owned, including Miami's Dolphin Stadium, Charlotte's Bank of America Stadium, Landover's FedEx Field, and Foxborough's Gillette Stadium. Thus, another 27 stadiums are the property of cities, counties, municipalities, and/or states while more than 100,000 shareholders own the Green Bay Packers franchise but not Lambeau Field.

As denoted in column two of the table, three (nine percent) of these stadiums were built before 1960 and another three during the 1960s. Furthermore, six (19 percent) of them were constructed in the 1970s, two (six percent) in the 1980s, eight (25 percent) in the 1990s, and 10 (32 percent) in the 2000s. As such, approximately 43 percent of these 31 NFL stadiums opened before 1990 and 57 percent since that year.

Besides differences in these proportions before and after 1990, there were recent and major renovations completed to Soldier Field, Jacksonville Municipal Stadium, Lambeau Field, Arrowhead Stadium, and the Louisiana Superdome, and then during 2009–2011, the construction of a new facility in Dallas for the Cowboys and another in the New York area for the Giants and Jets. Consequently, it will be several years or even a decade before the majority of NFL teams request any additional financial assistance from U.S. taxpayers and/or sponsors to upgrade their facilities or build them a new stadium.

Column four in Table 4.1 contains the various capacities of these 31 venues. It denotes, for instance, that the average size of the three stadiums

TABLE 4.1 NATIONAL FOOTBALL LEAGUE
CHARACTERISTICS OF TEAM STADIUMS, SELECTED YEARS

Team	Year	Stadium	Capacity	Cost
Jacksonville Jaguars	1946	Jacks. Municipal Stadium	67,164	145
Green Bay Packers	1957	Lambeau Field	72,515	295
San Francisco 49ers	1960	Candlestick Park	69,734	25
Oakland Raiders	1966	Oakland-Alameda Stadium	63,132	100
San Diego Chargers	1967	Qualcomm Stadium	71,500	27
Chicago Bears	1971	Soldier Field	61,500	660
Dallas Cowboys	1971	Texas Stadium	65,675	35
Kansas City Chiefs	1972	Arrowhead Stadium	79,451	53
Buffalo Bills	1973	Ralph Wilson Stadium	73,967	22
New Orleans Saints	1975	Louisiana Superdome	69,703	134
New York Giants	1976	Giants Stadium	78,741	78
New York Jets	1976	Giants Stadium	78,741	78
Minnesota Vikings	1982	Hubert H. Humphrey Met.	63,000	55
Miami Dolphins	1987	Dolphin Stadium	75,192	115
Atlanta Falcons	1992	Georgia Dome	71,228	210
St. Louis Rams	1995	Edwards Jones Dome	66,000	248
Carolina Panthers	1996	Bank of America Stadium	73,400	248
Washington Redskins	1997	FedEx Field	91,000	251
Baltimore Ravens	1998	M&T Bank Stadium	70,107	220
Tampa Bay Buccaneers	1998	Raymond James Stadium	65,647	169
Cleveland Browns	1999	Cleveland Browns Stadium	73,200	300
Tennessee Titans	1999	LP Field	67,000	292
Cincinnati Bengals	2000	Paul Brown Stadium	65,600	334
Denver Broncos	2001	Invesco Field at Mile High	76,125	401
Pittsburgh Steelers	2001	Heinz Field	64,450	281
Detroit Lions	2002	Ford Field	65,000	440
Houston Texans	2002	Reliant Stadium	69,500	449
New England Patriots	2002	Gillette Stadium	68,756	325
Seattle Seahawks	2002	Qwest Field	67,000	360
Philadelphia Eagles	2003	Lincoln Financial Field	68,532	360
Arizona Cardinals	2006	University of Phoenix Stad.	63,000	395
Indianapolis Colts	2008	Lucas Oil Stadium	63,000	719

Note: The first column contains the names of NFL teams while column two denotes the year these club's stadiums opened. In column three, the word Jacks. refers to "Jacksonville" while

Met. means "Metrodome" and Stad. is an abbreviation of "Stadium." Capacity is in thousands of seats for these stadiums as of the early 2000s. In column five, the costs of construction are estimates in millions of dollars.

Source: *The World Almanac and Book of Facts* and "The Business of Football" at http://www.forbes.com.

constructed before 1960 was approximately 69,800 or 69.8. For those built in the 1960s, 1970s, 1980s, 1990s and 2000s, these averages in thousands were, respectively, about 68.1, 73.4, 69.0, 72.1, and 67.0. Thus, the smallest group of stadiums in capacities opened in the 1960s and 2000s, while the largest emerged in the 1970s and 1990s.

In other words, the average sizes of new NFL stadiums varied each decade, that is, increase and decrease twice between 1960 and 2008. In part, expansion of the U.S. economy, growth of city and area populations, increased amounts of tax revenues collected by municipal governments and their ability to issue new debt had each, in some way, contributed to the construction of large, midsized, or small facilities for this group of 32 professional football teams.

Another interesting feature of column four is the distribution of capacities across teams. The largest stadiums in 2008 existed for home games of the Redskins, Chiefs, Giants and Jets, while the Vikings, Cardinals, and Colts each played single games within their venues before hometown crowds of no more than 63,000. With respect to other facilities that hosted NFL clubs, such popular and successful teams as the Broncos, Packers, and Panthers competed in home games within relatively large stadiums, as did some clubs that were less prominent, like the Bills, Dolphins, and Falcons. Alternatively, undersized venues appear to be the case for the Bears, Patriots and Steelers, and oversized stadiums existed for the 49ers, Saints, and Texans. Therefore, the distribution of these stadiums' capacities in 2008 was not necessarily consistent or matched with the performance and popularity of some superior, mediocre, and inferior teams in the league.

Column five of the table, meanwhile, depicts the estimated costs that were initially required to build each of these 31 stadiums in various years. Because of price and wage inflation and thus higher payments for equipment, materials and workers, the average construction cost of NFL stadiums changed each decade as follows: $50 million in the 1960s, $64 million in the 1970s, $85 million in the 1980s, $242 million in the 1990s, and $406 million in the 2000s.

Despite these expenditures, stadiums of the Bills, 49ers, Chargers, and Vikings still need major renovation or perhaps replacement. Moreover, the amounts spent for the construction of Dallas' Texas Stadium, Miami's Dolphin Stadium, and Tampa Bay's Raymond James Stadium were a bargain compared to the relatively high costs of stadiums built during the same decade. Even so, the cost of each NFL building is less important to investors than how much revenue they generate for their respective franchise. As such, some stadiums that cost less than $200 million to build or renovate may have generated more revenue in 2008 for their hometown teams than others with total payments at or above $200 million.

In 2008, the gate receipts of teams who played regular season games at home in these 31 stadiums ranged from $84 million for the Redskins at FedEx Field in Landover to $39 million for the 49ers at Candlestick Park in San Francisco and Raiders at Oakland-Alameda Stadium (renamed McAfee Coliseum) in Oakland. Two other stadiums that provided high and low gate receipts included, respectively, Gillette Stadium in Foxborough at $80 million and Invesco Field at Mile High in Denver at $59 million, and then Ralph Wilson Stadium in Buffalo at $40 million and the Louisiana Superdome in New Orleans at $41 million.

Because they were attractive, entertaining, and/or popular clubs during 2008, the Redskins, Patriots, and Broncos played well enough in games before spectators within their home stadiums to earn the highest amounts of gate receipts among all NFL clubs. In contrast, the 49ers, Raiders, Bills, and Saints failed to attract many local football fans to home games and thus the amounts they collected from receipts at their venues each summed to less than 50 percent of what the Redskins had earned at FedEx Field.

During 2008, *Forbes* magazine published an interesting article titled "The Business of Football." Among various topics within this article, the authors reported the initial cost to build NFL stadiums and the dollar amounts of these facilities in 2008 as a proportion of each team's estimated market value that year. According to this study, the cost to construct 21 (67 percent) of these stadiums exceeded the amount of their financial worth as a fraction of the respective franchise. For example, it cost $449 million to build Houston's Reliant Stadium in 2002. However, its worth in 2008 was $185 million (16 percent) of the Texans estimated market value of $1.125 billion. In fact, such differences in worths and values existed primarily for any stadiums built or renovated since the mid–1990s, like Lambeau Field in Green Bay, Paul Brown Stadium in Cincinnati, and M&T Bank Stadium in Baltimore. Thus, it will be several years or perhaps one or two decades before individuals and groups in the private and public sectors recoup their initial investment in each of these 21 venues.[4]

Besides those particular facilities, the article in *Forbes* also denoted the reverse for nine (30 percent) of the NFL stadiums. That is, their estimated worth in 2008 was greater than the initial cost of constructing the facility. To illustrate these differences in amounts, Kansas City's Arrowhead Stadium was valued at $145 million in 2008 but it cost only $50 million in 1972 to build it. Since they opened before the early 1990s, three other venues that belong in this category included Dolphin Stadium, Giants Stadium, and Qualcomm Stadium.

In other words, because of inflation or decline in the purchasing power of a U.S. dollar, the amounts and financial returns on nine NFL stadiums exceeded the original investment of dollars in them. Interestingly, the $365 million worth in 2008 of 12-year-old FedEx Field in Landover is greater than its cost by $114 million. For sure, Redskins proprietor Daniel Snyder owns the most efficient, productive, and profitable stadium in the league.

In comparison to the two previous groups of teams facilities, the initial cost and estimated amount to replace 27-year-old Hubert H. Humphrey Metrodome in the Minneapolis–St. Paul area equaled $55 million in 2008. That year the Vikings franchise was valued at $839 million, and approximately seven percent of this amount applied to the club's stadium. Besides the Vikings, two other NFL clubs whose stadiums' cost and their market value almost equaled each other in dollars during 2008 included the Buccaneers and Raiders, whereas the largest differences in these amounts existed for home stadiums of the Bears, Colts, and Lions. In short, the oldest stadiums in the league have appreciated in value above their initial cost while a majority of the 31 will require many years of use before they provide more value and return as investments for their owners.

Recently *Sports Illustrated* conducted a study of all NFL stadiums by forwarding a questionnaire to its readers in order to determine how happy they were as fans with their local professional football team's facility. About one-third of the responses returned from readers to the magazine were from season-ticket holders who had attended at least three home games per year. After measuring these results, *Sports Illustrated* ranked each stadium based on five criteria. In no specific order, these were affordability/food, tailgating, team quality, atmosphere, and accessibility. To establish the rank of each stadium, the five criteria were equally weighted. Thus, when concluded, the study revealed the level of satisfaction that each of the league's fan base had with its home stadium and the respective team's year-to-year success.[5]

Based on the results of this survey, a ranking of these stadiums appears in Appendix J. It indicates, for example, football fans ranked the Packers' Lambeau Field, the Steelers' Heinz Field, and the Broncos' Invesco Field at Mile High as stadiums that most satisfied them. More specifically, Lambeau Field in Green Bay finished first or second among all stadiums in three (60 percent) of the categories while Heinz Field in Pittsburgh scored relatively high in four of them, but not in accessibility. Meanwhile, Broncos fans did not appreciate the tailgating that occurred before, during, and after games played at the team's stadium in Denver.

At the lowest end of the distribution, the Vikings' HHH Metrodome, the Lions' Ford Field, and the Rams' Edward Jones Dome placed thirtieth, thirty-first, and thirty-second, respectively, among 31 stadiums in the study. Because of problems that affected fans, these three NFL facilities ranked below average in each of the five categories. Furthermore, the Jets' Giants Stadium in East Rutherford finished last on the list in affordability/food and in accessibility, but so did Minneapolis' HHH Metrodome in tailgating, Detroit's Ford Field in team quality, and Oakland's McAfee Coliseum in atmosphere.

Some rankings were interesting and therefore revealed information in the study. For example, the Colts' Lucas Oil Stadium in Indianapolis, Indiana, ranked sixth despite its opening in 2008. FedEx Field, which is the league's most lucrative stadium in revenue, placed near the bottom because the Redskins charge high ticket and food prices at its regular season games in Landover. Surprisingly, however, Bank of America Stadium in Charlotte did not rank above thirteenth, although Panthers fans are dissatisfied with the availability and opportunity to tailgate and the team's quality and overall atmosphere at home games.

Another observation derived from Appendix J is that the Cowboys' new stadium will likely rank lower in affordability/food in 2009 but higher in tailgating and accessibility. Furthermore, if the team wins a division title in the NFL's National Conference, then the Cowboys' stadium will rank at least fifteenth if *Sports Illustrated* performs another survey in 2010.

This concludes the first major section of Chapter 4. To continue with analyzing and evaluating the facilities of NFL clubs, the next part discusses how well various teams in the league played before and after they moved into new stadiums, and comparatively, whether their home attendances marginally increased or decreased in regular season games within each of these venues.

Stadiums and Teams

After the construction and opening of a new NFL stadium, any host team that plays there expects more fans from that area to attend its home games, which in turn may or may not affect the team's performances against its rivals. That is, the intensity, morale, and motivation of coaches and players on a hometown club will not necessarily improve when they perform during home games before more spectators in a new stadium than in front of smaller crowds within the former facility. Although several cultural, demographic, and economic factors affect the home attendance and quality of teams and the attitudes and performances of their athletes in regular season and postseason games, I made an effort to determine whether any relationships existed between the results of NFL teams before and then after they had played in a new stadium.

To identify and reveal any important facts, insights, and/or theories about types of relationships, I created Table 4.2 from data contained in the sports literature as published by reputable sources. As a result, the table includes such specific information as the current (and not former) names of NFL stadiums and the years in which they opened. Furthermore, it lists the average home attendances and winning percentages across three regular seasons of the specific teams that occupied these facilities.

The first entry in the table, for example, is the opening of Lambeau Field in Green Bay in 1957 and the average home attendances and winning percentages of the Packers during three seasons before and then three after this franchise's team had moved into its new stadium. In part, the table indicates some major or minor changes in attendances and win-loss percentages that occurred based on when each of these NFL clubs had performed prior and subsequent to playing in a new venue while at home. For the Packers, the three prior years (columns labeled Before) were 1954–1956 while in Milwaukee County Stadium, and then subsequently (columns labeled After) were 1957–1959 while in Lambeau Field.

Of the 31 venues listed in column one of Table 4.2, the expansion teams in Jacksonville, Cleveland, and Houston opened their initial seasons in them and not in other stadiums of these cities. The nicknames and years of these clubs were the Jaguars in 1995, Browns in 1999, and Texans in 2002. Thus, the remaining 29 teams moved from a stadium into their current facility and played there during the first year listed in bold in column three. The Chargers, for example, vacated Balboa Stadium in 1966 to compete in San Diego Stadium in 1967 (renamed Jack Murphy Stadium in 1981 and Qualcomm Stadium in 1997). To be sure, the majority of these NFL clubs had performed at home at least three regular seasons in each of two stadiums. Indeed, the exceptions to this arrangement were the Panthers and Colts who, respectively, played at home for one year in Clemson's Memorial Tigers Stadium and in Lucas Oil Stadium, which opened in 2008.

After they transferred into a new facility, the average three-year attendance at home increased for 23 (79 percent) of the NFL teams, declined for another five (17 percent), and did not change when the Cowboys moved from the Cotton Bowl in Dallas to Texas Stadium in 1971. The most significant increases in attendances, on average, occurred for such home teams as the Bills at Ralph Wilson Stadium in 1973–1975, Redskins at FedEx Field in 1997–1999, and Titans at LP Field in 1999–2001. In contrast to these results, the Bengals, Broncos, Seahawks, and Eagles had only marginal improvements in home attendances in years following the opening of their new stadiums

TABLE 4.2 NFL STADIUMS: AVERAGE ATTENDANCE AND
WIN-LOSS OF HOME TEAMS, SELECTED YEARS

Stadiums	Years Before	Years After	Average Attendance Before	Average Attendance After	Average Win-Loss Before	Average Win-Loss After
Lambeau Field	1954–1956	1957–1959	22.2	28.6	49.9	33.3
Candlestick Park	1957–1959	1960–1962	54.3	49.3	72.2	45.2
Oakland-Alameda Stad.	1963–1965	1966–1968	18.3	40.7	76.1	76.1
Qualcomm Stadium	1964–1966	1967–1969	26.9	42.3	61.8	61.3
Soldier Field	1968–1970	1971–1973	45.4	52.1	28.5	28.5
Texas Stadium	1968–1970	1971–1973	63.0	63.0	80.9	80.9
Arrowhead Stadium	1969–1971	1972–1974	50.1	65.6	80.9	42.8
Ralph Wilson Stadium	1970–1972	1973–1975	41.1	75.7	18.7	61.8
Louisiana Superdome	1972–1974	1975–1977	62.3	48.2	52.3	28.5
Giants Stadium (Giants)	1973–1975	1976–1978	54.1	67.6	19.3	45.2
Giants Stadium (Jets)	1973–1975	1976–1978	50.8	47.3	30.1	30.9
H.H.H. Metrodome	1979–1981	1982–1984	45.2	56.9	62.5	47.5
Dolphin Stadium	1984–1986	1987–1989	64.0	57.0	79.1	47.6
Georgia Dome	1989–1991	1992–1994	47.1	61.1	58.3	54.1
Edward Jones Dome	1992–1994	1995–1997	46.6	62.4	41.6	41.6
Jacks. Municipal Stadium	NA	1995–1997	NA	68.4	NA	66.7
Bank of America Stadium	1995–1995	1996–1998	55.2	67.2	62.5	50.0
FedEx Field	1994–1996	1997–1999	52.1	76.5	37.5	62.5
M&T Bank Stadium	1996–1997	1998–2000	59.1	68.6	43.7	58.3
Raymond James Stadium	1995–1997	1998–2000	56.2	65.4	62.5	79.1
Cleveland Browns Stad.	NA	1999–2001	NA	72.6	NA	25.0
LP Field	1996–1998	1999–2001	32.3	67.7	45.8	75.0
Paul Brown Stadium	1997–1999	2000–2002	53.1	56.0	37.5	33.3
Heinz Field	1998–2000	2001–2003	53.4	61.0	45.8	66.7
Invesco Field at Mile High	1998–2000	2001–2003	73.2	75.2	70.8	75.0
Ford Field	1999–2001	2002–2004	74.4	61.3	50.0	45.8
Gillette Stadium	1999–2001	2002–2004	58.6	68.5	58.3	87.5
Qwest Field	1999–2001	2002–2004	60.6	64.5	58.3	66.7
Reliant Stadium	NA	2002–2004	NA	70.3	NA	33.3
Lincoln Financial Field	2000–2002	2003–2005	65.5	67.7	62.5	66.7
UOP Stadium	2003–2005	2006–2008	36.8	64.0	50.0	62.5
Lucas Oil Stadium	2005–2007	2008–2008	57.1	66.3	87.5	75.0

Note: Names of these stadiums existed in 2008. The years displayed in bold are when the stadiums opened. Attendance (in thousands per game) and Win-Loss (in percentage per season) are each three-year averages before and after the construction of these NFL stadiums. For example, Lambeau Field in Green Bay opened for the Packers home games in 1957. The columns labeled Before include the Packers' average attendance per game and winning percentages at home during the 1954–56 NFL regular seasons. The columns labeled After are averages of these two variables for the Packers in 1957–59. The Rams, for example, played at home in California's Anaheim Stadium during 1992–94 and then in St. Louis' Edward James Stadium in 1995–97. Jacks. is Jacksonville, H.H.H. means Hubert H. Humphrey, and Stad. is Stadium and UOP, the University of Phoenix. NA indicates "not applicable" since the Jaguars were an expansion team in 1995, Browns in 1999, and Texans in 2002. The Carolina Panthers played its home games as an expansion team before in Clemson University's Memorial Tigers Stadium during 1995 and then after in Ericsson Stadium (renamed Bank of America Stadium) in 1996–98.

Source: *The Pro Football Encyclopedia: The Complete and Definitive Record of Professional Football*; *The ESPN Pro Football Encyclopedia*; *2008 NFL Record & Fact Book*; "Sports Business Data" at http://www.rodneyfort.com; "Team Games & Schedules" at http://www.pro-football-reference.com

within, respectively, the metropolitan areas of Cincinnati, Denver, Seattle, and Philadelphia.

Meanwhile, the average home attendances fell across three regular seasons for the 49ers after the team entered Candlestick Park in 1960, for the Saints at the Louisiana Superdome in 1975–1977, for the Jets at Giants Stadium in 1976–1978, for the Dolphins at Dolphin Stadium in 1987–1989, and for the Lions at Ford Field in 2002–2004. With respect to a decline in a team's numbers of spectators per year and its percentage changes at home, these two variables were each approximately 5,000 spectators (a ten percent decline) for the 49ers in San Francisco; 14,000 (23 percent) for the Saints in New Orleans; 3,500 (seven percent) for the Jets in New York; 7,000 (11 percent) for the Dolphins in Miami; and 13,100 (18 percent) for the Lions in Detroit.

From a business perspective, the previous attendance data suggests that at least 23 NFL clubs experienced higher gate receipts at their new stadiums because fans purchased more tickets to regular season games. Furthermore, five other franchises sold fewer seats to their homes games but earned more or perhaps less receipts based on the percentage changes in their average ticket prices (see Chapter 3).

Columns six and seven of Table 4.2 are, respectively, the average winning percentages of these 29 teams at home before and after they had moved into their new stadiums. According to the data listed in these columns, the average winning percentages increased for 13 (45 percent) of the clubs during three regular seasons at their new home sites but decreased for 12 (41 percent) of other teams. Otherwise, the number of wins remained the same in their new facilities for the Raiders of the AFL at Oakland-Alameda Stadium in 1966–1968, Bears at Soldier Field in 1971–1973, Cowboys at Texas Stadium in 1971–1973, and Rams at Edward Jones Dome in 1995–1997.

More specifically, some of the largest increases in attendances occurred for the Bills in 1973–1975 at Ralph Wilson Stadium in Buffalo, Steelers in 2001–2003 at Heinz Field in Pittsburgh, and Patriots in 2002–2004 at Gillette Stadium in Foxborough. In contrast, significantly fewer fans attended games of the Chiefs in 1972–1974 at Arrowhead Stadium in Kansas City, Saints in 1975–1977 at the Louisiana Superdome in New Orleans, and Dolphins in 1987–1989 at Dolphin Stadium in Miami. Besides these relatively major changes in the teams' attendances within their new venues, only modest differences in the number of spectators affected the Jets in 1976–1978 at Giants Stadium in New York, Falcons in 1992–1994 at the Georgia Dome in Atlanta, and Bengals in 2000–2002 at Paul Brown Stadium in Cincinnati.

In other words, about the same number of the league's teams had increases and decreases in their performances during the three years following their entry into new stadiums. These results denote, in part, that playing in a new facility did not improve some teams' goal of winning more games and attracting fans at home than what they had achieved within their former stadiums.

After excluding the average home attendances and winning percentages of the Jacksonville Jaguars, Cleveland Browns and Houston Texans because they were expansion franchises that each played in one stadium at home, Table 4.2 indicates that both variables had declined for the 49ers, Saints, Dolphins, and Lions when these teams moved into their new venues. Thus, their exceptional performances in one or more of the previous regular seasons (column two) and/or poor execution in games after moving into other stadiums (column three) contributed to a drop in their home attendances (column five) and win-loss percentages (column seven) and perhaps these clubs' income from ticket sales.

To illustrate, the 49ers won 13 of 18 games at Kezar Stadium during 1957–1959 but only 9 of 20 in 1960–1962 at Candlestick Park. Meanwhile, the Dolphins went undefeated in Miami by winning its eight home games in 1985 at the Orange Bowl but then finished with only eight total victories at Dolphin Stadium in 1988–1989. Furthermore, the Saints won more home games at New Orleans' Tulane Stadium in 1972–1974 than at the Louisiana Superdome in 1975–1977, as did the Lions at Detroit's Pontiac Superdome in 1999–2001 than at Ford Field in 2002–2004. In other words, the opening of new stadiums failed to attract more football fans to home games in San Francisco, New Orleans, Miami, and Detroit because of inferior performances by the coaches and players of these four NFL teams.

The most frequent result, however, for the majority of NFL teams represented in Table 4.2 was that a dozen experienced higher average attendances and winning percentages in the years after they had vacated their former premises to play in another stadium. As listed in order for the stadiums in column one of Table 4.2, this group consisted of the Bills, Giants, Redskins, Ravens, Buccaneers, Titans, Steelers, Broncos, Patriots, Seahawks, Eagles, and Cardinals. In most cases, each of these teams performed increasingly better at home, in part, because of the support they received from their hometown fans, additional exposure and publicity from the local media, and the excitement of playing games before more spectators in attractive and larger venues.

Except for the Giants, Redskins, Patriots and Eagles, the other eight teams discussed in the previous paragraph thrived for at least a few regular seasons despite their being located in small or midsized sports markets. For various reasons, such legendary stadiums as the War Memorial Coliseum in Buffalo, Houlihan Stadium in Tampa Bay, and Husky Stadium in Seattle did not appeal to local sports fans as sites for their professional football clubs. Thus, in the short run, the business activities, operations, and revenues of these 12 NFL franchises had likely increased at the home games played in their new stadiums.

The third relationship that affected another eight clubs in stadiums of the table was an increase in average attendances at home even though they performed relatively worse within their new facilities. During various groups of years in column three, this result occurred for the Packers, Chargers, Chiefs, Vikings, Falcons, Panthers, Bengals, and Colts. In other words, more fans attended the home games of these teams at their new stadiums but they won fewer of them. The Packers, for example, were more successful on average at Milwaukee County Stadium during three years prior to it transferring into Lambeau Field in 1957. To explain, the club won 83 percent of its home games in 1955 and finished third in the NFL's Western Conference, but then placed sixth in the conference during the 1957 and 1958 regular seasons. Nevertheless, the Packers attracted an additional 6,000 spectators per year at games of its teams that played in a new stadium.

Besides the Packers at Milwaukee County Stadium, other inferior venues of NFL clubs were the Chargers' Balboa Stadium, the Chiefs' Kansas City Memorial Stadium, the Vikings' Metropolitan Stadium, the Falcons' Atlanta-Fulton County Stadium, the Panthers' Clemson Memorial Tigers Stadium, the Bengals' Cinergy Field, and the Colts' RCA Dome. In comparison to these teams' new stadiums, more than one of their former facilities had fewer seats, inconvenient entries and exits, and parking lot problems, lacked enough bathrooms and concessions, and hosted local college football or other sports clubs. In short, the Packers and these seven other NFL teams realized more opportunities to increase business, cash flows, and profits from home and out-of-town fans who attended regular season games at their new stadiums.

After moving from the Meadowlands into Giants Stadium in 1976, the Jets' attendances at home games fell approximately 3,500 per year while their three-year winning percentage slightly increased from 30.1 to 30.9 percent. Apparently, New York football fans preferred to see the Giants perform at home during the mid-to-late 1970s and win considerably more games than attend those played by the Jets. Furthermore, the Jets were more competitive, popular, and successful as an AFL team in the late 1960s when quarterback Joe Namath led them to a great victory by defeating the NFL Baltimore Colts in Super Bowl III.

According to Table 4.2, other results affected some teams after they had moved into new stadiums. That is, the average attendances of the Raiders while in the AFL, and the Bears and Rams increased at home games even though their winning percentages in regular seasons remained unchanged at, respectively, Oakland-Alameda Stadium, Soldier Field, and Edward Jones Dome. Indeed, the Raiders more than doubled their attendances at home within three years while the Bears added 7,000 and Rams 16,000 more spectators per season.

In contrast, the Cowboys averaged 63,000 in attendances per season at both the Cotton Bowl and Texas Stadium and furthermore the franchise won the same proportion of its games played in these stadiums during the before and after years stated in the table. As such, the operating income of the Cowboys and Raiders, Bears, and Rams likely rose at their games because of more or the same number of people that paid higher ticket prices. Nevertheless, competitively, each of them won the same percentage of home games before and after they transferred into a new facility.

In total, the data in Table 4.2 provides historical information and also some interesting relationships about how various NFL (and two AFL) teams existed while playing a few years in their old and new stadiums. First, the average attendances at the home games of these clubs increased for 23 (79 percent) of them. Economists call this change the "honeymoon effect" because after a few years, the excitement of local sports fans about their new stadium gradually dissipates after which a team's regular season attendances tend to flatten or even decline. In fact, five clubs experienced a decrease in spectators at home games played in their new venues while the Cowboys' attendances remained constant after it vacated the Cotton Bowl for Texas Stadium in 1971.

Second, about the same number of these professional teams won more or less games in years before they had moved into their new facilities. That is, the performances of 13 of them increased, 12 decreased, and the other four did not change. This result suggests, in turn, that opening a new stadium will not necessarily improve the winning percentage of clubs at home games against their rivals. Nonetheless, these stadiums caused the business, revenue, and value of franchises to appreciate, which benefitted their owners, coaches, players, and investors.

Third, while the average attendances and win-loss percentages both declined for four teams and likewise increased for another 12 when they played games at home within their new venues, these variables changed in different directions for the other clubs. As a result, several of the NFL teams won more games before larger crowds at home and therefore improved their financial situation and reputation as sports businesses. Meanwhile, the clubs whose attendances and/or winning percentages declined were less likely to become more popular or profitable in the short run from the amenities available at games within their new stadiums. Even so, their estimated net worths probably increased since new football stadiums financed by government or private investors become prime real estate properties that potentially add value to sports enterprises that operate in their respective metropolitan areas.

Fourth, professional football clubs based in large urban cities receive more economic benefits from playing in their new publicly financed stadiums than do other clubs located in small and midsized markets. For sure, the total population, number of sports fans, broadcasters and sponsors, and the average income and wealth of households in areas are relatively greater for such teams as the Chicago Bears, New York Giants and Jets, and Houston Texans than, for example, the Cincinnati Bengals, Jacksonville Jaguars, and Kansas City Chiefs. Consequently, stadiums of the former franchises provide their tenants with significant amounts of cash flows from advertising, concessions, merchandise, parking fees, and ticket sales. In comparison, these sources of revenue are not as abundant or available at the games of professional clubs that play at home in smaller municipalities.

Fifth, since the early 1970s, new NFL stadiums have provided significant economic value for owners of franchises with a great tradition, enthusiastic fans, and a history of success. For example, these facilities and their home teams include Soldier Field for the Bears, Heinz Field for the Steelers and Texas Stadium for the Cowboys. With respect to the construction of new homes for other popular clubs, there were economic benefits and equity created for owners of teams from building Gillette Stadium for the Patriots, FedEx Field for the Redskins and Invesco Field at Mile High for the Broncos.

Sixth, the estimated market values of such expansion clubs as the Carolina Panthers, Cleveland Browns, and Houston Texans have dramatically risen during years of the early 2000s. This change in estimates partly occurred because, respectively, Bank of America Stadium, Cleveland Browns Stadium, and Reliant Stadium are expensive, modern, and plush facilities built to host games in professional football and thus generate millions in revenues for their hometown team and wealth for these clubs' owners. Furthermore, any commercial and residential property and vacant land located near these stadiums benefited because financially they increased in value.

Seventh, the construction and renovation of NFL stadiums generated business and the creation of many temporary jobs and growth of personal incomes of skilled and unskilled workers within metropolitan areas. Although not permanent throughout the year, these employment opportunities marginally increased the business of some local retail, industrial, and manufacturing enterprises and contributed to the development and renewal of a few neighborhoods. In other cases, however, stadium projects simply shifted income, jobs, and urban development from sections of cities to places surrounding these venues. Economists have analyzed and criticized such results and reported them in articles of the literature.

Eighth, the average home attendances and winning percentages of football teams that played in stadiums of Table 4.2 cover a period of up to six years. For a more accurate and comprehensive analysis of the economic, financial, and sport-specific effects of new NFL stadiums, these numbers and percents in the table need revision in order to include ten or more regular seasons of competition in the league. With this information, these luxurious sports structures may have had a different impact on each host team's attendances and win-loss percentages, and thus its operation, revenue, and value.

Ninth, how did financing and opening any of these new NFL stadiums influence the actual and potential venues in sports markets that also contained one or more MLB, NBA, NHL, and MLS franchises? In other words, at any time did government officials and local taxpayers approve or deny requests to construct or renovate some ballparks, arenas, ice rinks, and fields for clubs in other professional sports leagues? Indeed, the amounts of private and public funds and resources devoted to building a stadium for a club in the NFL were not available to erect a facility for another local professional sports team during years from the late 1950s to early 2000s. This implies that the real costs of NFL stadiums exceed those numbers reported and published in the news by team owners, politicians, and the media.

Tenth, besides the average attendances and winning percentages of teams before and after they played in new NFL stadiums, there are other ways to measure year-to-year changes in their performances during and across regular seasons of the league. These are, for example, yearly differences in the number of division and conference titles won by teams and their Super Bowl appearances and championships; number of points scored on offense and allowed on defense; home attendances per capita; amount of revenues franchises earned from operating in old and new stadiums; renewal rate of commercial partnerships and sponsorships; value of leases on stadiums; and improvements in broadcasting contracts. In short, these and other indicators reflect something important and measureable regarding NFL stadiums and their effects on teams' performances in regular seasons and postseasons.

To expose some interesting features and other matters about the distribution of costs to construct or renovate stadiums for various NFL teams, I organized Appendix K. Based on the research of a San Diego task force and published in an article during early 2000, this table reveals estimates of the dollar amounts contributed by the public and private sectors for each of 22 stadium projects. Furthermore, it includes the cost overruns and lease terms of these projects. According to the article, what are some important characteristics that highlight the conditions, specifications, and requirements with respect to these particular stadiums?

As of 2002, these NFL stadium projects were valued at $6.89 billion. The public sectors' estimated contribution amounted to $4.29 billion (62 percent) of the total cost. Businesses, franchise owners, investors, and other individuals and groups within the private sector provided the remaining $2.60 billion (38 percent) of the total. Within the group, the two largest projects were the renovation of Soldier Field in Chicago for the Bears at $590 million and a proposal to build a new $518 million stadium in Philadelphia for the Eagles. The only project valued less than $100 million was the installation and/or upgrade of concourses, club seats and luxury seats and other infrastructure changes at Ralph Wilson Stadium in Buffalo for the Bills.

For contributions made by the public sector, the entire amount or 100 percent allocation of funds involved the multimillion-dollar projects of the Falcons, Bills, Raiders and Rams. To complete their projects, they received money capital from such sources as revenue and lease bonds and city, county, and/or state taxes, hotel taxes, general funds, and other appropriations. In contrast, the four least proportions spent by the public for any projects included 17 percent or $70 million for the Patriots, 23 percent or $55 million for the Panthers, 26 percent or $125 million for the Lions, and 27 percent or $70 million for the Redskins. These franchises, in turn, obtained their relatively large amounts of private funds by selling permanent seat licenses and naming rights, issuing debt and different types of equity, receiving investment dollars from businesses, and requesting money from owners. In fact, the average contribution of money from the public sector equaled $195 million for a typical project included in the table.

In comparison to the public's contribution, the highest estimates in dollars from private sources consisted of between $325 million and $350 million for projects of the Lions, Patriots and Eagles, while the lowest amounts above zero dollars were for stadium projects of the Buccaneers and Jaguars each at $15 million, and the Ravens at $24 million and Bengals at $25 million. For the group of 22 clubs, the amount of private money per project was $118 million (40 percent) of the contributions from government.

The article also reported whose responsibility it was for cost overruns of each stadium's project and length of the lease terms. Regarding the former problem, nine (40 percent) of the teams paid any costs that exceeded budgeted amounts; public (city, county, state, and/or district) departments or divisions covered any overruns of ten (45 percent) of the 22 stadiums; guaranteed maximum price contracts were established for stadium projects of the Buccaneers and Texans; and a construction company was responsible for costs beyond a guaranteed maximum price to renovate Soldier Field for the Bears.

As denoted in column five of Appendix K, lease terms of these stadium projects varied from 15 to 35 years. Those of the Bills and Raiders, for example, had the shortest terms while the Lions' lease expired in 35 years. Moreover, the terms of 15 (68 percent) of the projects for teams ended in 30 years, or two years above an average of 28. Except for the Bengals, projects with the least expenditures had less lengthy lease terms than those that cost $150 million or more. In other words, the majority of local governments within municipalities prohibit NFL teams from moving operations to another city by requiring their owners to sign leases that extend beyond one-fourth of a century.

A typical example of projects within the group of 22 teams was the 30-year, $395-million expenditure to build a new stadium for the Arizona Cardinals. In a referendum passed during November 2000, the public's total contribution of $261.4 million consisted of $236 million in sports authority revenue bonds, $15.4 million from the City of Glendale, and $10 million provided by receipts at the Fiesta Bowl. The team contributed $133.6 million (34 percent of the cost) and a public authority in Arizona assumed responsibility for any overruns. Interestingly, the 63,000-seat University of Phoenix Stadium cost approximately $395 million when it opened for the Cardinals' home games in 2006 (see Table 4.1).[6]

The project for the Seahawks in Seattle, in turn, was more expensive and complex than Arizona's. Approved in a June 1997 referendum and then five years later estimated at $465 million, this project included $299 million for building a stadium, $45 million for purchasing land and preparing a site, $57 million for an exhibition facility and parking area, and $64 million for other costs. The public's $296 million in contributions derived, in part, from Washington State general obligation bonds, lottery revenues and sales tax credits, annual debt service supported by an extension of a two percent King County hotel-motel tax, and a facilities admission tax and parking tax. Of the private sector's $169 million contribution, the team provided $152 million (90 percent) of it with the remaining portion of the contribution collected from the sale of permanent seat licenses to fans in the area. Finally, a 30-year lease assigned any cost overruns to the Seahawks. As denoted in Table 4.1, 67,000-seat Qwest Stadium in Seattle eventually opened for Seahawk games in 2002.

Interestingly, since the mid–1990s, three of the most lucrative NFL facilities built include 13-year-old Bank of America Stadium in Charlotte, 12-year-old FedEx Field in Landover, and seven-year-old Gillette Stadium in Foxborough. In fact, each of these venues became football structures primarily with funds obtained from the private sector. As such, it is not likely that owners of the Panthers, Redskins, and Patriots franchises must or will request approval from local public officials with respect to any current and/or future renovations to their stadiums. This freedom from government oversight, in turn, suggests that any decisions regarding these stadiums depends on business factors and the expectation of generating more revenues for their teams at games from admissions, advertisements and promotions, concessions, sales of merchandise, parking fees, and miscellaneous products and services.

For buildings of clubs totally subsidized with public money, such as the Georgia Dome in Atlanta and Edward Jones Dome in St. Louis, it is likely that government officials play a different and more important role in the operation, renovation, and use of them. Thus, some of these franchise owners are or could be required to negotiate and coordinate with one or more local public officials in order to change their ticket prices and for other actions, policies, and/or rules relative to operating their home stadiums.

As a result, the Falcons and Rams may or may not succeed in achieving an economic goal of maximizing the revenues from their stadiums because of government involvement in decision-making and perhaps conflicts between them, and a concern for profits and not the interest and social welfare of a community. Most teams in professional sports leagues, including the NFL, play their games in publicly owned stadiums to avoid the immense cost of allocating precious resources and spending owners' financial capital to construct them.

This concludes an analysis of the data contained in previous tables of this chapter and a few in the Appendix, and a discussion of any unique economic, financial, and sport-specific relationships that existed between NFL teams and their respective performances while they each played in two different stadiums. To extend this part of Chapter 4, in the next section I examine another relevant but special aspect of NFL stadiums. The topic of interest is the business of naming rights of teams stadiums and how these rights affect the image, reputation, and value of some franchises in this 89-year-old professional football league.

Stadiums Naming Rights

Simply put, this concept generally means that a sponsor agrees to pay someone else for the right to place its name on a public or private building, and/or on a sign or video board within it. As such, there is an exchange of compensation for commercial value between two or more parties in a transaction. Based on a common usage of this concept, one of the earliest deals in the modern era of the NFL occurred in 1972 when Rich County, New York, signed a 25-year, $1.5 million naming rights agreement with the privately owned Rich Products Corporation. As a result, the league's Buffalo Bills proceeded to play their home games in 73,900-seat Rich Stadium.[7]

Besides the Bills and Rich Products and the county, a few other government officials and companies or teams signed similar agreements in the 1970s to name or rename NFL stadiums. These included the City of Pontiac, Michigan, and the Detroit Lions to perform at the 80,300-seat Pontiac Silverdome and the City of Foxborough, Massachusetts, and Schafer Brewery for the Patriots to play at Schaefer Stadium in Foxborough. According to reports, the Rich Stadium and Schaefer Stadium deals did not generate much attention among marketing experts nor did they interest civic leaders in America or excite the media since both of these agreements involved small, local businesses headed by families.

After the 1970s–1980s, however, the revenues from the sale of naming rights became increasingly lucrative to pursue by the owners of America's sports stadiums. This caused naming rights transactions to expand in professional sports because they involved different and more complex business relationships between stadium owners and teams besides placing signs on and within these buildings. That is, rights deals became sophisticated and intricate types of packages that contained benefits, communications with consumers and opportunities, including such commercial matters as advertising, coupons, event tickets, luxury suite and club seat usages, retail space, and various services. Therefore, in reality, the current naming rights contracts of sports venues not only involve a variety of revenues and values, they also establish cooperation, legal relationships, and partnerships between respective parties in the transaction.

During the 1990s and early 2000s, American companies in different industries became more aware, aggressive, and proactive to acquire naming rights from private and public stadium owners in order to promote and expand their businesses. To illustrate this activity, Table 4.3 lists the names of stadiums that hosted 17 NFL clubs in 2008 and reveals the types of rights agreements, which existed that year, between the owners of these facilities and various businesses.

An interesting fact about the agreements in the table is that the amount of rights in column four totaled $1.66 billion or $98 million per agreement while cumulatively the years in column five equaled 307 or an average of 18 years. With respect to the other 15 clubs in the league, their home stadiums

TABLE 4.3 NFL TEAMS STADIUM NAMING RIGHTS, BY TOTAL VALUE, 2008

Team	Stadium (Company)	*Naming Rights*		
		Amt.	Yrs.	Exp.
Houston Texans	Reliant Stadium (Reliant Energy)	300	30	2033
Washington Redskins	FedEx Field (FedEx Corporation)	205	27	2025
Arizona Cardinals	UOP Stadium (University of Phoenix)	154	20	2025
Carolina Panthers	BOA Stadium (Bank of America)	140	20	2024
Philadelphia Eagles	Lincoln Fin. Field (Lincoln National)	139	20	2022
Indianapolis Colts	Lucas Oil Stadium (Lucas Oil Corp.)	121	20	2028
Denver Broncos	Invesco Field at MH (Invesco Funds)	120	20	2021
New England Patriots	Gillette Stadium (Gillette Corporation)	115	15	2017
Baltimore Ravens	M&T Bank Stadium (M&T Bank Corp.)	75	15	2017
Seattle Seahawks	Qwest Field (Qwest Communications)	75	15	2016
Pittsburgh Steelers	Heinz Field (H.J. Heinz)	57	20	2021
Detroit Lions	Ford Field (Ford Motor Company)	40	20	2042
Tampa Bay Buccaneers	Raymond James (Raymond James Fin.)	32	13	2011
St. Louis Rams	Edward Jones Dome (Edward Jones)	31	12	2012
Tennessee Titans	LP Field (Louisiana Pacific)	30	10	2013
San Diego Chargers	Qualcomm Stadium (Qualcomm Corp.)	18	20	2017
Oakland Raiders	McAfee Coliseum (McAfee Inc.)	13	10	2008

Note: The UOP is University of Phoenix and BOA the Bank of America, while Fin. is Financial, MH is Mile High, Exp. is Expiration Year, and Inc. means Incorporated. During late 2008, McAfee Inc.— a company whose previous title was Network Associates — did not renew its naming rights agreement with the Oakland Raiders. Amount (Amt.) is in millions of dollars. Some fractional amounts, however, are rounded into millions. The other 17 NFL teams did not have naming rights with companies in 2008.

Source: "Naming Rights Online" at http://www.namingrigtsonline.com; "What's In a Name?" at http://www.forbes.com; *Sports Business Resource Guide & Fact Book 2006*.

had identities based on the names of various objects or subjects other than the titles of companies.

For some examples of other kinds of agreements, stadium names represented such different things as a former coach/owner (Lambeau Field of the Green Bay Packers); a team (Giants Stadium of the New York Giants and also the Jets); a state (Texas Stadium of the Dallas Cowboys); an animal (Dolphin Stadium of the Miami Dolphins); a city (Jacksonville Municipal Stadium of the Jacksonville Jaguars); a deceased politician (Hubert H. Humphrey Metrodome of the Minnesota Vikings); and a military person (Soldier Field of the Chicago Bears). In short, 53 percent of the NFL teams played at home during 2008 in stadiums named after U.S.-based companies while the other

47 percent of the league's franchises performed in facilities whose names were not the titles of commercial enterprises.

In 2009, companies and stadium owners negotiated and established two unique rights agreements. First, the new majority owner of the Miami Dolphins, Stephen Ross, agreed to rename Dolphin Stadium for one year to Land Shark Stadium. Ross signed this deal with entertainer Jimmy Buffet, who markets with Anheuser-Busch his Land Shark lager beer, which is a brand affiliated with Buffet's Margaritaville franchise. Second, the New York Giants agreed to name their new training and practice facility as the Timex Performance Center. Being valued at an estimated $35 million, this deal gives Timex a major presence on the Giants' radio broadcasts and on video-board advertising within the stadium. According to some marketers, Timex president Adam Gurian's strategy in the agreement is to transform his company into a timing technology leader while the Giants obtain a name for its practice facility located in New Jersey's Meadowlands Sports Complex.[8]

As published in the sports literature, several articles discuss the business implications and other aspects of naming rights assigned to the stadiums of some teams within the NFL. For example, Kate Macmillan's "NFL Stadiums: What's In a Name?" highlights the differences between naming rights agreements that existed before the 1990s and those in 2008. She mentions, for example, how big deals of the Carolina Panthers, Houston Texans, New England Patriots, Philadelphia Eagles, and Washington Redskins had changed the economics of the sport and exposed the business of companies like Ericsson, Reliant Energy, Gillette, Lincoln National, and FedEx. Moreover, in her article Macmillan introduces such marketing concepts as brand awareness, niche audience and client entertainment, and economics/financial terms as return on investments, markets, and profits. As stated by Bonham Group president Rob Vogel, "Today's companies look at how sponsorships [including naming rights] can drive their businesses and provide direct interaction with consumers."[9]

Regarding different sponsors of stadiums, some previous naming rights disappointed franchise owners and the NFL because these deals created costly and unnecessary problems. In an article titled "Lost Backers," Sheridan Prasso listed a few stadiums of teams that had troubles and thus changed or terminated their contracts with corporate sponsors of naming rights. These cases included three companies that folded during the early 2000s after implosion of the dot.com bubble. Specifically, the Cincinnati Bengals switched rights from Cinergy Field (1997–1999) to Paul Brown Stadium in 2000; St. Louis Rams from the Trans World Dome (1995–2001) to Dome at America's Center in 2002; Baltimore Ravens from PSI Net (1999–2001) to Ravens Stadium in 2002; and Tennessee Titans from Adelphia Coliseum (1999–2001) to The Coliseum in 2002.[10]

Also during 2002, a controversial issue emerged with the naming rights to the Broncos' new stadium in Denver, Colorado. As the issue evolved, an employee of a major financial company (Invesco Funds Group)—which committed $60 million of its group's funds for naming rights—told local sports columnist Woody Paige that the team's stadium would be nicknamed "The Diaphragm." Inevitably, Paige's newspaper printed this employee's statement. As a result, Invesco's chief executive officer threatened to sue Paige and his newspaper, the *Denver Post*. Nevertheless, the executive later made this remark when interviewed, "...his firm has learned that an employee did have a social conversation with Mr. Paige that subsequently formed the basis for his column." In turn, the *Post*'s editor Glenn Guzzo replied to Invesco's threats in this way, "...that the name diaphragm will be associated with Bronco stadium for generations longer than it would have otherwise."[11]

This completes my analysis of naming rights of NFL stadiums and the benefits, costs, opportunities, and risks associated with this concept as a type of sponsorship. Essentially, the discussion highlighted the names of most teams' stadiums within the league and revealed the amounts, years, and expiration dates of these facilities' rights. Furthermore, I identified some problems that had occurred for teams after their stadiums received naming rights.

New Palaces

In the fall of 2009, the Dallas Cowboys opened at home in a spectacular but unnamed state-of-the-art stadium located in Arlington, Texas (see Appendix L). Valued at $1 billion, this new ultramodern 80,000-seat venue includes several amenities and other attributes and attractions that involve spectators. In more detail, some of these features are as follows: 120-foot-long retractable glass doors at the main entrance and exit; a $35 million scoreboard that is approximately 160-to-180-foot-long with a high-definition screen; 15,000 premium seats that cost up to $340 per seat for each home game; and 300 luxury suites in which New Zealand baby lamb chops and Kobe beef are among items listed on the menu. For fans who acquired the most expensive tickets, they may park inside the stadium and relax within 200,000 square feet of clubs and lounges.[12]

For the right to purchase season tickets and attend all home games, Cowboys fans must buy a personal seat license that may cost up to $150,000 each. Nevertheless, some tickets in the stadium sell for $59 per game, but these seats are further away from the field than those at the former facility, Texas Stadium. Anyway, games appear in action on video boards within the stadium. The team's chief operating officer Stephen Jones, son of owner Jerry Jones, notes that as of mid–2009, families had already bought thousands of the affordable and premium seats, while corporations decided to lease several of the luxury suites. Despite an economic recession, the Cowboys franchise does not intend to reduce its published ticket prices at the stadium.

According to HKS Inc.'s Bryan Trubey, the style of this new Cowboys stadium reflects the future. In particular, two mammoth steel arches support a retractable roof, the façade and interiors are made of glass and steel rather than concrete and stone, and glass panels wrap around the exterior and become increasingly transparent when they rise. After reviewing a number of marketing and strategy studies, architect and designer Trubey attempted to capture the Cowboys brand, which executive Stephen Jones contends is about flash, glitz and glamour, and not checkered tablecloths, conformity, and tradition. In fact, the amenities of this expensive stadium will generate more revenues for the team and help Jerry Jones to maximum the profits of his franchise.

Besides the Cowboys palace, the New York Giants and Jets have agreed to share a new facility scheduled to open in 2010. Located in East Rutherford, New Jersey, this yet-to-be-named stadium will contain approximately 82,500 seats and at least 200 luxury suites. Moreover, its cost estimate is $1.6 billion. As reported in Appendix L, other NFL teams besides the Giants and Jets are attempting to build new stadiums or they expect to renovate their existing facilities. More specifically, as of mid–2009 the Vikings seek to replace the 28-year-old H.H.H. Metrodome in Minneapolis, the Saints the 35-year-old Louisiana Superdome in New Orleans, the Chargers the 43-year-old Qualcomm Stadium in San Diego, and the 49ers the 50-year-old Candlestick Park in San Francisco. Furthermore, for the Chiefs, the team plans to complete a $150 million upgrade of Arrowhead Stadium in Kansas City by adding new bathrooms and concessions and finishing other modifications within the stadium.

For each of these NFL stadium projects, some key issues may require discussions between — and decisions among — communities, local governments, and team owners. For example, these groups must determine whether the public and/or private sectors share any construction or renovation costs, and assign the total amount of budgeted expenditures, lease terms and length of the project, responsibility for overruns, and solve any environmental problems associated with construction or renovation. If these and other types of matters are not fully resolved before work on the project begins, there may be financial and/or legal conflicts, disputes, and mistrust among the parties that, in turn, jeopardize their investment and successfully complete it.

Given a thorough examination of professional football stadiums and their host teams, the primary topic in the next and final section of Chapter 4 is an analysis of the actual and potential markets of current and/or future

NFL clubs. When this section concludes, there is a summary of this chapter's contents followed by the notes.

Football Markets

Before the 1950s, several small and midsized urban places within the United States struggled as sites of NFL teams. A few of these clubs and their places at home in states were the Canton Bulldogs and Cincinnati Celts in Ohio, the Rock Island Independents in Illinois, the Hammond Pros and Muncie Flyers in Indiana, the Frankford Yellow Jackets and Pottsville Maroons in Pennsylvania, the Duluth Kelleys and Minneapolis Red Jackets in Minnesota, and the Kenosha Maroons and Racine Legion in Wisconsin. After playing one or more regular seasons in the league, each team folded, in part, because they played within inferior, undersized, and undeveloped football markets whose sports fans had rarely attended their home games. Furthermore, professional football was not a very popular team sport in America or elsewhere during early-to-mid twentieth century.[13]

After the NFL merged with a rival league in 1949 and again 20 years later, its franchises gradually established their operations in midsized and relatively large metropolitan areas, and likewise in small cities like Buffalo, New York, and Green Bay, Wisconsin. Besides these two mergers, the league also expanded into new markets while some of its teams shifted their operations from one area to another. Consequently, because of these and other business strategies, the NFL surpassed major league baseball during the 1980s–1990s to become America's most lucrative, popular, and prominent professional organization in team sports.

Since the NFL increased in size by adding the Houston Texans in 2002, its various clubs have played their regular season games at home within the same cities through 2008. Moreover, except for the Green Bay Packers and Jacksonville Jaguars, the league's clubs shared their home markets with at least one team from another major professional sports league. Indeed, Table 4.4 indicates this fact. That is, the 32 NFL teams as a group had sites that overlapped with 26 (86 percent) teams in MLB, with eight (57 percent) of those in MLS, with 20 (66 percent) of those in the NBA, and with 19 (63 percent) of those in the NHL. Thus, there were three metropolitan areas in MLB, five in MLS, nine in the NBA, and 11 in the NHL that failed to contain an NFL franchise during 2008.

To identify and discuss which of the unoccupied or vacant MLB, MLS, NBA, and NHL areas are potential markets for NFL clubs, the former leagues appear next in four separate parts. Within each of these league's part, I rank and justify the places where a current or new professional football team may or may not survive as a viable business enterprise in 2010 and years thereafter. As such, these choices of sites reflect my research of the sports industry and location theory, and knowledge of the business strategies of franchises during the history of the NFL.

MLB Sites

The three baseball areas without an NFL club in 2008 were Los Angeles, Milwaukee, and Toronto. This suggests that years after the Raiders and Rams had moved from Southern California subsequent to completing the 1994 NFL season, the Los Angeles area became a potential site to put an expansion or relocating professional football franchise. Before that occurs, however, the NFL requires that this city or its county or a private group of investors either build a new stadium for football games to replace the 85-year-old Los Angeles Memorial Coliseum or make major renovations to the facility.

This requirement is a problem since in May 2009, California governor Arnold Schwarzenegger threatened to sell the stadium to close an enormous budget shortfall of the state. Another complication is that in 2008, the University of Southern California signed a 25-year lease agreement for the property to host its home football games. Nonetheless, despite these and other matters, Los Angeles is the nation's second-largest media market, ranked only behind New York in population, and the home of two each MLB, MLS, and NBA franchises, and also the location of Hollywood celebrities and several millionaires.

In contrast to Los Angeles, the Milwaukee and Toronto areas are unprepared to host an NFL club. For the former, this city in southeast Wisconsin has a relatively small population with slow growth, Milwaukee's business executives and sports fans fail to adequately support and attend home games of the MLB Brewers and NBA Bucks, and the area lacks a football stadium that meets NFL standards. With respect to the latter city in Canada, ice hockey is undoubtedly Toronto's major and most popular sport while the local NBA Raptors team struggles to attract people for games in its arena. Besides, the area is home to the NHL Maple Leafs, CFL Argonauts, and MLS Toronto FC. In short, Los Angeles and not these two cities is a better sports market to be a potential site for any new or existing NFL teams.

MLS Sites

Columbus, Ohio, Los Angeles and San Jose, California, Salt Lake City, Utah, and Toronto, Canada, were MLS sites where an NFL team did not exist

TABLE 4.4 PROFESSIONAL SPORTS LEAGUES NUMBER
OF TEAMS, BY NFL METROPOLITAN AREAS, 2008

Area	*Professional Sports Leagues*					
	MLB	*MLS*	*NBA*	*NFL*	*NHL*	*Total*
Atlanta	1	0	1	1	1	4
Baltimore	1	0	0	1	0	2
Boston	1	1	1	1	1	5
Buffalo	0	0	0	1	1	2
Charlotte	0	0	1	1	0	2
Chicago	2	1	1	1	1	6
Cincinnati	1	0	0	1	0	2
Cleveland	1	0	1	1	0	3
Dallas	1	1	1	1	1	5
Denver	1	1	1	1	1	5
Detroit	1	0	1	1	1	4
Green Bay	0	0	0	1	0	1
Houston	1	1	1	1	0	4
Indianapolis	0	0	1	1	0	2
Jacksonville	0	0	0	1	0	1
Kansas City	1	1	0	1	0	3
Miami	1	0	1	1	1	4
Minneapolis–St. Paul	1	0	1	1	1	4
Nashville	0	0	0	1	1	2
New Orleans	0	0	1	1	0	2
New York	2	1	2	2	3	10
Oakland–San Francisco	2	0	1	2	0	5
Philadelphia	1	0	1	1	1	4
Phoenix	1	0	1	1	1	4
Pittsburgh	1	0	0	1	1	3
St. Louis	1	0	0	1	1	3
San Diego	1	0	0	1	0	2
Seattle	1	0	1	1	0	3
Tampa Bay	1	0	0	1	1	3
Washington	1	1	1	1	1	5

Note: The number of teams in each league appears in columns two-to-six. Columns two, three, four, and six exclude any clubs not located in NFL areas. Professional teams that play at home in nearby places are included in various columns such as the NFL Patriots of Foxborough in Boston and the NBA Nets and NHL Devils of New Jersey in New York.

Source: "2008 Major League Soccer Season" at http://en.wikipedia.org; "NBA Standings, 2008–2009 Season" at http://sports.espn.go.com; *2008 NFL Record & Fact Book*; *The World Almanac and Book of Facts*, 2008.

during 2008. Other than Los Angeles, the other cities are not attractive locations for a professional football team. The Columbus area ranks about thirtieth in population within the U.S., and it contains the NHL Blue Jackets, MLS Crew, and college's Ohio State Buckeyes. It would be difficult, therefore, for an NFL team to be successful and compete with the Buckeyes for football fans living in Columbus and those fans in other areas of Ohio who attend games of the league's Cincinnati Bengals and Cleveland Browns.

San Jose's population is slightly larger than in Columbus, Ohio, and the MLS Earthquakes play at home there. Because the city is only a short distance south of San Francisco, its sports fans tend to root for the 49ers, and also MLB Giants and Athletics. Thus, the market in San Jose is inferior demographically and economically to host an NFL team. Meanwhile, Salt Lake City is home to NBA and MLS teams, and its population is smaller than Columbus and San Jose. Since football is a minor sport played in the Salt Lake area, it is highly unlikely that an NFL franchise could succeed as a business in this region of northern Utah. Finally, Toronto was determined to be an inappropriate area for American football in the previous part subtitled MLB Sites. In other words, the most desirable location among MLS Sites for an NFL team is Los Angeles. Following that city in priority is Columbus and then the other three areas of current MLS teams.

NBA Sites

In 2008, eight U.S. metropolitan areas and one in Canada that hosted an NBA club did not contain an NFL team. Listed in alphabetical order, these places included Los Angeles, Memphis, Milwaukee, Orlando, Portland, Sacramento, Salt Lake City, San Antonio, and Toronto. As discussed in the parts named MLB Sites and/or MLS Sites, I evaluated and ranked the Los Angeles, Milwaukee, Salt Lake City, and Toronto areas as places to locate or not locate an NFL franchise. With respect to the other five cities among the list of nine NBA Sites, Portland and San Antonio are superior cities to put an NFL club than Memphis, Orlando, and Sacramento. As such, there are some major and minor differences in quality between these five as hosts of one or more professional football teams during and after 2010.

First, Portland and San Antonio each had a high population growth rate during most years of the 1990s and early 2000s. Moreover, they contain thousands of football fans and households whose personal incomes rank above average, would welcome and support another professional sports franchise, and serve as headquarters or branches for an increasing number of midsized and large businesses. Furthermore, the NBA Trailblazers in Portland and Spurs in San Antonio have successfully established their organizations in, respectively, regions of northwest Oregon and southeast Texas. Finally, a competitive NFL team in Portland may develop a strong rivalry with the Seattle Seahawks, and if located in San Antonio, with the Houston Texans and/or Dallas Cowboys.

Second, the latter three areas are marginally less attractive as NFL sites than Portland and San Antonio. That is, their sports fans and athletes likely prefer basketball and/or soccer games to those in football, have other popular outdoor events and activities for people to participate in and enjoy, and are less inclined to subsidize the construction of a new NFL stadium or renovate any of their existing venues. In short, these and other differences indicate why Los Angeles and then the Portland and San Antonio areas are currently the best NBA sites to host an NFL club.

NHL Sites

Eleven cities that contained an NHL team in 2008 may also be potential or inferior markets for a franchise of the NFL. Within the U.S. and Canada, respectively, there are hockey clubs in Anaheim, Columbus, Los Angeles, Raleigh and San Jose, and in Calgary, Edmonton, Montreal, Ottawa, Toronto, and Vancouver. Based on various demographic, economic, and financial factors mentioned before in this part and previous sections of the chapter, Los Angeles and Anaheim are superior sites to host an NFL franchise than Columbus, Raleigh and San Jose as well as these six Canadian cities.

Indeed, these two cities in California include within their metropolitan areas enough small, midsized, and/or large businesses to form partnerships and establish relationships with an NFL franchise. Furthermore, they encompass a sufficient number of middle and upper income households, and have a supply of experienced and knowledgeable sports fans that would attend the home games of a professional football team. At the other locations, ice hockey is the most popular sport in Canada, while CFL clubs currently exist in Calgary, Edmonton, Montreal, and Toronto. Thus, an area on the West Coast of the U.S. could serve as an adequate site for an NFL club.

To conclude this portion of Chapter 4, my research indicates that from a business perspective, Los Angeles and then Portland, San Antonio, or Anaheim are the most attractive, convenient, and lucrative markets for a new or current NFL team. Whether the league decides to evaluate and approve or reject one or more of these areas as expansion and/or relocation sites depends on several factors mentioned next.

Relative to the growth of professional football in the U.S., these factors involve such matters as (a) business conditions, economic growth, and prosperity of the national economy; (b) willingness of local taxpayers to pass a referendum in order to publicly finance the renovation of an existing football stadium or construction of a new facility for a future NFL team; and (c) number of opportunities available for local companies and other private and public sector organizations to become advertisers, partners, and/or sponsors of an NFL franchise's operations.

In addition to matters in (a)—(c), there are other considerations, such as (d) individuals and/or groups of investors within these metropolitan areas that would organize a syndicate to purchase, own, and operate an incoming NFL team; (e) distribution, location, and size of a sports fan base in an area; and (f) competition for these fans from any local MLB, MLS, NBA, and/or NHL teams within the marketplace.

Summary

Chapter 4 emphasized and discussed two vital elements of the NFL, especially with regard to the league's history and its organization, operation, and strategy. As contained in two major sections of this chapter, each of these elements was the identity and role of the teams' old and new stadiums and the location of current and potential football markets within North America.

In reference to the former topic, several characteristics and other information about football stadiums appeared in tables and were analyzed within the chapter's contents. For example, one table included the distribution of names, capacities, and costs of stadiums that existed in 2008. Another table denoted changes in the average home attendances and win-loss percentages of NFL (and two former AFL) clubs when they moved from one stadium into another and then performed there in regular seasons. When the discussion of this data concluded, I briefly described different benefits, risks, and values for those companies who acquire naming rights to pro football stadiums and whether or not these rights significantly matter to franchises in the league.

Within most local NFL markets, there is at least one team from MLB, MLS, the NBA, and/or the NHL. Based on the distribution of these teams across metropolitan areas in 2008, I explained why NFL clubs could or could not survive at sites in major sports cities where they currently do not perform. A few of these places include Los Angeles, Portland, and San Antonio in the U.S., and Calgary, Montreal, and Toronto in Canada. Because of various demographic, economic and sport-specific reasons, the former three markets were preferred as sites for existing and/or future NFL clubs than any located in Canada.

In sum, Chapter 4 essentially highlights why the construction of new stadiums became popular and thus increasingly lucrative for NFL franchises and how these structures contribute to the teams' home attendances, winning percentages, and their revenues, profits, and estimated market values. Then the chapter identifies the most attractive cities in metropolitan areas of the U.S. and Canada where clubs in other professional sports played in 2008, but not any teams in the NFL.

5

NFL Domestic and Foreign Affairs

Topics previously discussed involved the short- and long-term role of the National Football League within professional football and among organizations in the American sports industry. A few all-important goals and tasks of the league's officials include the following decisions: whether and when to contract, expand and/or merge; to evaluate and approve or reject the ownership of teams and process requests from them for relocation; to establish relationships and interact with member franchises; and, to authorize and financially support clubs who seek new football stadiums or the renovation of their current venue.

This environment, in turn, is similar to the mission of other leagues or organizations, such as major league baseball (MLB), Major League Soccer (MLS), the National Basketball Association (NBA) and the National Hockey League (NHL). The commissioner of the NFL and the league's franchise owners jointly consider and make decisions that affect the current and future operation and prosperity of the sport across the United States and around the world.

As discussed in Chapter 3, several types of team officials contributed specifically to the development and financial success of their franchises. Rather than the different offices and officials of football clubs within the league, this chapter focuses on some of the most important domestic and foreign affairs of the NFL, especially those adopted since the 1960s. As such, these affairs relate to various affiliates and divisions, and events, personnel, programs, or subsidiaries that affect and influence the league's corporate operations at its headquarters in New York.

To illustrate, fantasy football is a popular pastime associated with one in the league, in which thousands of sports fans thoroughly enjoy and actively participate. Likewise, NFL Productions and Publishing each contribute to the business performance of the league, although historically theirs have not been not well-publicized activities reported on by sportswriters or examined by researchers. Even so, the NFL is a powerful and prosperous organization because of these and many other internal elements. Chapter 5 examines a number of decisions that league and team officials implemented after the 1950s in order to expand the league's markets and increase its business prospects.

Domestic Affairs

Between 1920 and the early 1950s, the NFL dealt with several issues. The commissioner and other league officials became involved with specific matters during these decades, including the monitoring of franchises to determine which of them would or would not survive within their respective local markets, and they signed contracts to promote the broadcast of exhibition, regular season, and postseason games on radio stations and television networks throughout America. League officials successfully established business relationships with advertisers, partners and sponsors; periodically realigned divisions and conferences; revised the organization's by-laws; adopted new reforms, rules and standards; and determined schedules for teams that were meant to allow those teams to effectively compete. The league merged with the All-American Football Conference in late 1949, and seven years later, the NFL Players Association (NFLPA) organized, with attorney and former Cleveland Browns general manager Creighton Miller appointed as the union's first representative.

Regarding its formal and legal status as an organization, the NFL is a not-for-profit and unincorporated association constituted under the laws of New York State. That is, the league is a joint enterprise consisting of 32 member clubs that engage in the business of scheduling and exhibiting professional football games in places distributed throughout the U.S. In fact, the NFL administers the affairs of the league. Meanwhile, a distinct and separate entity named NFL Enterprises LP (NFLELP) is a limited partnership, created by statute, and constituted under the laws of the state of Delaware. The NFLELP's partners consist of the existing teams in the NFL. From a purely legal perspective, the NFLELP limits the liabilities of teams to no more than their investment in the company, functions as a vehicle to raise capital, and files taxes as a separate entity. Consequently, the NFL and NFLELP are unique and different but otherwise interrelated organizations.[1]

NFL Offices and Officials

The league consists of six divisions that delegate responsibilities and conduct operations. As indicated in a recent edition of the *Sports Business Resource*

Guide & Fact Book, these NFL divisions are business ventures, management council, broadcasting, international, public relations, and nfl.com. The following were some officials and job titles and functions included, respectively, within each division during 2006.[2]

In business ventures, there were an assortment of executive and senior vice presidents and vice presidents. They engaged in such activities as business affairs, consumer products, corporate development, events, finance, football operations, partnership marketing and corporate sales, security, and strategic transactions. Although somewhat different, several of these activities similarly appeared as titles of certain offices of teams in the American Football Conference and National Football Conference. NFL commissioner Roger Goodell served as an executive vice president and chief operating officer in business ventures, as did executives Eric Grubman and Jeff Pash. Of the six administrative divisions within the league, business ventures contained the most executive and senior vice presidents.

The management council members, on the other hand, consisted of one executive vice president, a few senior vice presidents and vice presidents, and some senior directors, directors, and managers. These personnel performed duties related to career transition and continuing education internships, and life skills programs; served as general counsels and counsels and labor relations and labor finance and operations, participated in player and employee development; and served together/perform information and research. Based on these types of jobs, this division included human resource specialists, lawyers, and labor relations experts who implemented programs to assist employees and players on teams. In 2006, Harold Henderson served as executive vice president–labor relations and chairman of the management council.

Broadcasting was the next major NFL division listed in the *Guide & Fact Book*. It consisted of fewer employees and positions than business ventures and the management council, and included one executive vice president, three senior vice presidents and vice presidents, two senior directors and directors, one manager, and an executive in charge of studio and remote production. These personnel completed such divisional tasks as consumer marketing and distribution of the NFL Network, formulating media strategy, and broadcast planning, programming and administration. The top official assigned here in 2006 was executive vice president–media, and president and CEO of the NFL Network Steve Bornstein. Relative to its power and priority among NFL divisions, the broadcasting unit ranked third after business ventures and the management council.

During 2006, NFL International consisted of seven employees. Within this division, there was vice president Gordon Smeaton and his staff of two senior directors and four managing directors. Reporting to Smeaton, these senior directors supervised international media and commercial development activities while the other directors managed international affairs in Canada, Europe, Japan, and Mexico. According to Commissioner Goodell, the NFL plans to expand its efforts and devote additional resources to schedule and promote fewer exhibitions but more regular season games at stadiums in these and other countries. If this effort continues after 2009, NFL International will become an increasingly important division and thereby generate more publicity and revenue for the league and its 32 member teams.

In 2006, 13 people worked within the league's public relations division. Besides an executive vice president, vice president and senior director, the group in this division also included three directors and seven managers. They in turn supervised jobs that involved community affairs, corporate communications, editorial projects, information for the AFC and NFL, media services, publicity, and the NFL Network. Meanwhile, the highest-ranking official in public relations during 2006 was executive vice president of communications and public affairs Joe Browne. He and vice president of public relations Greg Aiello occasionally provided statements to sports reporters and scheduled interviews with the media regarding any minor and major developments, plans, and policies of the league's business and its football operations, financial issues, labor relations, the NFL Network, player programs, public affairs, and other ventures.

The sixth and final division mentioned in domestic affairs is the NFL's online website, nfl.com. Recently, this group consisted of a senior manager, three general managers, and a coordinator. Their responsibilities primarily involved such matters as business development and content programming. During 2006, senior manager of content programming Mark Zimmerman supervised the staff of nfl.com. Zimmerman's role will likely expand in the future as the league puts more of its news online. This includes any information about franchise owners, teams and their coaches and players, and the NFL Network, Pro Football Hall of Fame, tickets for seats to preseason, regular season and postseason games, merchandise sales, and fantasy football for fans.

Given the league's corporate structure in New York and its divisions and their offices and types of officials, the next parts of this section identify and focus on some of the specific domestic affairs that significantly contributed to the development and growth of pro football in the U.S. and to the NFL's business and its increasing popularity across the world. Even so, other NFL organizations and programs relate to the sport and history of the game. Yet for various but special reasons, I decided not to thoroughly examine them here or elsewhere in the book. Among this list of subsidiary organizations and programs within the league are the NFL draft, enterprises, fantasy football, productions, and publishing. However, for more information about each of them and their history and purpose, see nfl.com or other websites and the readings contained in the bibliography of *Football Empire*.

NFL Properties

During 1963, the NFL experienced and dealt with several newsworthy affairs. For example, the league suspended Green Bay Packers halfback Paul Hornung and Detroit Lions defensive tackle Alex Karras for betting on games, and the Pro Football Hall of Fame opened in Canton, Ohio. Then after more than three years of litigation, the U.S. Fourth Circuit Court of Appeals reaffirmed the lower court's finding for the league in a $10 million suit brought by the rival American Football League (AFL). Finally, the NFL established NFL Properties, Inc. (NFLPI), as its official licensing agent.[3]

Essentially the league formed NFLPI as an unincorporated organization that consisted of independently owned teams whereby they owned and controlled such intellectual property as their name, logo, slogans, and other trademarks. Based on that purpose, NFLPI assumed the responsibility to develop, license, and market the intellectual property of these teams and conduct and engage in advertising campaigns and promotional ventures for the NFL and its member franchises. Therefore, within years after NFLPI had emerged as the legal entity that licenses the trademarks of all teams, several U.S. companies filed claims in courts that challenged the NFLPI and its right to represent and protect such property of teams within the league. The following are excellent examples of these cases and their legal implications.

For at least a decade, NFLPI had granted multiple nonexclusive licenses to a number of different vendors. In 2000, however, the league's clubs authorized NFLPI to issue an exclusive license for football headwear with Reebok for a period of ten years. Because of that deal, the NFL's former vendor of headwear, American Needle, sued the teams, NFLPI, and Reebok under Section 1 of the 1890 Sherman Antitrust Act. That is, this company claimed the group's licensing of the separately owned team trademark properties was a contract, combination, and/or conspiracy in restraint of trade.[4]

In a prior case titled *Copperweld*, a U.S. court of appeals held that for the purpose of licensing trademarks, the NFL is one source of economic power when it promotes professional football through the licensing of its teams' intellectual property and thus immune from a claim of conspiracy in restraint of trade. Henceforth, once the court had reached a conclusion that the league was a single entity, the exclusivity of licensing survived any claims filed in court under Section 1 and Section 2 of the Sherman Antitrust Act.

With respect to other intellectual property of teams, a security guard and football fan named Frederick Bouchat filed a complaint against the Baltimore Ravens and the NFLPI in federal district court for $10 million in damages. Indeed, he alleged that the Ravens and NFLPI had infringed upon his copyrights by using a "shield logo." Bouchat claimed he authored the logo by producing a drawing of it and then said he submitted the logo to the Ravens or someone else did on his behalf. By presenting his design of the logo to the court, Bouchat achieved the first step to win an amount of compensation from the defendants.[5]

The second step for the prosecution to win this case, however, was to prove the concept of "access." Therefore, rather than deny a similarity between Bouchat's design and the Ravens' actual logo, the NFL admitted the logos were alike but that there was no way the league could have seen or had access to Bouchat's design of it. In other words, the similarities were a coincidence and therefore no misappropriation occurred by the league in using the design. After each side presented their evidence, the jury returned a verdict against the NFL, stating there was access based on the designs being substantially similar in appearance. The league appealed the verdict twice, but lost its claims.

At the phase of the trial involving damages, the NFL claimed that the logo's name was the most important aspect of the transaction and thus damages should amount to the consultant's fee and not $10 million. In contrast, Bouchat's attorneys stated that a relationship existed between beer sales at games and the logo. Thus, they sought as damages a percentage of each beer sold in a cup that carried the Ravens' logo. After considerable negotiations over these dollar values, a new jury assigned to the case returned a verdict of no damages or any financial rewards to Bouchat. This outcome not only pleased owners of professional sports teams, it also restated the two-step process of substantial similarity and access in the determination of infringement.

There are two important lessons learned from this case. First, the owner of an NFL franchise must have an unsolicited submissions policy in place regarding the rights of intellectual property. Second, when a court offers a settlement to a plaintiff, he, she, or they should accept it since some juries are inconsistent in court cases. Although the finding of no damages is difficult to explain given the jury's first verdict, it was nevertheless legally correct as defined by the law.

During the 1990s, another intellectual property case involved a patent dispute between NFLPI and a Los Angeles-based clothing company named the Hawaii-Pacific (HP) Apparel Group Inc. More specifically, since the early-to-mid 1980s, the phrase "Dawg Pound" originally referred to the Cleveland Browns' defense and then later to fans who dressed in costumes and woofed like dogs at the club's home games. In fact, they sat together in bleachers at the city's old Municipal Stadium but now form as a group in the east end zone of the club's new stadium. Anyway, NFLPI claimed senior-user trademark rights to "Dawg Pound" because in 1988 the team officially registered itself as the "Cleveland Browns Dogs" and "Cleveland Browns Dawgs" with the State of Ohio Trademark Office. Thereafter, NFLPI issued licenses to vendors to sell Browns t-shirts and other apparel as well as Christmas cards and posters that displayed these phrases. However, when the Browns franchise moved from Ohio to Baltimore in late 1994, there was no longer a "Dawg Pound" located in Cleveland.[6]

Meanwhile, during the mid-to-late 1980s and early 1990s, HP president Donald Shepherd began to manufacture and distribute non-football-related apparel and other products bearing such phrases as "Dawg Pound," "Lil Dawg Pound," and "Top Dawg." He attempted, in fact, to register the "Dawg Pound" trademark with the U.S. Patent and Trademark Office (USPTO) in 1994, even though NFLPI adamantly opposed the company's application to register the trademark. Later, the USPTO denied HP's application.

In 1995–1996, Shepherd successfully registered the marks "Top Dawg" and "Lil Dawg Pound" but for some reason, the NFLPI did not oppose his company's action. As a result, HP sold approximately $10 million of its apparel with the trademark throughout the late 1990s. Subsequently, a new Browns team began to play home games in Cleveland in the early fall of 1999. Ironically, in the next few months, the USPTO rejected NFLPI's intent-to-use application for the "Dawg Pound" mark that it had filed because of its similarity to HP's "Lil Dawg Pound" mark.

Four years after a district court in Ohio had dismissed a suit filed by the NFLPI against HP in 2000, the claim reappeared as a court case in order to finally determine whether NFLPI or HP had senior-user status and prior use rights associated with the phrase "Dawg Pound" and to address the issue of trademark abandonment. With respect to the problem of prior use, the court found that no reasonable jury could find HP the senior-user of the mark because NFLPI had licensed merchandise containing the words "Dawg Pound" together with some reference to the Browns or NFL for several years prior to HP's use of the "Dawg Pound" mark in commerce. However, regarding abandonment, the court observed that the Browns and NFLPI had enforced what they perceived their rights in using "Dawg Pound" during 1995–1999, despite no NFL team existing then in Cleveland. Consequently, the court held that no reasonable jury could find that HLPI or the NFL had discontinued use of the mark or otherwise discontinued it with the intent not to resume use of the mark.

The court's decision suggested three implications for professional sports managers. First, these managers must be proactive and seek federal registration for any trademarks. Second, managers must keep their trademark registrations current and find ways to continue utilizing marks in commerce because infrequent use of them will defeat a claim of abandonment by a subsequent user of a mark. Third, managers must maintain sufficient control of the licensing process in order to avoid any minor or major evidence of abandonment.

Besides those special and publicized cases, the NFLPI and/or the league's teams have dealt in some way with other intellectual property rights issues. These involved, for example, trademark infringement and enforcement, licensing of the term "Super Bowl," an attempt by the New England Patriots to secure a patent on the phrase "19–0 The Perfect Season," and PBL Sport's agreement to develop, market, and distribute NFL licensed food products. Furthermore, the NFL established or renewed contracts for using trademarks with such companies as AOL, Nike, Oscar Mayer, Puma, Viacom, and Visa.[7]

In short, the 47-year-old NFLPI is an important and valuable organization in such matters as legal challenges and disputes involving different types of trademarks and the ownership and control of intellectual property rights. Thus, it plays a critical and prominent role in business for the NFL and its member franchises. In the future, I expect that NFLPI will expand its efforts to protect the league and register its teams' names, logos, slogans, and other marks.

NFL Films

Three years after entrepreneur Ed Sabol founded Blair Motion Pictures in 1962, NFL commissioner Pete Rozelle negotiated an agreement on behalf of the league's clubs to acquire this New Jersey-based company from Sabol and rename it NFL Films (NFLF). Besides filming, recording, and then selling the results of unrelated major events and award shows, the NFLF primarily produces commercials, documentaries, feature films, and television programs about the affairs of the league.[8]

In fact, NFLF films at least 270–300 professional football games during each of the league's regular seasons, and since the mid-to-late 1960s, this organization has shot more than 9,000 games. Furthermore, NFLF successfully completes other tasks. These include such matters as recording popular sports games like the World Series in MLB, producing content for the NFL Network, and offering commercial and corporate video services for various non-football events.

For the most part, NFLF promotes and truly preserves a history of the gridiron by being a pioneer and trendsetter in the motion picture industry. For example, this NFL subsidiary accomplished the following milestones. It was the first filmmaker to put a microphone on coaches, players, and referees during games; to display diagrams of defensive and offensive plays in games on a television screen; to use a reverse-angle replay of plays; to put popular music onto sports footage; to use 600-mm telephoto lenses in sports events; and to produce a bloopers video of mistakes made by teams, coaches, and players.

Experts admire NFLE's style for being creative, provocative, and remarkably effective. More specifically, it always occurs with film and a camera showing motion shots. Microphones placed on the sidelines and near the field pick up sounds of games and discussions among coaches and players on the sidelines, while narrators speak in deep, powerful and baritone voices. Other than these features, NFLF's unique style also includes dramatic shots of a spinning football as it travels from a quarterback's hand to a receiver as well as multiple camera angles, muscular orchestral scores, and film of coaches and players in a locker room after games. These techniques, in turn, transform football games into memorable events that resemble ballet, opera, and large-scale military battle stories.

For almost 50 years, Ed Sabol and his staff of filmmakers have produced a number of inspirational, original, and popular sports programs. Some of these are a *Greatest Moments* series, which focuses on classic football games during the 1960s–1990s, and a *Lost Treasures* series, which uses footage never shown on television to give an inside and uncut look at the behaviors of various coaches, players, and referees. Finally, there is *NFL Films Presents*, which features football games in their dramatic and traditional styles that ultimately appear on ESPN or the NFL Network.

Another program NFLF produced is the *NFL Game of the Week*, which highlights a previous game during the league's current regular season. This and other credits of NFLF are programs for NFL Total Access and football games presented on HBO's *Inside the NFL*, which now airs on Showtime. Moreover, Ed and his son Steve Sabol inject their sense of humor in *Football Follies*, a series that uses blooper plays, outtakes, and silly narration within the sport.

From artistic and financial perspectives, the NFLF is undoubtedly a great success. Through 2008, it had won more than 90 sports Emmy awards, and reportedly the company earned at least $50 million in revenue during recent years. According to some experts, the NFLF's real value reflects how teams' games become alive on film, commercially packaged, and then sold for a profit. Because of NFLF's achievements, fans enjoy the league's preseason, regular season, and postseason games. Thus, millions of households with athletes, children and adults frequently watch NFL events on television in sports markets across America.

During the late 1990s, former Dallas Cowboys quarterback Roger Staubach and his company provided project management skills and feasibility studies to expand audio and video space for additional technology equipment and rooms and studios at a new and larger complex for NFL Films in Mount Laurel, New Jersey. As of the early 2000s, NFL Films' 200,000-square-foot plaza consisted of technical and administration wings bridged by a two-story glass-and-steel connector. This modern facility now offers a wide range of audio services, which includes music composition and scoring, editing, mixing, live recording on location, dialogue cleanup, sound effects, transfer, record production, and archiving for the league and such clients as the A&E network, ESPN, FOX, the History Channel, and Sony Music.

At its home office, NFL Films employs more than 300 workers and owns over 100 million feet of football film stored as inventory in its vault. Indeed, within the building, *NFL Playbook* and *Showtime Inside the NFL*, after filming, eventually appear as programs on television. As such, the first program features former Denver Broncos all-pro wide receiver Sterling Sharpe as its host, while the latter show includes such entertaining commentators as James Brown, Cris Collinsworth, Phil Simms, and Warren Sapp.

Based on his impression and knowledge of the film and motion picture business, Sharpe said, "When you walk around and see all the pictures of the outstanding players, there is a sense of history, there is a sense of accomplishment, there is a sense that you want to be here. It seems like it was the place where football was born." Likewise, Steve Sabol offered this insight about the company's history and the sport of professional football, saying, "Dad wanted to show football the way Hollywood portrayed fiction. I wanted to portray football the way I experienced it as a (high school) player, with the eyeballs bulging and the veins sticking out and snot flying. We blended those two things together and that is how the NFL Films came about."[9]

NFL Network

Four years after the introduction of NBA TV, the NFL launched NFL Network (NFLN) on satellite provider DirecTV at a cost of $100 million and located this business in Culver City, California. Because of its brand power and production wherewithal to organize, finance, and operate a 24-hour, full-service entertainment network, the league had found its place in the multi-channel universe. Besides being available to DirecTV's 13 million subscribers, this relatively new football network had originally appeared on the digital tier of Charter Communications.[10]

For its daily, year-around programming of football events, NFLN offers standard and high definition and video-on-demand services through television providers, NFL Mobile content via Sprint, online video and editorial content through nfl.com, and downloadable video content through iTunes.

Annually the league's broadcast network televises more than 200 NFL games, including 52 in preseason, eight in primetime during the regular season, nearly 90 replays, and the Insight, Senior, Super, and Texas bowls plus any NFL Classic games. With a camera at the 32 teams' facilities and cooperation from the league's executives and franchise owners and their coaches and players, the audience of viewers receives access to action on the field and more inside information about games than they ever experienced before in the sport.

Besides *Playbook*, the league's network consists of such segments as *NFL Replay*, *GameDay*, and *Total Access*. As a group, the purpose of these programs is, in general, to increase sports fans' knowledge of, interest in and dedication to professional football and thereby expand the market for NFL teams across the U.S. and in cities abroad. Therefore, the following is a brief but insightful overview that highlights each NFLE program.[11]

Playbook is a show for sports fans interested in the strategy of football as a competitive game between two teams. In other words, such former and/or current analysts as Brian Billick, Brian Baldinger, and Solomon Wilcox combine their talents to break down and discuss each NFL game in a series of roundtable debates. During each of their shows, these analysts look ahead to next week's games and provide details of key match-ups using footage supplied by the league's teams. *Playbook* gives fans an in-depth understanding of how these clubs exploit the weaknesses of their opponent's defense, offense, and/or special teams. *Playbook* appears in the evenings on Thursdays and Fridays, but also is televised on Sundays prior to that day's games.

NFL Replay features broadcasts of regular season games played during the previous weekend complete with original television announcers and cameras. More specifically, these games originate in a 90-minute fast-paced format without halftime ceremonies and other elements not critical to the outcome of them. To provide context, the NFL Network furnishes sideline and on-the-field sound bites captured during a game and in the post-game press conference. Other program enhancements include exclusive shots and camera angles from NFL Films, which allows fans an inside look at any action within games they did not see earlier on Sunday afternoon or evening. In fact, this feature gives fans a much deeper appreciation of team rivalries, and relationships between coaches and players. Normally a game on *NFL Replay* presents itself on television each Monday evening followed by other NFL contests on Tuesday and Wednesday with kickoff times after 8 P.M.

NFL GameDay follows the final game played on Sundays. As such, this program includes highlights of that day's games, post-game press conferences and interviews, on-the-field discussions by coaches and players, and more analysis to sum up each NFL Sunday. Furthermore, it provides unlimited access to the highlights of all games plus any analyses, interviews, and late scores. In previous years, such hosts as Rich Eisen, Deion Sanders, and Steve Manucci entertained fans with the most comprehensive recaps of games from a state-of-the-art studio in Los Angeles, California. In short, *NFL GameDay* shows such key highlights as post-game press conferences, interviews from the field and locker room, exclusive audio captured throughout game day, and updates of player and team statistics.

NFL Total Access is perhaps the league's most entertaining showcase of record because it provides daily news and information about professional football in a structured and unique way. With 60-minute editions during the evenings of each Monday through Saturday, this program especially appeals to sports fans who demand only football news and interviews of coaches and players. For example, hosts like veteran sportscaster Rich Eisen interviews a "who's who" from around the league each of these nights to inform fans of any happenings that occurred among them and their teams.

Moreover, insiders like Jason La Canfora gives breaking news and up-to-the-minute reports on one or more of clubs while the NFL vice president of officiating provides the audience with their insights about referees' calls from the preceding weekend games. Among other contributors to the *NFL Total Access* program are a features reporter, draft and college football gurus, and some former players. Since this program is the only year-round show dedicated to fans of the NFL, it provides live on-site coverage of such events as kickoff and the playoffs, and the combine, draft, Hall of Fame, league meetings, training and mini-camps, Pro Bowl, and the Super Bowl.

Between early 2004 and mid–2009, the NFL Network was involved in some affairs that affected the business, growth, and future of the league. During certain years, these matters created a number of commercial opportunities as well as publicity and revenue for the NFL and its member teams. The following discussion highlights a few of them from a historical perspective.

In 2004, for instance, the NFLN signed a potentially lucrative contract with cable giant Comcast Corporation. This six-year deal committed Comcast to carry all NFL regular season games for a monthly fee of 20 cents per subscriber and that amount increased each year by about a penny or five percent. According to this arrangement, cable operators pledged to keep the league's network away from their low-circulation digital tiers. Furthermore, Comcast placed NFLN on its digital plus platform, which extended into six million homes or 75 percent of its total subscribers. Besides Comcast, other distributors of NFL programs in 2004 were Charter Communications, DirecTV, and Insight Communications.

Then in 2006, three other events occurred regarding more business and the communication and distribution of professional football programs to fans in markets across the U.S. First, the league awarded its late-season, eight-game primetime package to the NFLN despite a generous offer of $300 million for the package from Comcast's OLN network. This decision of the league, in turn, created competition among — and programming challenges between — cable systems supplied by Cablevision, Charter, Cox, and Time Warner.[12]

Second, the NFLN initiated a multimillion-dollar marketing campaign in 2006 to transform its regular season game package into improved carriage across the U.S. These advertisements and promotions spanned the print, radio and television media, and they included broadcasts on giant in-stadium screens and such team assets as websites and coaches shows. This campaign's primary goal was to drive consumers to a telephone number that routed calls to the local cable carrier by area code.

Third, the NFLN strongly requested that four cable operators charge a monthly license fee of 20 cents per subscriber for its service, as opposed to 20 cents before the NFL's primetime eight-game schedule became part of the roster. This decision, in part, reflects the NFLN's attempt to collect more revenue for its teams and achieve wider basic distribution of games played from late November through the end of the regular season.

Several interesting but controversial business problems, meanwhile, continued to challenge the economic power of the NFLN during 2007. In the summer of that year, for example, the football network mailed Comcast's customers and urged them to demand NFLN on their current cable package. Otherwise, they should ask for a rebate because of a loss of the NFL channel's programming that had resulted when Comcast began to bounce NFLN from its no-extra-charge digital platform for a sports tier that cost an additional $4.95 per month. In effect, the NFLN wanted Comcast's customers to cancel their cable subscriptions and enroll in DirecTV or EchoStar, both of which carried the channel on widely circulated tiers.[13]

During November and December of 2007, other important events had occurred with respect to the NFLN's development and its current and future business. That is, lawmakers in Illinois, Ohio, Texas, and Wisconsin threatened to introduce legislation that forced cable networks and operators to settle carriage disputes and other programming conflicts through arbitration. Although risky for these groups, a spokesperson for the NFLN agreed to this type of intervention by an impartial arbitrator to resolve such problems. Shortly thereafter, however, Comcast filed a breach of contract with the Federal Communications Commission (FCC) against the NFL for encouraging the company's customers to drop their current service and essentially destroy Comcast's right to put the NFLN channel on its sports tier. The FCC, in turn, stalled and failed to issue a decision in the case.

Because of intense pressure and opinions from politicians within the nation's capital, in December 2007 the NFLN signed the CBS and NBC networks to carry a telecast of a primetime Saturday game between the undefeated New England Patriots and New York Giants. This simulcast was a significant event since it indicated the football channel's fear that the FCC and/or Congress would interfere in disputes and perhaps force the NFLN to expand the distribution and broadcast of NFL prime-time and other regular season games, thereby limiting the league's monopolistic control of filming them. Clearly, such cable operators as Cablevision, Charter, and Time Warner viewed the channel's decision in December as a breakthrough in their quest to offer more pro football games to subscribers on their sports tiers and thereby avoid a pricey deal and perhaps an unprofitable multiyear commitment with the NFLN.

Even so, some local television stations in the Boston and New York areas protested the NFLN's agreement with CBS and NBC because these stations planned to carry the Patriots-Giants game within their markets after bidding for and winning exclusive broadcast rights and then selling advertising to customers based on those rights. According to NFLN representative Seth Palansky, "Going wide with the broadcast was a business decision based on the magnitude of the game and the fact that the league [NFL] could not make any progress with the holdout cable operators. The [league's] commissioner made a decision to do what's best for fans and all these other issues are unintended consequences of the initial decision."[14]

From a business perspective, the NFLN had other experiences reported in the media during 2007–2008. Indeed, some of the football network's affiliates ended 2007 with double-digit increases in their sales after forwarding advertising to subscribers, participating in sweepstakes prizes and programming promotions, and receiving marketing support from the NFLN. Because of this momentum in business during November–December, the NFLN successfully signed more deals with carriers in 2008, which in turn expanded its subscriber base to an estimated 43 million people.

Furthermore, in 2008, the FCC agreed with the league and its complaint of discrimination against Comcast since the latter company had unfairly placed the NFLN on its premium tier rather than on basic service. Consequently, some communication experts suggested that the FCC's decision actually protected consumers and encouraged competition by enforcing carriage rules that offset potentially bad managerial practices of vertically integrated cable distributors. In a letter addressed to the U.S. Senate, NFL commissioner Roger Goodell condemned some cable operators for denying consumers reasonable access to the league's programs or charging exorbitant fees to watch pro football games on the NFLN.[15]

Despite negotiations between the league and Comcast, the bickering over broader distribution and fees of NFLN programming continued into early 2009. In April, for example, former NFL commissioner Paul Tagliabue accused Comcast CEO Brian Roberts of threatening the league if it did not license a live eight-game package to Comcast's OLN (renamed Versus) network. Roberts claimed that Tagliabue's remarks were simplistic and inaccurate because of this issue's complications and murky relationship between contractual rights, subscription fees and prices, program distribution, and business aspects of the cable and sports industries.[16]

After three years of legal hostilities, in spring 2009 the adversaries signed a nine-year contract for Comcast to make available to approximately 11 million of its digital-basic subscribers any games on the NFLN before August 1 of that year. For Goodell and Roberts to settle their dispute, the league decided to reduce the price of its network by 28 percent, or in amount, from a monthly subscriber fee of 70 cents to an average of 50 cents. Comcast, meanwhile, obtained a better deal for its customer base because it carried the Red Zone Channel, which is a part of DirecTV's Sunday Ticket package. Moreover, that channel will be available by 2012 for a fee charged to cable operators, telephone companies, and other carriers that cannot get the league's Sunday Ticket.

In the end, this was a lucrative and special television deal for the NFL. A larger mass of Comcast subscribers now may watch more of the league's games on cable for the next nine years and, presumably, the NFL will soon offer similar opportunities as Comcast's to Cablevision, Charter, and Time Warner. Thus, this strategy appears to be a victory for the NFL, Comcast and its subscribers, and to some extent, for CBS and FOX, who each received a two-year extension of their current contracts to broadcast all Sunday afternoon games simultaneously packaged into the Sunday Ticket. Finally, the NFL did not cede or sell equity in its channel to sweeten the agreement in comparison to what happened with MLB when it awarded ownership of one-third of its channel to DirecTV, Comcast, Cox, and Time Warner.

Super Bowl

For more than three decades, the Super Bowl has been the most popular event viewed on television within American professional team sports. Between 1966 and 1969 inclusive, the champion of the NFL's Eastern and Western conferences played the best club from the AFL's Eastern and Western divisions. After these leagues merged following their 1969 postseasons, the Super Bowl became the NFL Championship Game.[17]

For a few minor but relevant facts about this event's origin, former NFL commissioner Pete Rozelle preferred to call the league's final postseason game "The Big One" while Kansas City Chiefs owner Lamar Hunt decided to identify it as a Super Bowl after watching his children play with a toy labeled Super

Ball. In fact, the title Super Bowl was consistent with college football's post-season bowl games whereas the term "bowl" originated from a Rose Bowl Game played in a circular football stadium located in Los Angeles, California. Anyway, the game's name of Super Bowl became permanent in 1966.

Throughout the NFL's postseasons, various major television networks have won the exclusive right to broadcast a number of Super Bowl games. Because of the event's increasing popularity and status of being an undeclared but de facto national holiday in America, the most expensive commercial ads in television history have appeared during these championship football games. For example, despite an economic recession, NBC earned $3 million for broadcasting each 30-second spot that appeared while the Pittsburgh Steelers defeated the Arizona Cardinals, 27–23, in February 2009. This amount for a single ad represented an increase of 11 percent from 2008. While General Motors (GM) purchased time to advertise before and after — but not during — the 2009 game, such traditional U.S.-based companies as Anheuser-Busch, Coca-Cola, Monster.com, and PepsiCo filled the gap in advertising that GM had abandoned.

There are other interesting facts to report about the history of this great event. One, Super Bowl Sunday ranks each year as the second-highest food consumption day within the U.S., following Thanksgiving Day in late November. Two, GM spent $46 million to advertise its automobiles during the Super Bowls played in 2004–2008 while Anheuser-Busch's expenditures totaled $115 million. Three, approximately 100 million people watched commercials and the halftime show of Super Bowl XLIII held in 2009, but not the actual game played between teams.

Four, more than 97 million people across the world watched the Super Bowl game played between the New York Giants and New England Patriots in 2008, while the Denver Broncos-San Francisco 49ers contest in 1990 was the least popular of them at 73.8 million. Five, one sports website estimated that $10 billion in bets occurred on the 2009 Super Bowl game, or five percent less than the total wagered on the Seahawks-Steelers match-up in 2006. In fact, sports books have reportedly won at least $100 billion from bettors on Super Bowl games played since 1990.

To summarize the facts and outcomes of 43 Super Bowls, including numeral XLII played in Tampa Bay in 2008, I prepared Table 5.1. It denotes, in part, some specific information. To illustrate, 15 different U.S. cities have hosted Super Bowls, ranging from nine each in Miami, Florida, and New Orleans, Louisiana, to one each in Detroit, Michigan, Glendale and Tempe, Arizona, and Jacksonville, Florida. Regarding the number of games within states, 14 took place in Florida, 11 in California, nine in Louisiana, two each in Arizona, Georgia, Michigan and Texas, and one in Minnesota.

TABLE 5.1 NATIONAL FOOTBALL LEAGUE SUPER BOWL
GAMES AND RESULTS, 1966–2008 SEASONS

	Games		*Results*	
NFL Season	*City*	*Attendance*	*Champion*	*Runner-up*
1966	Los Angeles	61,946	Green Bay Packers	Kansas City Chiefs
1967	Miami	75,546	Green Bay Packers	Oakland Raiders
1968	Miami	75,389	New York Jets	Baltimore Colts
1969	New Orleans	80,562	Kansas City Chiefs	Minnesota Vikings
1970	Miami	79,204	Baltimore Colts	Dallas Cowboys
1971	New Orleans	81,023	Dallas Cowboys	Miami Dolphins
1972	Los Angeles	90,182	Miami Dolphins	Washington Redskins
1973	Houston	71,882	Miami Dolphins	Minnesota Vikings
1974	New Orleans	80,997	Pittsburgh Steelers	Minnesota Vikings
1975	Miami	80,187	Pittsburgh Steelers	Dallas Cowboys
1976	Pasadena	103,438	Oakland Raiders	Minnesota Vikings
1977	New Orleans	75,583	Dallas Cowboys	Denver Broncos
1978	Miami	79,484	Pittsburgh Steelers	Dallas Cowboys
1979	Pasadena	103,985	Pittsburgh Steelers	Los Angeles Rams
1980	New Orleans	76,135	Oakland Raiders	Philadelphia Eagles
1981	Pontiac	81,270	San Francisco 49ers	Cincinnati Bengals
1982	Pasadena	103,667	Washington Redskins	Miami Dolphins
1983	Tampa	72,920	Los Angeles Raiders	Washington Redskins
1984	Stanford	84,059	San Francisco 49ers	Miami Dolphins
1985	New Orleans	73,818	Chicago Bears	New England Patriots
1986	Pasadena	101,063	New York Giants	Denver Broncos
1987	San Diego	73,302	Washington Redskins	Denver Broncos
1988	Miami	75,129	San Francisco 49ers	Cincinnati Bengals
1989	New Orleans	72,919	San Francisco 49ers	Denver Broncos
1990	Tampa	73,813	New York Giants	Buffalo Bills
1991	Minneapolis	63,130	Washington Redskins	Buffalo Bills
1992	Pasadena	98,374	Dallas Cowboys	Buffalo Bills
1993	Atlanta	72,817	Dallas Cowboys	Buffalo Bills
1994	Miami	74,107	San Francisco 49ers	San Diego Chargers
1995	Tempe	76,347	Dallas Cowboys	Pittsburgh Steelers
1996	New Orleans	72,301	Green Bay Packers	New England Patriots
1997	San Diego	68,912	Denver Broncos	Green Bay Packers

| | *Games* | | | *Results* |
NFL Season	City	Attendance	Champion	Runner-up
1998	Miami	74,803	Denver Broncos	Atlanta Falcons
1999	Atlanta	72,625	St. Louis Rams	Tennessee Titans
2000	Tampa	71,921	Baltimore Ravens	New York Giants
2001	New Orleans	72,922	New England Patriots	St. Louis Rams
2002	San Diego	67,703	Tampa Bay Bucs	Oakland Raiders
2003	Houston	71,525	New England Patriots	Carolina Panthers
2004	Jacksonville	78,125	New England Patriots	Philadelphia Eagles
2005	Detroit	68,206	Pittsburgh Steelers	Seattle Seahawks
2006	Miami	74,512	Indianapolis Colts	Chicago Bears
2007	Glendale	71,101	New York Giants	New England Patriots
2008	Tampa Bay	72,500	Pittsburgh Steelers	St. Louis Cardinals

Note: Each Super Bowl was played in the year following the NFL seasons listed in column one. Pasadena and Stanford are cities in California while Pontiac is in Michigan and Glendale and Tempe are in Arizona. The states of other cities listed in column two are well known.

Source: *2008 NFL Record & Fact Book* and *The World Almanac and Book of Facts*.

For teams and their total Super Bowl championships through 2008, the Pittsburgh Steelers have won six, the Dallas Cowboys five, the New York Giants, Green Bay Packers, New England Patriots, and Washington Redskins each with three, and 12 other teams each with one or two titles. As of the 2008 NFL postseason, five (15 percent) active clubs had never participated in a Super Bowl. These were the Cleveland Browns, Detroit Lions, Houston Texans, Jacksonville Jaguars, and New Orleans Saints. Nonetheless, both the Browns and Lions won more than one NFL Championship before 1966.

Besides earning millions for the NFL, some civic boosters estimate that a Super Bowl improves the host city's local economy by $300–400 million. Therefore, during the early 2000s, two economists decided to evaluate these boosters' claim. Indeed, they studied the financial results of 32 Super Bowls to determine a typical game's contribution to these cities' economies by quantifying their predicted and actual growth in income from hosting this NFL event.[18]

Based on a regression analysis, the study revealed that the numerous Super Bowls had created an average of $92 million in income gains for the various host cities, or roughly 25 percent of the amount estimated by boosters but not accepted or refuted by the league. In short, the authors suggest that cities should be very suspicious about any economic impact estimates performed by independent consultants or the NFL and supported by local businesses, politicians, and other special interest groups who overinflate the financial benefits of a Super Bowl.[19]

The Super Bowl concludes a discussion of the business relations and activities, operations, and results regarding several interesting, prominent, and relevant domestic affairs of the NFL and its teams. Therefore, in the next and final section of this chapter, I describe the league's affairs with respect to its events and business deals that occur in a few foreign countries.

Foreign Affairs

From 1995 to 2007, the NFL subsidized the World League of American Football or WLAF (renamed NFL Europe or NFLE in 1998). The league failed, unfortunately, because teams did not attract enough local fans to home and away games. Moreover, some teams had financial problems and competitive pressures at their home sites due to the presence of popular team sports in Europe, such as basketball, cricket, ice hockey, rugby and soccer. Furthermore, they received poor exposure of their football games on foreign television and radio networks and in the print media. Due to these problems, the defunct professional football league is not among the NFL's commercial entities and its most recent international affairs.

Before and while the league existed, however, the NFL had periodically scheduled exhibition and/or preseason football games in stadiums of various nations. During the 1950s and 1960s, for example, the cities of Hamilton, Montreal, Ottawa, and Toronto in Canada hosted NFL games, and in the 1970s–1980s, other games took place at stadiums in London, Mexico City, and Tokyo. Generally, these competitions attracted large and enthusiastic audiences despite relatively high ticket prices for admission. Even so, these events encouraged NFL teams to begin playing a few regular season games abroad during the early 2000s. Thus later in this section, a discussion of the league's American Bowl and International Series includes the results of football games played in other countries. Consequently, the following parts highlight an organization previously established by the NFL to coordinate foreign affairs and then describe the role of American football as a sport and business in a few nations of the world.

NFL International

After the WLAF began its regular season schedule of games in 1995, executives of NFL Properties Inc. (NFLPI) decided one year later to be aggressive but efficient and therefore extend the NFL brand from areas within the

U.S. into sports markets abroad. That is, the NFLPI consolidated its operations and various offshore marketing campaigns and assigned them to a new division titled the NFL International (NFLI). As such, this new organizational unit assumed responsibility and received authority for the following matters: to unify the operations and business activities of the league's increasingly important foreign markets; streamline the goals, plans, and tasks of NFLPI; and provide the league with innovative marketing and grassroots programs that, for a profit, may be sold to existing and/or potential affiliates, licensees, partners, sponsors, and/or vendors in America but preferably across the globe.

To strategically expand the league's games internationally and sell more football merchandise, especially since the mid-to-late 1990s, NFLPI reorganized as a unit and implemented a number of its business plans in order to become more successful. To illustrate, in 1998 Germany's SATI and Spain's TV3 television networks agreed to broadcast key segments of the former NFLE's games for the first time. In addition, both networks joined with five other European broadcasters to provide highlights from the NFL teams' regular season games.

Then in 1999, the NFLI signed a lucrative and well-publicized commercial agreement with Keith Prowse International (KPI), which was the world's leading entertainment travel company that had provided services for concerts, theaters, and a number of high-profile marketing projects. According to its contract with the NFLI, KPI became an authorized ticket agent for foreign sports fans who wanted to purchase tickets and ticket-inclusive packages to any NFL preseason, regular-season, and postseason games.

For other business activities to market and promote American professional football events, including those of the NFL before and throughout the early 2000s, the NFLI successfully enrolled more than one million children and/or teenagers from foreign countries in various flag football programs. Also, the league's international unit coordinated football promotions with more than 65 sponsors, scheduled nearly 56,000 hours of NFL programming to be broadcast on television in 24 languages to households in 182 countries, and created links to football-related websites expressed in German, Japanese, and Spanish. Another important innovation, during January 2003, the NFLI sponsored a $1.6 million Super Bowl advertising campaign to attract athletes and appeal to adult sports fans and television viewers from the United Kingdom, which was the world's second-most valuable market for television sports rights fees.

According to a statement issued in 2002 by NFLI senior vice president and managing director Douglas Quinn, "Our focus for the future is to continue to provide our existing and potential new fans with the highest quality entertainment experience while delivering our business partners the maximum value from their NFL association." To help fulfill its executives' visions, the NFLI proceeded to establish business partnerships with at least 30 corporate sponsors and 18 multinational companies, earn an estimated $100 million in consumer sales, and maintain strategic business partnerships with such leading retailers as Foot Locker, Deportes Marti, Japan Sports Vision, and Wal-Mart.[20]

In short, because of creative and grassroots business, marketing and football programs as well as corporate alliances and other types of deals, the NFLI continues to promote the NFL's brand worldwide. As such, this effort generates an enormous amount of extra revenue for the league and its teams from the advertisement, sale, and distribution of NFL merchandise, programming, and video games to corporations, households, and avid sports fans located in many foreign nations.

During the mid–1990s, the NFLI decided to initiate and establish regional branch offices in three geographically dispersed countries: Japan in 1996; Canada in 1997; and, Mexico in 1998. Because these three offices represent, in part, examples of the NFL's global long-term priorities and most valuable international investments, I discuss the league's historical football activities, partnerships and sponsorships, and its events and business developments within these nations followed by the important and unique alliances, events, and ventures proposed and/or established within the United Kingdom, Spain, and China.[21]

Japan

In 1934, American football games came to fruition in Japan when U.S. schoolteacher Paul Rusch organized some local amateur teams. Years later, while the Allied armies maintained a military presence throughout Asia during the mid-to-late 1940s, the sport gradually grew more popular and expanded in the 1950s and 1960s. Therefore, to provide competitive football games across Japan in the 1970s, the nation's largest companies formed a league. This group included approximately 71 teams, each of which played in one of four tiers.

Between the late 1970s and 1980s, the Japanese economy boomed. Thus, football attracted more sports fans, who supported their local team's games. Then in 1989, Tokyo hosted the fourth annual American Bowl Series in which the Los Angeles Rams defeated the San Francisco 49ers, 16–13, in overtime, which thrilled Asian spectators attending that game in the Tokyo Dome. Nevertheless, by the early-to-mid 1990s, Japan's economy fell into a severe recession caused by overinflated asset values and, subsequently, a crash of the country's real estate and stock markets.

These unfortunate events significantly restricted the opportunities for Japanese consumers to spend their diminishing disposable incomes on entertainment activities, including sports. As a result, attendances at football games declined, although ticket prices remained relatively high despite unemployment problems and financial hardships experienced then by households and companies that struggled from a deteriorating economy. Consequently, millions of Japan's sports fans gradually shifted their attention and support of existing football leagues, teams, and players to local amateur soccer leagues and national professional baseball clubs.

Although Japan's economy remained sluggish while its consumers became increasingly pessimistic about prospects for the future, the NFL continued to schedule football programs in Japan during the mid-to-late 1990s to early 2000s. The league marketed the sport by implementing new grassroots activities, such as flag football programs for Japanese kids, negotiating licensing agreements and signing sponsorship deals with local businesses, and establishing television and radio contracts with broadcasting companies. From its office in Tokyo, which opened in June 2001, the NFLI restructured and streamlined its business strategies and thus profitably exploited any economic opportunities available in Japan.

For examples of these deals, the NFL and its NFLI unit willingly provided programming services to such broadcast partners as the NHK-BS, NTV terrestrial, Gaora and SkyPerfectTV networks. Additionally, the league promoted various fan and player development programs for teenagers and adults in some Japanese cities and smaller rural towns. More specifically, the NFLI formed strategic alliances with Toyota and VISA and arranged partnerships with Japan Sports Vision, Marubeni, and Reebok. Because of these marketing campaigns and business relationships, during the early 2000s an estimated 9,000 Japanese athletes played in football games on teams in more than 200 colleges while nearly 160,000 elementary and junior high school students participated in flag football programs.

Notwithstanding the NFLI's marketing campaigns and programming since the mid-to-late 1990s, and the league's investments in grassroots football programs, the most popular team sports events within Japan are baseball and soccer games, while ping-pong and sumo wrestling dominate as competitions between individual athletes. In comparison to the availability and popularity of these four latter sports, scheduling football seasons for teams and operating a league requires expenditures of yen by local governments and/or businesses for equipment, facilities, and payments to administrators, coaches and players. Meanwhile, football games are played on relatively large areas of land, which is a very scarce resource, particularly within and surrounding Japan's densely populated cities. Moreover, many Japanese people believe

American football spectacles involve too much contact and encourage brutality, injuries and violence.

Since the sport's fan base is relatively small in Japan, a number of the nation's corporations must support their football team or teams, albeit with miniscule budgets, in order to operate. Furthermore, to remain in business, thousands of Japanese firms reduced their payrolls during the late 1990s and early 2000s. Realistically, these circumstances have made it rather difficult to organize football teams and assign employees from business organizations in Japan to practice, compete in, and win games. In fact, Japanese football players receive no special privileges or recognition from their employers and, unfortunately, sports fans do not admire or greatly respect them for their athletic skills, competitiveness, and willingness to train hard and participate in games.

In short, the feelings toward this team sport by Japanese companies and sports fans indicates why the formation of any high quality, full-fledged football leagues in the country is only a remote possibility. Perhaps Japan's NFL managing director Hikaru Machida was overly optimistic in 2002 when he declared, "Japanese fans embrace the NFL with a unique blend of awareness and emotion. Participants play the game at an increasingly competitive level. This combination bodes well for the NFL and the sport of football [in Japan]."[22]

Canada

To expand the sport beyond the U.S., the NFL and its business associates and subsidiaries have sponsored marketing campaigns and scheduled television broadcasts of the league's football games in Canada since the late 1990s. The following examples illustrate a few of these activities and programs. In order to broadcast NFL preseason, regular season, and postseason games into thousands of households within various provinces and/or cities of Canada, the NFLI initiated and formed partnerships with such Canadian telecommunications companies and cable television networks as Global, The Score, RDS, and Rogers Cable. Besides those broadcasters, the NFLI established commercial relationships with some international consumer goods companies, like Frito-Lay, Gatorade, Pepsi, and Pizza Hut. These businesses, in turn, used the NFL brand and publicized the league's image, history, and reputation as popular entertainment in the advertisements and sales promotions of their beverages and/or food products.

Similar marketing and sales projects as mentioned before continued into 1999 when the NFLI signed a four-year, seven-figure contract with Canadian beer company John Labatt Ltd., which agreed to advertise Budweiser beer in four television spots during some of the league's regular season games. Then during 2003, the NFLI concluded a lucrative two-year deal with Craig Media Inc. The contract specified that this communications company provide broadcasts of at least 17 *NFL Monday Night Football* games to various Canadian stations located in Alberta, Manitoba and Ontario, with Toronto/One, which was the first over-the-air television station launched in that city since the early 1970s.

Despite some minor concerns and objections stated by a few Canadian network executives, the NFL Network broadcasted NFL games and other programs of the league into regions of Canada during 2004–2005. When these programs appeared on cable and satellite systems within the country, this football channel's contents consisted of NFL game analysis and replays, archival footage, and home shopping shows. Invariably, these and other television network programming alliances, and such fan and player events as the American Bowl series, NFL Canada Days, and "Practice With The Pros," were each initiatives that required significant financial investments, leadership roles, and trustworthy relationships between various NFL officials in New York, NFLI executives, and their respective affiliated broadcasters in Canada. Regarding the league's management and business of its Canadian office, NFLI vice president Gordon Smearton said, "The integrated marketing programs from our top partners have taken the NFL to a new level in Canada. Our local office provides the creative and promotional support to drive the NFL's development across the country."

In short, the increase in exposure of American professional football in Canada, the marketing campaigns of the NFLI, and the broadcast of games played by NFL teams for Canadian fans have been commercially profitable long-term ventures for the league. Besides these efforts, the NFL established a five-year alliance in 1997 with the Canadian Football League (CFL) to jointly cooperate and build people's awareness of and an interest in the sport of professional football. As a result, these two leagues' business relationships and their shared responsibilities have stabilized such that they amicably co-exist and interact, yet compete for shares of each other's local sports markets.

Mexico

Although this American sport and league have never significantly threatened the market share and success of the country's baseball and soccer programs and teams, any amateur and semiprofessional games and other football events are increasingly popular entertainment activities in Mexico, which according to some experts in the sport is the NFL's largest and most lucrative international market. Indeed, numerous Mexican athletes have organized local teams and played football games since the early 1900s. Besides a college group of clubs that refers to its organization as major league, Latino teenagers and young adults tend to participate on teams in football leagues within neighborhood areas that are located in midsized and large cities of the country.

Established during the early 2000s, for example, a two-year-old Mexican football league named *Tochito* encompasses an estimated 100,000 enthusiastic youngsters who are between eight and 18 years old. This sports organization also includes a special 48-team league for emerging athletes who are 12–14 years old. Thus, Mexican kids and teenagers who join teams at the grassroots level enjoy and play American-style football games in addition to competing in baseball and soccer events. Based on the nation's close proximity to the U.S. border states of Arizona, California, New Mexico and Texas, the growth of such leagues as *Tochito* and NFL games broadcast on television partially explain why football became more popular in Mexico, particularly in the late 1990s and early 2000s.

Since its regional office opened below the border in 1998, the NFLI has aggressively advertised and promoted American professional football games and other league events, including its Super Bowl and Pro Bowl and fantasy football to households within the Mexican economy. Many of these marketing efforts succeeded to redistribute and energize the sport's fan base. To illustrate, during 2002 the DirecTV, ESPN, Fox Sports, Grupo Imagen, Televisa, and/or TV Azteca networks broadcast all regular season and postseason NFL games in Mexico on various cable and satellite channels as well as urban radio networks. Then three years later, more than 103,000 spectators watched the Arizona Cardinals trounce the San Francisco 49ers in a game at Azteca Stadium in Mexico City.

According to reports published by the NFLI, during one year of the early 2000s, a number of the league's U.S. business partners, such as Campbell's Inc., Gatorade, Nestlé, and VISA, spent an estimated $10 million on NFL-themed advertisements, promotions, and other sales projects in various Mexican cities. The NFL also sponsored integrated marketing displays that appeared in Mexican retail stores like Deportes Marti, Suburbia, and Wal-Mart. Furthermore, other events and programs such as non-contact flag football, player and cheerleader events, and American Bowl series games exposed the NFL's products within the country and thereby provided male teenagers and adults with entertainment options to play and/or watch games and therefore appreciate, learn, and respect the challenges and excitement of American football.

Because of the growth in Mexico's amateur and professional football fan bases since the late 1990s, the NFL sold approximately $16 million of NFL-franchised goods and merchandise to 20 million or more Mexicans in recent years. With respect to one of the NFL's business strategies, when that nation's economy improves and new marketing opportunities emerge there, the league plans to grant more of its licenses to small-to-midsized Mexican companies that can efficiently produce, promote, sell, and distribute quality football products. These retailers understand and value the preferences of local customers and know how to effectively merchandise and deliver NFL products to those who live in Mexico's urban areas and rural communities.

When a devaluation of the Mexican peso occurred during the mid–1990s, the country experienced an economic crisis. Because of that problem, many local retailers went bankrupt while other consumer-oriented companies moved their businesses from Mexico to China, India, Indonesia, and other very low-wage nations. However, for the majority of Mexican firms that manufactured and/or marketed NFL goods on a full-time basis, they survived that economic crisis, and during the late 1990s and early 2000s, these business firms realized greater revenues and higher profits from selling the league's football products.

According to football statistics published in 2003, a couple of Mexican players appeared on NFL teams while 27 Latino players qualified for training camp rosters. Before their tryouts at NFL-sponsored camps, these athletes probably played on independent Mexican clubs or for U.S. Division II and III college football teams where their outstanding performances attracted the attention of professional football coaches, general managers and/or scouts. When these NFL mini-camps concluded, generally the most promising Mexican and other Latino players signed contracts and received assignments to play for a team in the former NFLE for one or more regular seasons. As such, this experience exposed these foreign players to various game conditions and provided them with an opportunity to become competent professionals by improving their offensive and defensive skills for preparation to qualify for another team and perform in the NFL.

To demonstrate the league's interest in international affairs, in 2002 some NFL officials attended the inauguration of the prestigious Mexican Football Hall of Fame, which is located in Mexico City. Besides honoring many of the American and foreign players who were top performers, this ceremony celebrated professional football for its long and storied history in Mexico. To that end, a number of NFL teams containing Latinos have excelled to win football championships, including Super Bowls. Thus, sports fans who reside in Mexico and other nations below America's southwest border adore these clubs and their former and current coaches and players.

Because of such factors as their geographic locations, winning traditions and superstars, the most popular NFL teams for sports fans in Mexico have been the Dallas Cowboys, Miami Dolphins and Oakland Raiders. If, as a professional football team, it continues to play competitively within the South Division of the American Conference and establishes a larger regional fan base, the Houston Texans will likely become an increasingly popular team in Mexico and perhaps throughout other countries in Latin America.

The NFLI and its parent in New York City, and since 1998, the league's office located in Mexico City, have collectively aroused a passionate and grassroots group of football fans of all ages within that country. This excitement has occurred in Mexico due to several reasons. These factors include the competition displayed between teams at American Bowl series games and in Super Bowls, extensive foreign television coverage and other media programming of professional football, and NFL business alliances with local and regional retailers, partners, and sponsors within Mexico and nationwide with affiliates, corporations, and civic institutions.

To highlight the sport's global progress, the NFL's managing director in Mexico, Will Wilson, summarized the efforts to promote professional football and the league's games south of the U.S. border. He said, "With our continued investment in the market through integrated marketing programs, we expect to continue to build our fan base and deliver value for a growing list of partners."

United Kingdom

For various cultural, economic, and sports-related reasons, during the mid-to-late 1980s American professional football — as exhibited and played by teams in the NFL — became more accepted as a sport and entertainment event in western European countries and specifically within Great Britain. Consequently, when some prominent British amateur and professional soccer teams experienced a modest contraction of their fan bases because of hooliganism, illegal drug use, and rowdy behavior by spectators who attended their games and international tournaments in London, the NFL suddenly grew more popular while the league's games appeared throughout England on various terrestrial television channels. Furthermore, the American Bowl series games played in Wembley Stadium attracted large and enthusiastic crowds in 1983 and again in 1986(1989.

During the early 1990s, however, the novelty of the sport waned in Europe and as a result Britain's passion for and interest in American-style football games and the NFL began to fade. This dilemma for the NFL occurred, in part, when England's professional soccer leagues revised their marketing strategies and retargeted soccer events to attract and entertain social and commercial groups, such as families and businesses. Likewise, British sports commentators who announced professional football games on the country's terrestrial channels failed to inform and educate their television viewers about team strategies, player performances, and the entertainment value of American-style competitiveness and the NFL. Meanwhile, the U.S. Dream Team composed of professional basketball players became an international success after winning a gold medal at the 1992 Summer Olympic Games in Barcelona, Spain. Therefore, when American-style basketball became popular and penetrated England's national sports market, a significant portion of the country's football fans shifted their allegiance and support from the NFL to the NBA.

During August 1993, London hosted an American Bowl series game played between the Dallas Cowboys and Detroit Lions at Wembley Stadium. When this event concluded, and after the league's revenue streams from the sales of football merchandise had gradually diminished, the NFL decided to shrink its presence and the sport's exposure in Britain. To reallocate its resources and funds elsewhere during the mid-to-late 1990s, the league invested in other countries and thus opened regional football offices in Japan, Canada, and Mexico.

Based on various newspaper articles and other research findings published about the league, in 2003 the NFL apparently changed its strategy regarding the development and growth of professional football programs in England. According to NFL vice president for planning and development Alistair Kirkwood, the new goals established by commissioner Paul Tagliabue and 32 franchise owners became "to push the league into popular culture" and "make football stars to be household names within a few years."

The league implemented a multimillion-dollar, five-year marketing plan in England to increase British consumers' demand for American football and establish the NFL as one of the leading sport brands in the nation. Interestingly, the league's plan contained four unique characteristics. First, the NFL signed a contract with a British terrestrial television network named *Five*, which assumed responsibility to broadcast a prime-time U.S. professional football show each week. Second, different types of outdoor, print, and radio advertising were used as methods to promote the NFL and its clubs to sports fans throughout the country. Third, the league concluded some key partnerships with such consumer product firms as Budweiser, EA Sports, and Reebok in which these companies highlighted the NFL brand and its football games and programs in their advertising. Fourth, the league sold in London and other major European cities a new line of women's clothing and redesigned NFL accessories, equipment, and merchandise.

In addition to the strategy revisions adopted in 2003, the NFL continued to sponsor a number of flag football programs and other activities organized at the grassroots level to appeal to British kids, teenagers and young adults, and to prospective athletes throughout the nation. As created by the NFL, these programs and activities attempted to teach youngsters in England how to train and develop specific football-related skills, and how to interpret the basic procedures and rules of this American football game. In fact, during June 2003, football teams in England composed of 12-to-14-year-old British and Scottish gridiron players competed against each other in regularly scheduled games until there was a group champion. When this tournament concluded, the winning club advanced to the eight-team European School Final, which took place that year in Glasgow, Scotland.

Spain

After sports officials settled their negotiations in March 2002, the NFL endorsed a three-year marketing agreement to exchange benefits with a very popular and successful Spanish soccer club named FC Barcelona. Essentially, the contract required that America's elite football league promote FC Barcelona and its activities within the U.S., and inversely, for this foreign professional soccer team to promote games of the former NFLE's Barcelona Dragons in Spain and inform Spanish sports fans about the performances of NFL teams in the U.S.

Besides these transactions, there were other important business and sports-related matters included in the two groups' agreement. One of these actions, for example, recommended that some NFL teams and FC Barcelona play exhibition games in each other's stadium. Additionally, the agreement specified that these teams display shields on their uniforms, share advice about broadcasting, licensing and sponsorship deals, and allow each of them the right to use trademarks in their sales promotions. Lastly, they expected to cooperate by coordinating, advertising, and scheduling American football games in Spain and to provide amateur soccer programs for students in U.S.-based elementary and secondary schools.

To highlight the historic significance of this marketing agreement with FC Barcelona, NFL commissioner Paul Tagliabue stated to the media, "We're doing this as part of the growing globalization of sports, combining the best of American and European sports." Besides these remarks by Tagliabue, NFL executive Alistair Kirkwood graciously expressed his sentiments about the league's relationship with this prominent Spanish club when he said, "The NFL's historic alliance with FC Barcelona represents the first time the two leading sports in their respective countries have joined forces to promote each other's activities. This groundbreaking relationship, along with our close ties with local government, sports federations, and commercial partners throughout Europe, are examples of the kinds of partnerships that are keys to our continued success."

An aside, Major League Soccer commissioner Don Garber voiced an opinion about this business affair when he proposed that his organization join and participate in the NFL-FC Barcelona alliance. "We're in the soccer business," Garber stated. "We want to be part of the growth of the sport [soccer] in this country [U.S.] and are ready to do what's necessary to accomplish this." Paul Tagliabue, however, focused his efforts on the NFL's presence in Europe instead of any relationship or involvement with another U.S. professional sports league.

China

During January 1987, an audience estimated at 300 million Chinese watched an NFL regular season game broadcasted on the China Central Television (CCTV) network. Lyric Hughes, the president of a Chicago-based company named TL International, viewed the game on television in Peking with some prominent Chinese sports journalists. "They were very, very enthusiastic," remarked Hughes. "They cheered all the good plays and touchdowns, although I'm not sure they understood what was happening. They asked a lot of questions about the crowd — what the people were wearing and eating."

Hughes' observations, in part, relate to how words connected with a particular sport translate from English into Chinese. In China, for example, the term football translates into "ganlanqiu," which means "olive ball," while the sacking of a quarterback translates into "capture and kill." Anyway, after being encouraged by the huge Chinese audience that watched the league's game on television, TL International prepared a ten-week NFL postseason package of games that aired on the CCTV network from February to May in 1987.

Prior to the 2008 Summer Olympic Games in Beijing, NFLI managing director Douglas Quinn had negotiated various deals with top Chinese business, government and sports officials, and various promoters in the country, beginning in the early 2000s. Besides television broadcasts, the topics of these negotiations included scheduling NFL preseason games for teams to play at stadiums in Shanghai during 2005 and two years later, in Beijing. Based on his interest to communicate with these officials and thereby establish a business relationship with them, Quinn believed China had powerful economic incentives to further develop and upgrade its national sports programs and to modernize the country's football facilities. China welcomed and supported the proposed NFL football games and other professional and international amateur sports events played in Shanghai and Beijing, and perhaps in other Chinese cities.

To successfully reach an agreement with government officials in China and thus arrange for the broadcast and/or scheduling of the league's games to fans in that nation, Quinn spent numerous hours in 2004–2005 completing volumes of paperwork and securing commitments from the Chinese sports authorities to conclude legal contracts with them. Interestingly, the proposed football games performed in Shanghai and Beijing fulfilled the NFL's strategy of scheduling games, programs, and other football events in countries that successfully built or planned to build large and modern stadiums to host popular global competitions, such as the Summer and Winter Olympic Games. Moreover, NFLI executives believed that the exposure from televising and/or playing professional football games somewhere in China further expanded the NFL's fan base and boosted its business, image, and reputation with respect to Asia's corporate community and the continent's media and other service companies.

The previous part of this section completes an overview of how the NFLI and NFL had existed and commercially operated in several nations during the early 2000s. As emphasized before in this chapter, it is crucial that each U.S.-based professional league in team sports develop strategies and then plan, design, sponsor, and manage international grassroots activities and outreach programs. These, in turn, consist of such innovations as providing sports training to young athletes and supervising camps and clinics for them, counseling football coaches and players, distributing healthcare information, conducting tours and workshops, and scheduling football championship series and other types of tournaments.

To be productive, profitable, and popular, the NFL's foreign activities and events must be fun yet challenge players, entertain spectators, and attract sports fans to professional football. Moreover, these programs should inform, educate, and teach children, teenagers, and young adults from non-U.S. nations how football games occur and what rules apply in this rigorous contact sport. To that end, the next section describes two unique football projects the NFL organized and invested in for years at sports stadiums in major cities of Asia, Europe, and other regions of the world.

Events

American Bowl

To promote American-style football in other countries, the NFL established a series of preseason games at sites outside the U.S. for 18 consecutive years and then again in 2005. Named the American Bowl, these contests of the league served as its teams' fifth preseason game played the same weekend as the Pro Football Hall of Fame Game in Canton, Ohio. For where and when American Bowl games happened, I created Table 5.2 and Appendix M.[23]

According to Table 5.2, England hosted the first three games during 1986–1988 at Wembley Stadium in London. In 1989, one game occurred

TABLE 5.2 AMERICAN BOWL SERIES—COUNTRY, CITY, YEARS, AND GAMES, 1986–2003, 2005

Country	City	Years	Games
Australia	Sydney	1999	1
Canada	Montreal	1990	1
	Toronto	1995/1997	2
	Vancouver	1998	1
England	London	1986–1993	8
Germany	Berlin	1990–1994	5
Ireland	Dublin	1997	1
Japan	Osaka	2002	1
	Tokyo	1989–1996/1998/2000/2003/2005	12
Mexico	Mexico City	1994/1997–1998/2000–2001	5
	Monterrey	1996	1
Spain	Barcelona	1993–1994	2

Note: Three NFL preseason games occurred during years of the American Bowl but did not qualify for the series because the league decided not to organize them. These included a game in Montreal, Canada, and Gothenburg, Sweden, in 1988 and then five years later in Toronto, Canada.

Source: "American Bowl" at http://en.wikipedia.org and "NFL International Historical Results" at http://www.nfl.com.

again in London and another at the Tokyo Dome in Japan. Then during the 1990 series, 200,000 total football fans attended games played in London and Tokyo, and one each at the Stade Olympique (Olympic Stadium) in Montreal, Canada, and Olympia Stadion (Olympic Stadium) in Berlin, Germany. Subsequently, because of the large number of spectators who attended these games and the excitement, publicity, and success generated by the series during 1986–1990, several cities in other nations decided to open their sports stadiums and welcome NFL teams to perform there in American Bowl games.

The following are a few interesting facts about the history of the American Bowl. First, most NFL clubs had competed in one or more of the 40 total games at stadiums in 12 different foreign cities. As of 2008, the Arizona Cardinals, Baltimore Ravens, Carolina Panthers, Cincinnati Bengals, Jacksonville Jaguars, St. Louis Rams, and Tennessee Titans were the only NFL teams not to perform in an American Bowl. Second, 30 (75 percent) games occurred in Tokyo, London, Berlin and Mexico City, and six (15 percent) of the 40 in Dublin, Monterrey, Montreal, Osaka, Sydney, and Vancouver.

Third, for some reason American Bowl games did not occur in four cities where former NFLE teams had existed. These were the Rhein Fire in Dusseldorf and Frankfurt Galaxy in Frankfurt, Germany, Amsterdam Admirals in the Netherlands, and Scottish Claymores in Glasgow, Scotland. In contrast, the former NFLE's Barcelona Dragons, Berlin Thunder, and London Monarchs each played in their stadiums at home where NFL teams had competed in at least one American Bowl game.

Fourth, based on information in Appendix M, nine NFL teams went undefeated and won 19 total games in various series of the American Bowl. Regarding these clubs, the most successful of them included the Los Angeles Rams and Miami Dolphins. Furthermore, the Houston Oilers beat the Dallas Cowboys, 34–23, at the Tokyo Dome in 1992 and two years later conquered the Cowboys again at the Azteca Stadium in Mexico City. However, as a group, the Cleveland Browns, Detroit Lions, New York Jets, Oakland Raiders, and Seattle Seahawks played and lost six total games. Surprisingly, such former Super Bowl champions as the Dallas Cowboys, Denver Broncos, and Pittsburgh Steelers each won less than 50 percent of their American Bowl games.

The Atlanta Falcons defeated the Indianapolis Colts, 27–21, in August 2005 at the Tokyo Dome to complete the NFL's final American Bowl series. After that game and the termination of the league's NFLE operations in Europe two years later, NFL commissioner Roger Goodell decided to switch the league's strategy and schedule teams' regular season games in different foreign countries.

At a meeting in mid–2009, Goodell and franchise owners conscientiously discussed whether to reduce the number of preseason games and if NFL teams should or should not play consecutive regular season games at a stadium in another nation like Germany, Great Britain and/or Japan. Furthermore, during the meeting, Goodell suggested the NFL establish a developmental league overseas whose mission would be to teach and train players rather than promote professional football internationally while trying to achieve financial goals as attempted unsuccessfully by the former NFLE throughout the mid-to-late 1990s and early 2000s. As of late 2009, these issues have not been resolved.

International Series

While the NFLE existed as a league in cities of Western Europe, some NFL teams scheduled and began to play one of their regular season games at a stadium within a foreign country. Thus far, these include the following years, competitors, and places: in 2005, the Arizona Cardinals and San Francisco 49ers met at Azteca Stadium in Mexico City; and in 2007–2008 and 2009, respectively, the Miami Dolphins and New York Giants, San Diego

Chargers and New Orleans Saints, and New England Patriots and Tampa Bay Buccaneers each performed at Wembley Stadium in London.[24]

To highlight each year, the 2005 Cardinals-49ers game — being the first played in a regular season outside the U.S.— attracted more than 103,000 spectators in Mexico City. Then within 90 minutes, fans had purchased 40,000 tickets to the 2007 Dolphins-Giants game in London, which was the first held outside of North America. Although not available in most cities across the U.S., Fox broadcasted it to viewers who tuned into the network. Similarly, the 2008 game between the Chargers and Saints in London received only regional and not national coverage in America by CBS. Finally, the 2009 Patriots-Buccaneers game in London appeared on CBS in the U.S. and Sky Sports and the BBC television networks in the United Kingdom while the BBC Radio 5 Live carried it live there on the radio.

After 2009, I expect more NFL teams to compete in regular season games abroad within cities with large populations and an abundance of dedicated, enthusiastic, and grassroots sports fans, such as in Beijing, Toronto, and Tokyo.

Summary

Chapter 5 included two major sections about relationships between football business and the marketing, operation, and promotion of the NFL and its member franchises in the U.S. and outside its borders. Titled Domestic Affairs and Foreign Affairs, these sections each included some facts, statistics, and other historical information about how the league had established itself as a commercial organization across America and in several nations of the world, especially since the 1950s.

In domestic affairs, officials within the NFL's six divisions perform tasks necessary for the league to continue its operations as an enterprise. As such, some tasks appear within Business Ventures, an NFL division that contains the largest number of experienced and important executives. Meanwhile, other assignments finish within nfl.com, the division that includes the fewest and probably least significant directors. Besides the league's offices and officials, this section includes the critical affairs of NFL Properties Inc., Films, and Network. Formed prior to 2009, each of these units or subsidiaries plays a key role in the legal aspects, and filming and broadcasting the league's activities, news and programs, and its franchises' preseason, regular-season, and post-season games. The final domestic but popular affair highlighted here is the Super Bowl and its history of teams and results of games, and the advertisements and marketing campaigns associated with it since 1966.

In foreign affairs, there is information about such topics as the operation of a division titled NFL International, league's offices in six foreign nations and their goals and successes, and games played by teams in the American Bowl and International Series. Certainly, these topics matter to the league, in part, because sports fans in several countries watch professional football games on television and each year the sport's audiences expand in areas throughout Asia, Europe, and Latin America. In sum, these domestic and foreign affairs contribute to the current and future business, organization, and strategy of the NFL and its franchises.

Appendix A. APFA-NFL
Teams and Seasons, 1920–2008

Teams	Seasons
Akron Pros/Indians	1920–22/1923–26
Atlanta Falcons	1966–2008
Baltimore Colts→Indianapolis Colts	1950, 1953–83→1984–2008
Boston Patriots/New England Patriots	1970/1971–2008
Boston Braves/Redskins→Washington Redskins	1932/1933–36→1937–2008
Boston Yanks→New York Bulldogs/Yanks	1944–48→1949/1950–51
Brooklyn Lions	1926
Buffalo All-Americans/Bisons/Rangers/Bisons	1920–23/24–25/1926/1927, 1929
Buffalo Bills	1970–2008
Canton Bulldogs	1920–23, 1925–26
Card-Pitt	1944
Carolina Panthers	1995–2008
Chicago Cardinals→St. Louis→Phoenix/Arizona	1920–59→1960–87→1988–2008
Chicago Tigers	1920
Cincinnati Bengals	1970–2008
Cincinnati Celts	1921
Cincinnati Reds/St. Louis Gunners	1933/1934
Cleveland Browns	1999–2008
Cleveland Browns→Baltimore Ravens	1950–95→1996–2008
Cleveland Indians	1931

Teams	Seasons
Cleveland Indians/Bulldogs	1923/1924–25, 1927
Cleveland Rams→Los Angeles→St. Louis Rams	1937–42,44–45→46–94→95–08
Cleveland Tigers/Indians	1920/1921
Columbus Panhandles/Tigers	1920/1923–26
Dallas Cowboys	1960–2008
Dallas Texans	1952
Dayton Triangles→Brooklyn Dodgers/ Tigers	1920–29→1930–43/1944
Decatur Staleys→Chicago Staleys/Bears	1920→1921/1922–2008
Denver Broncos	1970–2008
Detroit Heralds	1920
Detroit Panthers	1925–26
Detroit Tigers	1921
Detroit Wolverines	1928
Duluth Kelleys/Eskimos→Orange Tornadoes→Newark	1923–25/1926–27→1929→ 1930
Evansville Crimson Giants	1921–22
Frankford Yellow Jackets	1924–31
Green Bay Packers	1921–2008
Hammond Pros	1920–26
Hartford Blues	1926
Houston Oilers→Tennessee Oilers→ Tennessee Oilers/Titans	1970–96→1997→1998/99–2008
Houston Texans	2002–2008
Jacksonville Jaguars	1995–2008
Kansas City Blues/Cowboys	1924/1925–26
Kansas City Chiefs	1970–2008
Kenosha Maroons	1924
Los Angeles Buccaneers	1926
Louisville Brecks/Colonels	1921–23/1926
Miami Dolphins	1970–2008
Milwaukee Badgers	1922–26
Minneapolis Marines/Red Jackets	1921–24/1929–30
Minnesota Vikings	1961–2008
Muncie Flyers	1920–21

Teams	Seasons
New Orleans Saints	1967–2008
New York Giants	1921
New York Giants	1925–2008
New York Jets	1970–2008
New York Yankees	1927–28
Oakland Raiders→Los Angeles→Oakland Raiders	1970–81→1982–94→1995–2008
Oorang Indians	1922–23
Philadelphia Eagles	1933–2008
Phil-Pitt Steagles	1943
Pittsburgh Pirates/Steelers	1933–39/1940–2008
Portsmouth Spartans→Detroit Lions	1930–33→1934–2008
Pottsville Maroons→Boston Bulldogs	1925–28→1929
Providence Steam Roller	1925–31
Racine Legion/Tornadoes	1922–24/1926
Rochester Jeffersons	1920–25
Rock Island Independents	1920–25
San Diego Chargers	1970–2008
San Francisco 49ers	1950–2008
Seattle Seahawks	1976–2008
Staten Island Stapletons	1929–32
St. Louis All-Stars	1923
Tampa Bay Buccaneers	1976–2008
Toledo Maroons	1922–23
Tonawanda Kardex	1921
Washington Senators	1921

Note: APFA and NFL are, respectively, the American Professional Football Association and National Football League. Some teams in column one joined the newly-named NFL originally in 1922 or as expansion franchises, or as a result of mergers between the All-American Football Conference and NFL in 1950 or between the American Football League and NFL in 1970. An arrow (–) indicates franchise relocation. A slash (/) is a change in a team's nickname. A few clubs did not play in the NFL during some seasons but reentered the league later. The mergers of teams in Philadelphia and Pittsburgh in 1943 and Chicago and Pittsburgh in 1944 are also included in Appendix A.

Source: *2008 NFL Record & Fact Book*; "National Football League Franchise Histories" at http://www .profootballhof.com; *Pay Dirt: The Business of Professional Team Sports*; *Relocating Teams and Expanding Leagues in Professional Sports: How the Major Leagues Respond to Market Conditions*.

Appendix B. Number of
Seasons Played, 1922–2008

Original in 1922 Teams	Seasons	AAFC-NFL Merger Teams	Seasons	AFL-NFL Merger Teams	Seasons
Akron Pros	5	Baltimore Colts	32	Boston Patriots	39
Buffalo All-Americans	7	Cleveland Browns	46	Buffalo Bills	39
Canton Bulldogs	2	San Francisco		Cincinnati	
Chicago Bears	87	49ers	59	Bengals	39
Chicago Cardinals	38			Denver Broncos	39
Columbus				Houston Oilers	27
Panhandles	5			Kansas City	
Dayton Triangles	8			Chiefs	39
Evans. Crimson				Miami Dolphins	39
Giants	1			New York Jets	39
Green Bay Packers	87			Oakland Raiders	12
Hammond Pros	5			San Diego	
Milwaukee Badgers	5			Chargers	39
Minneapolis Marines	6				
Oorang Indians	2				
Racine Legion	3				
Rochester Jeffersons	4				
Rock Island					
Independents	4				
Toledo Maroons	2				

Note: Column one lists the 18 original NFL teams as of 1922. AAFC and AFL are, respectively, the All-American Football Conference and American Football League. The AAFC-NFL merger occurred in 1950 and AFL-NFL merger in 1970. Group one represents the number of seasons played by the original NFL clubs through 2008. The number of seasons includes those of any teams that changed their nicknames, such as the Akron Pros to Akron Indians in 1923. It excludes those of franchises that had relocated, such as the Decatur Staleys to Chicago in 1921 and Chicago Cardinals to St. Louis in 1960. The city of Evansville is abbreviated Evans. The second column of teams includes those that joined the league from the All American Football Conference in 1950. The teams in the third column came from the American Football League, which merged with the NFL in 1970.

Source: *2008 NFL Record & Fact Book*, 2008.

Appendix C.
NFL Performances of Former
AFL Franchises, 1970–2008

Franchises	Performances			
	Playoffs	*Divisions*	*Conferences*	*Super Bowls*
Boston/New England Patriots	15	11	6	3
Buffalo Bills	17	10	4	0
Cincinnati Bengals	8	6	2	0
Denver Broncos	17	10	6	2
Houston/Tennessee Oilers/Titans	16	5	1	0
Kansas City Chiefs	11	5	0	0
Miami Dolphins	22	13	5	2
New York Jets	10	2	0	0
Oakland/Los Angeles Raiders	18	12	4	3
San Diego Chargers	11	9	1	0

Note: Columns two through five are, respectively, the number of former American Football League franchises' playoff appearances, division and conference titles, and wins in Super Bowls. The table excludes the four Super Bowls played before 1970 between the champion AFL and NFL teams.

Source: *2008 NFL Fact & Record Book*; *The World Almanac and Book of Facts*; "National Football League" at http://www.nfl.com; "National Football League Franchise Histories."

Appendix D.
Paid Attendance, Selected Years

Year	Regular Season Average	Regular Season Total	Postseason Average	Postseason Total	Season Average	Season Total
1937	17.5	963.0	15.8	15.8	33.3	978.8
1942	16.1	887.9	36.0	36.0	52.1	923.9
1947	30.6	1837.4	33.1	66.2	63.7	1903.6
1952	28.5	2052.1	48.7	97.5	77.2	2149.6
1957	39.3	2836.3	59.7	119.5	99.0	2955.8
1962	40.8	4003.4	64.8	64.8	105.6	4068.2
1967	53.0	5938.9	55.4	166.2	108.4	6105.1
1972	57.3	10445.8	60.4	483.3	117.7	10929.1
1977	56.2	11018.6	66.8	534.9	123.0	11553.5
1982	58.4	7367.4	64.5	1033.1	122.9	8400.5
1987	54.3	11406.1	65.6	656.9	119.9	12063.0
1992	61.7	13828.8	67.9	815.9	129.6	14644.7
1997	62.3	14967.3	66.8	801.8	129.1	15769.1
2002	65.7	16833.3	65.1	781.9	130.8	17615.2
2007	67.7	17345.2	66.0	792.0	133.7	18137.2

Note: Year is the league's season. Average and total attendance are in thousands. In 2007, for example, the average regular season attendance was 67,700 per game while the total attendance that year equaled 18,137,200. Paid attendance is not the number of spectators that actually attended games since these attendances exclude no-shows. There was a 57-day players strike in 1982 and a 24-day players strike in 1987.

Source: 2008 NFL Record & Fact Book.

Appendix E. Team Home-Site Statistics, Selected Years

Team	Seasons	Area Population	Stadium Age	Home Attendance
Arizona Cardinals	21	3.2	3	64.1
Atlanta Falcons	43	4.2	17	64.0
Baltimore Ravens	13	2.5	11	71.2
Buffalo Bills	39	1.1	36	71.4
Carolina Panthers	14	1.3	13	73.2
Chicago Bears	87	9.1	85	62.0
Cincinnati Bengals	39	2.0	9	64.6
Cleveland Browns	10	2.1	10	72.7
Dallas Cowboys	49	5.1	38	63.4
Denver Broncos	39	2.2	8	75.5
Detroit Lions	75	4.4	7	54.5
Green Bay Packers	87	.2	52	70.6
Houston Texans	7	4.7	7	70.4
Indianapolis Colts	25	1.5	2	66.3
Jacksonville Jaguars	14	1.1	63	65.1
Kansas City Chiefs	39	1.8	37	74.1
Miami Dolphins	39	5.0	22	65.4
Minnesota Vikings	48	2.9	27	63.2
New England Patriots	39	4.3	7	68.7
New Orleans Saints	43	1.3	34	70.1
New York Giants	84	18.3	33	79.1
New York Jets	39	18.3	33	78.4

Team	Seasons	Area Population	Stadium Age	Home Attendance
Oakland Raiders	12	4.1	43	57.8
Philadelphia Eagles	76	5.6	6	69.1
Pittsburgh Steelers	76	2.4	8	62.8
San Diego Chargers	39	2.8	42	68.1
San Francisco 49ers	59	4.1	49	67.4
Seattle Seahawks	33	3.0	7	67.9
St. Louis Rams	14	2.6	14	59.9
Tampa Bay Buccaneers	33	2.3	11	64.5
Tennessee Titans	11	1.3	10	69.1
Washington Redskins	72	4.8	12	88.6

Note: Seasons are these teams' number of years in the NFL through the league's 2008 season. Area Population is in millions for the year 2000. Stadium is the number years from when the stadium opened to 2008. Home Attendance is each team's per game attendance while playing at home in the 2008 NFL season.

Source: *2008 NFL Record & Fact Book*; *The World Almanac and Book of Facts, 2007*; "Ballparks" at http://www.ballparks.com; "NFL Attendance" at http://sports.espn.go.com.

Appendix F.
Ownership Characteristics, 2008

	Characteristics		
Franchise (Owner)	Year Purchased	Cost	2008 Value
Arizona Cardinals (Bill Bidwill)	1962	7M	914M
Atlanta Falcons (Arthur Blank)	2002	545M	872M
Baltimore Ravens (Steve Bisciotti)	2000	600M	1.062B
Buffalo Bills (Ralph Wilson)	1959	25,000	885M
Carolina Panthers (Jerry Richardson)	1993	206M	1.040B
Chicago Bears (McCaskey Family)	1920	100	1.064B
Cincinnati Bengals (Mike Brown)	1967	8M	941M
Cleveland Browns (Randy Lerner)	1998	530M	1.035B
Dallas Cowboys (Jerry Jones)	1989	150M	1.612B
Denver Broncos (Pat Bowlen)	1984	78M	1.061B
Detroit Lions (William Clay Ford, Sr.)	1964	5M	917M
Green Bay Packers (Green Bay Packers, Inc.)	1923	NA	1.023B
Houston Texans (Robert C. McNair)	1999	700M	1.125B
Indianapolis Colts (Jim Irsay)	1972	15M	1.076B
Jacksonville Jaguars (Wayne Weaver)	1993	208M	876M
Kansas City Chiefs (Lamar Hunt Family)	1960	25,000	1.016B
Miami Dolphins (Wayne Huizenga)	1994	138M	1.044B
Minnesota Vikings (Zygi Wilf)	2005	600M	839M
New England Patriots (Robert Kraft)	1994	172M	1.324B
New Orleans Saints (Tom Benson)	1985	70M	937M
New York Giants (John Mara/Steve Tisch)	1991	150M	1.178B
New York Jets (Robert Wood Johnson IV)	2000	635M	1.170B

Franchise (Owner)	Year Purchased	Cost	2008 Value
Oakland Raiders (Al Davis)	1966	180,000	861M
Philadelphia Eagles (Jeffrey Lurie)	1994	185M	1.116B
Pittsburgh Steelers (Dan Rooney)	1933	2,500	1.015B
San Diego Chargers (Alex Spanos)	1984	70M	888M
San Francisco 49ers (Denise DeBartolo York)	1977	13M	865M
Seattle Seahawks (Paul Allen)	1997	194M	1.010B
St. Louis Rams (Chip Rosenbloom)	1972	19M	929M
Tampa Bay Buccaneers (Malcolm Glazer)	1995	192M	1.053B
Tennessee Titans (Bud Adams)	1959	25,000	994M
Washington Redskins (Dan Snyder)	1999	750M	1.538B

Note: Columns one-three are self-explanatory. M and B are, respectively, millions and billions of dollars. NA is Not Available. To interpret the table's data, for example, Bill Bidwill acquired an NFL franchise nicknamed the Cardinals in 1932 for $50,000. In 2008, its estimated market value was $914 million.

Source: "NFL Team Valuations" at http://www.forbes.com and "List of NFL Franchise Owners" at http://en.wikipedia.org.

Appendix G.
Coaching Staff Statistics, 2008

| Team | | | **Coaching Staff** | | | |
	Head	Defense	Offense	Special Teams	Other	Total
American Football Conference						
Baltimore Ravens	1	6	8	2	3	20
Buffalo Bills	1	7	8	1	2	19
Cincinnati Bengals	1	5	6	1	4	17
Cleveland Browns	1	6	10	2	2	21
Denver Broncos	1	7	6	2	4	20
Houston Texans	1	8	9	2	0	20
Indianapolis Colts	1	7	6	1	3	18
Jacksonville Jaguars	1	6	6	2	3	18
Kansas City Chiefs	1	4	7	1	4	17
Miami Dolphins	1	5	7	1	4	18
New England Patriots	1	3	4	1	5	14
New York Jets	1	6	7	2	4	20
Oakland Raiders	1	6	7	2	7	23
Pittsburgh Steelers	1	4	6	2	0	13
San Diego Chargers	1	6	7	1	2	17
Tennessee Titans	1	6	6	2	1	16
National Football Conference						
Arizona Cardinals	1	6	6	1	2	16
Atlanta Falcons	1	5	7	2	3	18
Carolina Panthers	1	6	5	2	2	16

Team	Head	Defense	Offense	Special Teams	Other	Total
Chicago Bears	1	6	8	2	2	19
Dallas Cowboys	1	6	6	1	2	16
Detroit Lions	1	6	7	2	4	20
Green Bay Packers	1	6	8	2	2	19
Minnesota Vikings	1	7	10	2	4	24
New Orleans Saints	1	5	6	2	3	17
New York Giants	1	6	8	2	2	19
Philadelphia Eagles	1	6	8	2	1	18
St. Louis Rams	1	6	8	2	2	19
San Francisco 49ers	1	6	8	2	3	20
Seattle Seahawks	1	6	8	2	2	19
Tampa Bay Buccaneers	1	5	7	1	4	18
Washington Redskins	1	5	8	1	3	18

Note: Head is head coach. Other includes those staff that specialize in strength and conditioning, quality control, and serves as assistant head coaches.

Source: *2008 NFL Record & Fact Book.*

Appendix H.
Average Ticket Price, Selected Years

Team	1991	1993	1995	1997	1999	2001	2003	2005	2007	2008
Bears	28	29	35	38	38	42	65	68	84	88
Bengals	25	24	31	34	37	56	47	55	65	69
Bills	27	28	33	34	40	46	42	39	46	51
Broncos	24	27	33	35	46	77	57	63	71	76
Browns	22	27	32	NA	44	45	45	48	48	54
Buccaneers	20	24	29	35	64	70	49	63	72	90
Cardinals	30	27	31	35	39	37	35	44	56	65
Chargers	19	29	37	42	53	58	46	54	73	81
Chiefs	20	27	31	38	41	52	58	66	73	80
Colts	22	26	28	34	42	54	47	60	70	81
Cowboys	28	32	38	43	48	50	53	66	84	84
Dolphins	25	28	32	41	43	56	46	51	66	66
Eagles	30	35	40	42	37	46	64	66	69	69
Falcons	24	28	32	31	40	39	34	52	60	63
49ers	35	35	39	45	50	50	58	64	62	70
Giants	24	28	35	40	45	55	61	71	81	88
Jaguars	NA	NA	35	36	57	62	62	40	49	55
Jets	22	25	25	30	41	57	62	71	80	86
Lions	18	25	28	34	35	39	53	56	59	66
Oilers	23	29	31	NA	NA	NA	NA	NA	NA	NA
Packers	20	26	26	34	42	53	54	56	63	63
Panthers	NA	NA	37	39	55	60	42	54	60	63

Team	1991	1993	1995	1997	1999	2001	2003	2005	2007	2008
Patriots	29	28	34	39	39	47	75	90	90	117
Raiders	23	31	51	51	51	51	58	58	62	62
Rams	21	29	33	33	33	49	54	60	68	68
Ravens	NA	NA	NA	37	42	50	53	62	77	77
Redskins	32	35	35	52	74	81	68	67	79	79
Saints	23	27	32	34	41	49	43	51	54	62
Seahawks	27	27	28	32	35	44	43	44	54	61
Steelers	29	25	30	35	40	62	54	59	65	67
Texans	NA	NA	NA	NA	NA	NA	50	56	62	66
Titans	NA	NA	NA	40	55	60	43	47	54	58
Vikings	25	29	33	40	44	52	59	67	70	73
Average	25	28	33	38	45	53	53	58	67	72

Note: The NA means not applicable since an NFL team with that nickname did not exist in the league during the year. The Oilers, however, played home games in Houston, Texas, in 1991, 1993 and 1995, and in Tennessee in 1997–2008. Nevertheless, the average ticket price of $40 appears for the Titans in 1997 although the team's nickname that year was Tennessee Oilers.

Source: "Fan Cost Index" at http://www.teammarketing.com and "Sports Business Data" at http://www.rodneyfort.com.

Appendix I.
Team Valuations, Selected Years

Team	Revenue 1999	Revenue 2008	Operating Income 1999	Operating Income 2008	Value 1999	Value 2008
Arizona Cardinals	100	203	11	20	301	914
Atlanta Falcons	99	203	17	31	306	872
Baltimore Ravens	120	226	33	23	408	1062
Buffalo Bills	102	206	11	12	326	885
Carolina Panthers	128	221	19	22	488	1040
Chicago Bears	101	226	20	34	313	1064
Cincinnati Bengals	92	205	4	22	394	941
Cleveland Browns	NA	220	NA	19	NA	1035
Dallas Cowboys	162	269	57	31	663	1612
Denver Broncos	99	226	5	19	427	1061
Detroit Lions	98	204	16	8	293	917
Green Bay Packers	103	218	16	22	320	1023
Houston Texans	NA	239	NA	44	NA	1125
Indianapolis Colts	98	203	16	16	305	1076
Jacksonville Jaguars	116	204	29	28	419	876
Kansas City Chiefs	110	214	31	12	353	1016
Miami Dolphins	128	212	33	36	446	1044
Minnesota Vikings	100	195	5	19	309	839
New England Patriots	110	282	14	39	460	1324
New Orleans Saints	102	213	11	22	315	937
New York Giants	108	214	25	41	376	1178
New York Jets	104	213	12	26	363	1170

Team	Revenue 1999	Revenue 2008	Operating Income 1999	Operating Income 2008	Value 1999	Value 2008
Oakland Raiders	100	205	17	27	299	861
Philadelphia Eagles	103	237	19	34	318	1116
Pittsburgh Steelers	97	216	16	14	397	1015
San Diego Chargers	104	207	8	19	323	888
San Francisco 49ers	109	201	13	4	371	865
Seattle Seahawks	100	215	6	9	399	1010
St. Louis Rams	111	208	33	26	390	929
Tampa Bay Buccaneers	129	224	41	39	502	1053
Tennessee Titans	90	216	4	25	369	994
Washington Redskins	152	327	49	58	607	1538

Note: Revenue is net of stadium revenues used for debt payments. Operating income is earnings before interest, taxes, depreciation, and amortization. Value is the current (2008) stadium deal without deductions for debt. These numbers are in millions of dollars. NA means not available since revenue, operating income, and value were unreported for the Cleveland Browns in 1999 while the Houston Texans did not exist until 2002.

Source: "NFL Team Valuations" at http://www.forbes.com.

Appendix J. Stadium Rankings, by Category, 2008

Stadium	Rankings				
	Afford-ability/ Food	*Tail-gating*	*Team Quality*	*Atmos-phere*	*Accessi-bility*
Lambeau Field (Packers)	1	2	5	1	4
Heinz Field (Steelers)	4	5	2	6	11
Invesco Field at Mile High (Broncos)	7	13t	8	7	3
M & T Bank Stadium (Ravens)	9	7	12	11	2
Municipal Stadium (Jaguars)	3	17	11	12	1
Lucas Oil Stadium (Colts)	8	19	3	3	12
Qwest Field (Seahawks)	5	28	4	4	8
Ralph Wilson Stadium (Bills)	2	1	19	15	13
LP Field (Titans)	11t	20	13	2	5
Lincoln Financial Field (Eagles)	10	4	7	26	9t
Gillette Stadium (Patriots)	25	8	1	13	16
Arrowhead Stadium (Chiefs)	16	3	22	5	25
Bank of America Stadium (Panthers)	11t	24t	16	17	7
Cleveland Browns Stadium (Browns)	11t	6	25	28	6
Louisiana Superdome (Saints)	6	27	17	10	18
Reliant Stadium (Texans)	15	15	26	9	14
Soldier Field (Bears)	18	13t	15	16	20
Raymond James Stadium (Bucs)	17	16	14	19	23
Qualcomm Stadium (Chargers)	26	12	9	21	21
Texas Stadium (Cowboys)	23	24t	6	8	28
UOP Stadium (Cardinals)	14	23	23	22	15

Stadium	Afford-ability/ Food	Tail-gating	Team Quality	Atmos-phere	Accessi-bility
Giants Stadium (Giants)	30	10	10	18	31
McAfee Coliseum (Raiders)	22	9	29	32	9t
Georgia Dome (Falcons)	20	29	24	27	17
FedEx Field (Redskins)	31	18	18	20	30
Candlestick Park (49ers)	27	26	27	14	29
Paul Brown Stadium (Bengals)	21	21	31	30	22
Dolphin Stadium (Dolphins)	24	22	28	25	26
Giants Stadium (Jets)	32	11	21	31	32
HHH Metrodome (Vikings)	28	32	20	24	24
Ford Field (Lions)	19	30	32	23	27
Edward Jones Dome (Rams)	29	31	30	29	19

Note: The t means a tie in rank between teams in this category. Bucs is Buccaneers. HHH is Hubert H. Humphrey.

Source: "NFL Stadium Rankings" at http://sportsillustrated.cnn.com.

Appendix K. Stadium Projects Characteristics, Selected Years

Team	Contributions			Lease Term
	Total	Public	Private	
Arizona Cardinals	395.0	261.4	133.6	30
Atlanta Falcons	214.0	214.0	0.0	20
Baltimore Ravens	224.0	200.0	24.0	30
Buffalo Bills	63.2	63.2	0.0	15
Carolina Panthers	240.0	55.0	185.0	31
Chicago Bears	590.0	390.0	200.0	30
Cincinnati Bengals	449.8	424.8	25.0	26
Cleveland Browns	300.0	212.0	88.0	30
Denver Broncos	370.0	230.0	140.0	30
Detroit Lions	471.0	125.0	346.0	35
Green Bay Packers	295.2	169.1	126.1	30
Houston Texans	424.0	309.0	115.0	30
Jacksonville Jaguars	161.0	146.0	15.0	30
New England Patriots	406.0	70.0	336.0	25
Oakland Raiders	100.0	100.0	0.0	16
Philadelphia Eagles	518.7	188.7	330.0	30
Pittsburgh Steelers	234.0	138.0	96.0	30
St. Louis Rams	257.0	257.0	0.0	30
Seattle Seahawks	465.0	296.0	169.0	30
Tampa Bay Buccaneers	168.0	153.0	15.0	30

Team	Contributions			Lease Term
	Total	*Public*	*Private*	*Lease Term*
Tennessee Titans	292.0	220.0	72.0	30
Washington Redskins	259.0	70.0	189.0	30

Note: Some of these 22 stadium projects ended before, during, or after 2002. Contributions are in millions of dollars. Lease terms are in years.

Source: "Representative NFL Stadium Public/Private Partnerships" at http://www.sandiego. gov.

Appendix L. New, Proposed, or Renovated Stadiums, 2009

Team	City	Date	Cost	Stadium Public	Seats
Dallas Cowboys	Arlington	2009	1B	No	80,000
Kansas City Chiefs	Kansas City	2010	150M	Yes	79,500
Minnesota Vikings	Minneapolis	TBD	800M	TBD	TBD
New Orleans Saints	New Orleans	2011	450M	Yes	70,000
New York Giants	East Rutherford	2010	1.6B	No	82,500
New York Jets	East Rutherford	2010	1.6B	No	82,500
San Diego Chargers	Chula Vista	TBD	400M	Yes	70,000
San Francisco 49ers	Santa Clara	TBD	900M	No	68,500

Note: Cost and Seats are estimates. TBD indicates these characteristics of stadiums are To Be Determined and unavailable. B and M are, respectively, billions and millions of dollars. The Chiefs' Arrowhead Stadium in Kansas City is a renovation.

Source: "Ballparks" at http://www.ballparks.com.

Appendix M.
American Bowl Wins/Losses,
by Team, 1986–2003, 2005

Team	Wins	Losses	W-L %
Atlanta Falcons	2	0	1.000
Buffalo Bills	2	2	.500
Chicago Bears	1	2	.333
Cleveland Browns	0	1	.000
Dallas Cowboys	2	7	.222
Denver Broncos	3	4	.428
Detroit Lions	0	1	.000
Green Bay Packers	2	0	1.000
Houston Oilers	2	0	1.000
Indianapolis Colts	1	1	.500
Kansas City Chiefs	1	3	.250
Los Angeles Raiders	1	2	.333
Los Angeles Rams	3	0	1.000
Miami Dolphins	4	0	1.000
Minnesota Vikings	2	0	1.000
New England Patriots	1	1	.500
New Orleans Saints	2	0	1.000
New York Giants	1	0	1.000
New York Jets	0	1	.000
Oakland Raiders	0	1	.000
Philadelphia Eagles	1	2	.333
Pittsburgh Steelers	2	3	.400

Team	Wins	Losses	W-L %
San Diego Chargers	1	2	.333
San Francisco 49ers	4	4	.500
Seattle Seahawks	0	2	.000
Tampa Bay Buccaneers	1	0	1.000
Washington Redskins	1	1	.500

Note: Team is self-explanatory. The W–L% is each team's winning percentage.
Source: "American Bowl" at http://en.wikipedia.org.

Appendix N. Pro Bowl Games and Results, 1971–2009

		Game		Results	
Year	City	Stadium	Attendance	Winner	Runner-up
1971	Los Angeles	Memorial Coliseum	48,222	NFC	AFC
1972	Los Angeles	Memorial Coliseum	53,647	AFC	NFC
1973	Irving	Texas Stadium	37,091	AFC	NFC
1974	Kansas City	Arrowhead Stadium	66,918	AFC	NFC
1975	Miami	Orange Bowl	26,484	NFC	AFC
1976	New Orleans	Superdome	30,546	NFC	AFC
1977	Seattle	Kingdome	64,752	AFC	NFC
1978	Tampa	Tampa Stadium	51,337	NFC	AFC
1979	Los Angeles	Memorial Coliseum	46,281	NFC	AFC
1980	Honolulu	Aloha Stadium	49,800	NFC	AFC
1981	Honolulu	Aloha Stadium	50,360	NFC	AFC
1982	Honolulu	Aloha Stadium	50,402	AFC	NFC
1983	Honolulu	Aloha Stadium	49,883	NFC	AFC
1984	Honolulu	Aloha Stadium	50,445	NFC	AFC
1985	Honolulu	Aloha Stadium	50,385	AFC	NFC
1986	Honolulu	Aloha Stadium	50,101	NFC	AFC
1987	Honolulu	Aloha Stadium	50,101	AFC	NFC
1988	Honolulu	Aloha Stadium	50,113	AFC	NFC
1989	Honolulu	Aloha Stadium	50,113	NFC	AFC
1990	Honolulu	Aloha Stadium	50,445	NFC	AFC
1991	Honolulu	Aloha Stadium	50,345	AFC	NFC
1992	Honolulu	Aloha Stadium	50,209	NFC	AFC

Year	City	Stadium	Attendance	Winner	Runner-up
1993	Honolulu	Aloha Stadium	50,007	AFC	NFC
1994	Honolulu	Aloha Stadium	50,026	NFC	AFC
1995	Honolulu	Aloha Stadium	49,121	AFC	NFC
1996	Honolulu	Aloha Stadium	50,034	NFC	AFC
1997	Honolulu	Aloha Stadium	50,031	AFC	NFC
1998	Honolulu	Aloha Stadium	49,995	AFC	NFC
1999	Honolulu	Aloha Stadium	50,075	AFC	NFC
2000	Honolulu	Aloha Stadium	50,112	NFC	AFC
2001	Honolulu	Aloha Stadium	50,301	AFC	NFC
2002	Honolulu	Aloha Stadium	50,112	AFC	NFC
2003	Honolulu	Aloha Stadium	50,125	AFC	NFC
2004	Honolulu	Aloha Stadium	50,127	NFC	AFC
2005	Honolulu	Aloha Stadium	50,225	AFC	NFC
2006	Honolulu	Aloha Stadium	51,190	NFC	AFC
2007	Honolulu	Aloha Stadium	50,410	AFC	NFC
2008	Honolulu	Aloha Stadium	50,044	NFC	AFC
2009	Honolulu	Aloha Stadium	49,958	NFC	AFC

Note: In column one, Year corresponds consecutively to the NFL regular seasons of 1970–2008. Attendance is in thousands. AFC and NFC are, respectively, the American Football Conference and National Football Conference.

Source: *2008 NFL Record & Fact Book* and "History of the Pro Bowl" at http://www.nfl.com.

Chapter Notes

Introduction

1. For the websites of these American professional sports leagues and specific information about them and their teams, see "Major League Baseball" at http://www.mlb.com, cited 22 February 2009; "National Hockey League" at http://www.nhl.com, cited 22 February 2009; "National Football League" at http://www.nfl.com, cited 22 February 2009; "National Basketball Association" at http://www.nba.com, cited 22 February 2009; "Major League Soccer" at http://www.mlb.com, cited 22 February 2009.

2. The histories of some former sports leagues and the performances of their clubs are discussed in James Quirk and Rodney D. Fort, *Pay Dirt: The Business of Professional Team Sports* (Princeton, NJ: Princeton University Press, 1992); Phil Schaaf, *Sports, Inc.: 100 Years of Sports Business* (Amherst, NY: Prometheus Books, 2004); "Professional Sports Leagues" at http://www.hickoksports.com, cited 22 February 2009; *Idem.* at http://en.wikipedia.org, cited 22 February 2009.

3. The identifications of these five football books as contained in the Bibliography are, respectively, Peter King, *75 Seasons: The Complete Story of the National Football League, 1920 to 1995* (Atlanta: Turner Publishing, 1994); Will McDonough, *The NFL Century: The Complete Story of the National League, 1920–2000* (New York: Smithmark Publishers, 1999); Michael MacCambridge, *America's Game: The Epic Story of How Football Captured a Nation* (New York: Random House, 2004); Mark Yost, *Tailgating, Sacks, and Salary Caps: How the NFL Became the Most*

Successful Sports League in History (Chicago: Kaplan Business, 2006); Michael Oriard, *Brand NFL: Making and Selling America's Favorite Game* (Chapel Hill: University of North Carolina Press, 2007).

4. Different reviews and other comments about Michael Oriard's book are contained in "Brand NFL: Making and Selling America's Favorite Sport" at http://www.publishersweekly.com, cited 17 February 2009; Roger Anderson, "Brand NFL: Making and Selling America's Favorite Sport," *Journal of American Cultures* (June 2008), 210–211; L.J. Burton, "Brand NFL: Making and Selling America's Favorite Sport," *Choice* (1 May 2008), 1; Gilles Renaud, "Brand NFL: Making and Selling America's Favorite Sport," *Library Journal* (July 2007), 97; Travis Vogan, "Brand NFL: Making and Selling America's Favorite Sport," *Journal of Popular Culture* (October 2008), 908–909.

5. See Frank P. Jozsa, Jr., *American Sports Empire: How the Leagues Breed Success* (Westport, CT: Praeger, 2003), and *Big Sports, Big Business: A Century of League Expansions, Mergers, and Reorganizations* (Westport, CT: Praeger, 2006). The third book here is Frank P. Jozsa, Jr., and John J. Guthrie, Jr., *Relocating Teams and Expanding Leagues in Professional Sports: How the Major Leagues Respond to Market Conditions* (Westport, CT: Quorum Books, 1999). Furthermore, other books and articles that discuss league expansions and team relocations appear in the Bibliography of *Football Empire*.

6. Besides these articles as reported in the literature, the two media guides are *2008 NFL Record & Fact Book* (New York, NY: Time Inc.

Home Entertainment, 2008), and David Boss and Bob Oates, Jr., *First Fifty Years: A Celebration of the National Football League in Its Fiftieth Season* (New York, NY: Ridge Press/Benjamin, 1969).

7. These titles are Paul Downward and Alistair Dawson, *The Economics of Professional Team Sports* (New York: Routledge, 2000); Roger G. Noll, ed. *Government and the Sports Business: Studies in the Regulation of Economic Activity* (Washington, D.C.: Brookings Institution, 1974); Brad R. Humphreys and Dennis R. Howard, eds. *The Business of Sports* (Westport, CT: Praeger, 2008); Frank P. Jozsa, Jr., *Sports Capitalism: The Foreign Business of American Professional Leagues* (Aldershot, England: Ashgate, 2004); Jon Morgan, *Glory For Sale: Fans, Dollars and the New NFL* (Baltimore, MD: Bancroft Press, 1997). Also, see Note 2 above for the authors and publishers of *Pay Dirt* and *Sports, Inc.* Prominent economists report the theoretical and/or empirical results of their studies about professional sports, for example, in Robert A. Baade and Victor A. Matheson, "Have Public Finance Principles Been Shut Out in Financing New Stadiums For the NFL?" *Public Finance & Management* (September 2006), 284–320; Dennis Coates and Brad Humphreys, "The Economic Impact of Post-Season Play in Professional Sports," *Journal of Sports Economics* (3 March 2002), 291–299; Rodney Fort and James Quirk, "Rational Expectations and Pro Sports League," *Scottish Journal of Political Economics* (July 2007), 374–387; Mike Mondello and Joel Maxcy, "The Impact of Salary Dispersion and Performance Bonuses on NFL Organizations," *Management Decision* (December 2008), 110–123; John Siegfried and Andrew Zimbalist, "A Note on the Local Economic Impact of Sports Expenditures," *Journal of Sports Economics* (3 April 2002), 361–366; John Vroom, "Theory of the Perfect Game: Competitive Balance in Monopoly Sports Leagues," *Review of Industrial Organization* (February 2009), 5–44.

Chapter 1

1. For the history of professional football, see "Birth of Pro Football" at http://www.profootballhof.com, cited 18 March 1009; "NFL Franchise Year-by-Year Genealogy" at http://www.nflteamhistory.com, cited 9 March 2009; "National Football League" at http://www.nfl.com, cited 22 February 2009; "National Football League (NFL) History" at http://www.rauzulusstreet.com, cited 12 August 2005.

2. Several books describe the APFA's two years as a league in professional football before being renamed National Football League in 1922. For example, there is Peter King, *75 Seasons: The Complete Story of the National Football League, 1920–1995* (Atlanta: Turner Publishing, 1994); Will McDonough, *The NFL Century: The Complete Story of the National Football League, 1920–2000* (New York: Smithmark Publishers, 1999); David S. Neft and Richard M. Cohen, *The Sports Encyclopedia: Pro Football 5th ed.* (New York: St. Martin's Press, 1997); Robert W. Peterson, *Pigskin: The Early Years of Pro Football* (New York and London, England: Oxford University Press, 1996).

3. This book's Bibliography contains several books and readings about expansion within the NFL. Among them are Frank P. Jozsa, Jr., and John J. Guthrie, Jr., *Relocating Teams and Expanding Leagues in Professional Sports: How the Major Leagues Respond to Market Conditions* (Westport, CT: Quorum Books, 1999); Roger G. Noll, ed. *Government and the Sports Business: Studies in the Regulation of Economic Activity* (Washington, D.C.: Brooking Institution, 1974); James Quirk and Rodney D. Fort, *Pay Dirt: The Business of Professional Team Sports* (Princeton, NJ: Princeton University Press, 1992); Ken Peters, "Houston Rejoins NFL With Expansion Team" at http://sports.yahoo.com, cited 6 October 1999; T.J. Simers, "Ovitz Confident LA Will Win NFL Expansion Bid" at http://sports.yahoo.com, cited 30 September 1999.

4. Other readings about league expansion and/or expansion of teams that I researched online are Cliff Christi, "Texans Have a Headstart Over Other Expansion Teams" at http://www.jsonline.com, cited 12 July 2005; Jeff Goodman, "Expansion Candidates Meet With NFL in New York" at http://sports.yahoo.com, cited 14 September 1999; Michael Lutz, " McNair's Determination Rewarded With NFL Franchise" at http://sports.yahoo.com, cited 6 October 1999; "NFL Expansion

Fees" at http://www.profootballhof.com, cited 18 March 2009; Ken Peters, "Houston Rejoins NFL With Expansion Team" at http: //sports.yahoo.com, cited 6 October 1999; Travis Poling, "Is San Antonio Big Enough to Play in the Economic NFL Game(s)?" at http: //www.sportsbusinessnews.com, cited 26 September 2005; T.J. Simers, "Ovitz Confident LA Will Win NFL Expansion Bid" at http:// sports.yahoo.com, cited 30 September 1999. For a scholarly study, see Frank P. Jozsa, Jr., "An Economic Analysis of Franchise Relocation and League Expansion in Professional Team Sports, 1950–1975," Ph.D. diss., Georgia State University, 1977.

5. The reports of regular season and postseason performances of teams in the former APFA during 1920–1921 and then in the NFL appear in various publications. A few of these include the *2008 NFL Record & Fact Book* (New York: Time Inc. Home Entertainment, 2008); Tod Mayer and Bob Gill, eds. *The Pro Football Encyclopedia: The Complete and Definitive Record of Professional Football* (New York: Macmillan, 1997); "NFL Team History" at http://www.nflteam history. com, cited 9 March 2009; "National Football League Franchise Histories" at http: //www.profootballhof.com, cited 18 March 2009.

6. The topic of mergers in professional football is discussed in such books cited previously as *Government and the Sports* Business and *Pay Dirt*. See also Frank P. Jozsa, Jr., *Big Sports, Big Business: A Century of League Expansions, Mergers, and Reorganizations* (Westport, CT: Praeger, 2006), and Larry Felser, *The Birth of the New NFL: How the 1966 AFL/NFL Merger Transformed Pro Football* (Guilford, CT: Lyons Press, 2008). Historical data, statistics, and other information about the AAFC and/or AFL, and their respective teams are contained in various editions of *The World Almanac and Book of Facts* (New York: World Almanac Books, 1930–2007). For articles on aspects of the NFL's market power, see Gregg Easterbrook, "Why Congress Should Look At the NFL's TV Deal," *Wall Street Journal* (2 October 2002), D12; Paul D. Staudohar, "The Scope of Pro Football's Antitrust Exemption," *Labor Law Journal* (Spring 1999), 34–42; Stefan Fatsis, "Can Socialism Survive?" *Wall Street Journal* (20 September 2004), R1–R5.

Chapter 2

1. For some references on the history of professional football in America and the National Football League, see Frank P. Jozsa, Jr., *American Sports Empire: How the Leagues Breed Success* (Westport, CT: Praeger, 2003); Peter King, *Football: A History of the Professional Game* (Birmingham, AL: Oxmoor House, 1993); Michel MacCambridge, *America's Game: The Epic Story of How Football Captured a Nation* (New York: Random House, 2004); Will McDonough, *The NFL Century: The Complete Story of the National Football League, 1920–2000* (New York: Smithmark Publishers, 1999); Sal Paolantonio, *How Football Explains America* (Chicago: Triumph Books, 2008).

2. Information about NFL franchises between the 1920s and early 2000s and their territories is contained in several readings. These include, for example, "National Football League" at http://www.nfl.com, cited 22 February 2009; "National Football League Franchise Histories" at http://www.profootball-hof.com, cited 18 March 2009; "NFL Team History" at http://www.nflteamhistory.com, cited 9 March 2009; Bob Carroll, *Total Football II: The Official Encyclopedia of the National Football League* (New York: Harper-Collins, 1999); David S. Neft and Richard M. Cohen, *The Sports Encyclopedia: Pro Football*, 5th ed. (New York: St. Martin's Press, 1997).

3. The relocation of various NFL teams and their success or failure is discussed in Frank P. Jozsa, Jr., and John J. Guthrie, Jr., *Relocating Teams and Expanding Leagues in Professional Sports: How the Major Leagues Respond to Market Conditions* (Westport, CT: Quorum Books, 1999), and James Quirk and Rodney D. Fort, *Pay Dirt: The Business of Professional Team Sports* (Princeton, NJ: Princeton University Press, 1992). Different types of historical and business data used to analyze the relocations of football teams were obtained from such sources as Tod Maher and Bob Gill, eds. *The Pro Football Encyclopedia The Complete and Definitive Record of Professional Football* (New York: Macmillan, 1997); *2008 NFL Record & Fact Book* (New York: Time Inc. Home Entertainment, 2008); *The World Almanac and Book of Facts* (New York: World Almanac Books, 1930–2007); "NFL Attendance" at http://sports.espn.go.com,

cited 24 April 2009; "NFL Team Valuations" at http://www.forbes.com, cited 9 February 2009; "Sports Business Data" at http://www.odneyfort.com, cited 27 February 2009. For a scholarly study, see Frank P. Jozsa, Jr., "An Economic Analysis of Franchise Relocation and League Expansion in Professional Team Sports, 1950–1975," Ph.D. diss., Georgia State University, 1977.

4. The performances of NFL clubs during their years in the league are reported in *The World Almanac and Book of Facts, 1930–2007*; *2008 NFL Record & Fact Book*, 2008; Pete Palmer, ed. *The ESPN Pro Football Encyclopedia*, 2nd ed. (New York: Sterling Publishing, 2007); "NFL Teams Playoff Histories" at http://www.sportsencyclopedia.com, cited 3 March 2009; Frank P. Jozsa, Jr., *Big Sports, Big Business: A Century of League Expansions, Mergers, and Reorganization* (Westport, CT: Praeger, 2006).

5. The construction, cost, and return on investment of new football stadiums for NFL teams are important topics discussed in the sports literature. See, for example, such articles as Robert Baade, "Professional Sports as a Catalyst For Metropolitan Economic Development," *Journal of Urban Affairs* (18 January 1996), 1–17; Dennis Coates and Brad Humphreys, "Proximity Benefits and Voting on Stadiums and Arena Subsidies," *Journal of Urban Economics* (March 2006), 285–299; John Siegfried and Andrew Zimbalist, "A Note on the Local Economic Impact of Sports Expenditures," *Journal of Sports Economics* (3 April 2002), 361–366; Michael K. Ozanian, "Football Fiefdoms" at http://www.forbes.com, cited 17 March 2009; "Specter of Change: NFL Leaders Oppose Legislation on Financing New Stadiums" at http://www.cnnsi.com, cited 28 June 2009. For details about past, current, and future NFL stadiums see "Ballparks" at http://www.ballparks.com, cited 12 March 2009.

Chapter 3

1. For some books and readings about the history of NFL franchises, see Frank P. Jozsa, Jr., *Big Sports, Big Business: A Century of League Expansions, Mergers, and Reorganizations* (Westport, CT: Praeger, 2006); Tod Maher and Bob Gill, eds. *The Pro Football Encyclopedia: The Complete and Definitive Record of Professional Football* (New York: Macmillan, 1997); James Quirk and Rodney D. Fort, *Pay Dirt: The Business of Professional Team Sports* (Princeton, NJ: Princeton University Press, 1992); "National Football League Franchise Histories" at http://www.profootballhof.com, cited 18 March 2009; "NFL Franchise Chronology" at http://www.hickoksports.com, cited 27 August 2005; "NFL Franchise Year-by-Year Genealogy" at http://www.nflteamhistory.com, cited 9 March 2009.

2. See the *2008 NFL Record & Fact Book* (New York: Time Inc. Home Entertainment, 2008). Other references about various team franchise owners, officials and/or their staffs include Judy Battista, "Owners Agree to Steelers' Restructuring Ownership," *New York Times* (18 December 2008), 15; Stefan Fatsis, "The Battle For the NFL's Future: Team Owners Used to Share a Common Vision, But No More," *Wall Street Journal* (29 August 2005), R1–R3; James M. Gladden, Richard L. Irwin, and William A. Sutton, "Managing North American Major Professional Sport Teams in the New Millennium," *Journal of Sport Management* (October 2001), 297–317; Sherri A. McGee, "NFL Manager of On-Field Operations," *Essence* (November 2004), 112; Randy Mueller, "TSN NFL Executive of the Year," *Sporting News* (2 April 2001), 59–60.

3. Besides citations contained in Notes 1 and 2 above, other publications discuss facts and other information about NFL team owners. For example, see Frank P. Jozsa, Jr., *American Sports Empire: How the Leagues Breed Success* (Westport, CT: Praeger, 2003); Will McDonough, *The NFL Century: The Complete Story of the National Football League, 1920–2000* (New York: Smithmark Publishers, 1999); David S. Neft and Richard M. Cohen, *The Sports Encyclopedia: Pro Football*, 5th ed. (New York: St. Martin's Press, 1997).

4. The offices of NFL teams and the duties, responsibilities, and tasks of officials within them in 2008 were discussed based on information in the *2008 NFL Record & Fact Book* and my experiences, knowledge, and research of professional sports franchises and career in teaching from textbooks in business, economics, and finance in undergraduate and graduate classes for 35 years. In other words, I learned from a broad body of literature what

tasks these officials accomplished for their franchises and thus related them to basic principles of accounting, business administration, economics, finance, human resources, marketing, management, and operations. For a scholarly study, see Donald R. Latham, "An Analysis of the Organizational Structures of National Football League Teams," Ph.D. diss., University of Arkansas, 1979.

5. More facts and other details are available about business and the revenue, operating income, and/or valuations of NFL franchises in such readings as Dale Buss, "Football's Lean, Green Revenue-Generating Machine," *Wall Street Journal* (9 September 2004), 8; Stefan Fatsis, "Can Socialism Survive?" *Wall Street Journal* (20 *September* 2004), R1–R5; "In a League of Its Own," *Economist* (27 April 2006), 63–64; Michael K. Ozanian, "Selective Accounting," *Forbes* (14 December 1998), 124–134; "NFL Team Valuations" at http://www.forbes.com, cited 9 February 2009. For various costs and/or ticket prices of teams in the league, see "Fan Cost Indexes" at http://www.teammarketing.com, cited 26 February 2009 and such articles as Allen Barra, "$400 For a Day at the Ballpark," *Wall Street Journal* (11 May 2009), A17; Darren Everson, "Yankee Stadium's Ugly Start," *Wall Street Journal* (15 May 2009), W5; James T. Reese and Robin D. Mittelstaedt, " An Exploratory Study of the Criteria Used to Establish NFL Ticket Prices," *Sport Marketing Quarterly* (2001), 223–230; Bob Lubinger, "NFL Tickets: Where Does the Money Go?" at http://www.cleveland.com, cited 3 April 2003; "23 NFL Teams Freeze Ticket Prices as Global Meltdown Takes a Toll" at http://www.google.com, cited 3 April 2009; "Jaguars Introduce Half-Season Ticket Packages to Boost Sales" at http://www.nfl.com, cited 23 July 2009. For a theoretical study, see Juris Drayer, "An Analysis of the Primary and Secondary Ticket Markets For a National Football League Team: A Case Study of the Denver Broncos," Ph.D. diss., University of Northern Colorado, 2007.

6. Other viewpoints about business aspects of the league's franchises are discussed in Phil Breaux, "NFL Wrestles With Franchise Free Agency," *Greater Baton Rouge Business Report* (17 August 1999), A16–A17; Dave Cameron, "Trade the Face of the Franchise? It Might Help," *Wall Street Journal* (11 May 2009), B8;

Peter Onge, "Major League Sports Franchises Eye Future Uneasily," *Charlotte Observer* (7 March 2009), 10A; John Vroom, "Franchise Free Agency in Professional Sports Leagues," *Southern Economic Journal* (July 1997), 191–219.

Chapter 4

1. For information about the history of stadiums in the NFL, see Kevin Delaney and Rick Eckstein, *Public Dollars, Private Stadiums: The Battle Over Building Sports Stadiums* (New Brunswick, NJ: Rutgers University Press, 2003); Tod Maher and Bob Gill, eds. *The Pro Football Encyclopedia: The Complete and Definitive Record of Professional Football* (New York: Macmillan, 1997); James Quirk and Rodney D. Fort, *Pay Dirt: The Business of Professional Team Sports* (Princeton, NJ: Princeton University Press, 1992); Roger G. Noll, ed., *Government and the Sports Business: Studies in the Regulation of Economic Activity* (Washington, D.C.: Brookings Institution, 1974); *2008 NFL Record & Fact Book* (New York: Time Inc. Home Entertainment, 2008); "Ballparks" at http://www.ballparks.com, cited 12 March 2009.

2. See Thomas Owens, *Football Stadiums: Sports Palaces* (Brookfield, CT: Millbrook Press, 2001). For brief reviews of this book, see Michael McCullough, "Football Stadiums: Sports Palaces," *School Library Journal* (1 April 2001), 166–167, and Carolyn Phelan, "Football Stadiums: Sports Palaces," *Booklist* (1 April 2001), 5–8. McCullough recommended the book to serious sports fans while Phelan suggested it for kids who are curious about football fields as well as their favorite teams.

3. Robert C. Trumpbour, *The New Cathedrals: Politics and Media in the History of Stadium Construction* (Syracuse, NY: Syracuse University Press, 2006). Reviews of this book are contained with the same title in *Choice* (1 July 2007), 1948–1949, and *Reference & Research Book News* (1 May 2007), 82. The book's target market includes lower-/upper-division undergraduates, graduate students, and general readers.

4. This and other financial data of NFL teams appears in Kurt Badenhausen, Michael K. Ozanian, and Christina Settimi, "The Business of Football" at http://www.forbes.

com, cited 9 February 2009. Furthermore, miscellaneous business and financial information about the league and/or franchises are reported in such readings as "NFL Team Valuations (2004)" at http://www.forbes.com, cited 17 March 2009; Chris Harry, "NFL Continues to Thrive by Dividing Profits Among Teams," at http://www.sportsbusiness news.com, cited 27 March 2006; Matthew Futterman, "NFL Players Seek Bigger Slice of League's Revenue," *Wall Street Journal* (20 May 2008), B9; Michael K. Ozanian, "Selective Accounting," *Forbes* (14 December 1998), 124–134; Dale Buss, "Football's Lean, Green Revenue-Generating Machine," *Wall Street Journal* (9 September 2004), D8.

5. See "NFL Stadium Rankings" at http://sportsillustrated.cnn.com, cited 25 May 2005. Other facts and/or evaluations regarding all or specific football stadiums are available in Matthew Futterman, "Jets to Auction Seats on eBay," *Wall Street Journal* (17 September 2008), B1, B6; Thaddeus Herrick and Alex Frangos, "NFL Teams See Pay Dirt in Modern Stadium Designs," *Wall Street Journal* (3 January 2007), B1–B6; Matthew Johnson, "NJ, Agency Reach Deal With Teams Over Stadium," *Bond Buyer* (3 April 2006), 34; John Morrell, "NFL Teams Profiting From New Venues," *Amusement Business* (21 May 2001), 1–2; Chuck Ross, "Comfort, Diversity Hallmarks of NFL Stadiums," *Building Design & Construction* (September 2002), 12–14; David Stone, "New Homes Abound For NFL Teams," *Football Digest* (April 2001), 12–14.

6. Some financial and/or technical facts and features of NFL stadiums, such as for the Cardinals and other teams, are discussed in Ken Graber, "Arizona Cardinals' New State-of-the-Art Retractable Stadium Roof Employs Technology to Open and Close Panels," *Cost Engineering* (June 2006), 17–19; "Jurors Side With NFL in Oakland Raiders' Suit Over Lost Stadium Deal," *Wall Street Journal* (22 May 2001), B11; Joe LaPointe, "At Meadowlands Stadium, Lots of Bells and Whistles," *New York Times* (31 October 2008), 15; Tim O'Brien, "Work Begins on Houston's New Stadium," *Amusement Business* (27 March 2000), 18–19; Don Richards III, "Stadium Savvy," *Consulting-Specifying Engineer* (July 2002), 53–55; Dan Beighley, "Developer Appeals to Anaheim, OC With NFL Plan," *Orange County Business Journal* (2 June 2008),

1–14; "Specter of Change: NFL Leaders Oppose Legislation on Financing New Stadiums" at http://www.cnnsi.com, cited 28 June 1999.

7. This topic and others involving naming rights are discussed in Barry Janoff, "Naming Rights Deals Near $1B," *Brandweek* (21 April 2008), 18–20; Athena Schaffer, "FedEx Gives $205 Million to Name Redskins Stadium," *Amusement Business* (29 November 1999), 13; Jim Watts, "Arizona: Up Nabs Naming Rights," *Bond Buyer* (3 October 2006), 33–40; Joyce Cohen, "PSINet/Ravens Title Deal Sets Industry Benchmarks," *Amusement Business* (1 February 1999), 1–2; "Naming Rights Online" at http://www.namingrightsonline.com, cited 27 May 2009.

8. These agreements were discussed in Greg Cote, "Stadium Name a Mistake by Dolphins Owner," *Charlotte Observer* (13 May 2009), 2C; Simon Evans, "Dolphin Stadium Renamed Land Shark Stadium" at http://www.reuters.com, cited 18 June 2009; Adam Gretz, "Welcome to Land Shark Stadium, Home of the Miami Dolphins" at http://nfl.fanhouse.com, cited 18 June 2009. Potential naming rights agreements of proposed or new stadiums may or may not involve facts reported in Matthew Futterman, "A Safety For Giants as Clock Ticks Down on Stadium," *Wall Street Journal* (17 June 2009), B6; "Giants, Jets Will Wait For Right Price For New Stadium Naming Rights" at http://www.nfl.com, cited 23 July 2009; "Niners Show Santa Clara Officials Their Plans For New $937 Million Stadium" at http://www.nfl.com, cited 23 July 2009; "Deal That Would Keep Saints in New Orleans Through 2025 Nearly Done" at http://www.nfl.com, cited 23 July 2009; "Developer Abandons Plan to Build New Chargers Stadium" at http://www.nfl.com, cited 23 July 2009.

9. In Kate Macmillan, "NFL Stadiums: What's In a Name?" at http://sports.yahoo.com, cited 27 May 2009, several quotes appear from various marketers of companies. For example, these include "Naming rights have become the primary way, from a sponsorship perspective, to generate revenue." "Today companies can really look at how sponsorships can drive their business and provide direct interaction with consumers." "The reason to do naming rights was to increase brand awareness among consumers and financial advisors." "If you have your name on a stadium that isn't a

premier sports arena, that can detract from people's feeling for the product."

10. See Sheridan Prasso, "Lost Backers," *Business Week* (3 February 2003), 14–16. Besides those in the NFL, several stadiums in MLB, NBA, and the NHL have switched their corporate sponsorships since the height of the Internet industry boom in the late 1990s.

11. For more details about this controversy, see Felicity Barringer, "Private Sector: Going a Mile High and Back Over an Unwanted Nickname," *New York Times* (8 July 2001), 2. Besides express rage at the slur on your company's values and threaten to sue the columnist [Woody Paige] and his newspaper [Denver Post], other options for Invesco were to ignore the reference or explore the possibility of getting naming rights for other birth control devices.

12. The Cowboys fabulous new stadium is discussed in Kurt Badenhausen, Michael K. Ozanian, and Christina Settimi, "The Richest Game" at http://sport.yahoo.com, cited 27 May 2009; Ben Casselman, "Luxury Strikes Out," *Wall Street Journal* (6 March 2009), W1, W5; "The Cowboys New Stadium All That and a Great Deal More" at http://www.sportsbusinessnews.com, cited 13 December 2006; "Dallas Cowboys" at http://www.nfl.com, cited 18 March 2009.

13. The markets and histories of various NFL franchises — including their locations, performances, and stadiums — and the league since 1920 are contained, in part, online at such sources as "National Football League" at http://www.nfl.com, cited 22 February 2009; "National Football League Franchise Histories" at http://www.profootballhof.com, cited 18 March 2009; "NFL Franchise Chronology" at http://www.hickoksports.com, cited 27 August 2005; "NFL Team History" at http://www.nflteamhistory.com, cited 9 March 2009; "Team Games & Schedules" at http://www.pro-football-referenc.com, cited 11 June 2009. For similar information about franchises in other professional team sports, see "Major League Baseball" at http://www.mlb.com, cited 22 February 2009; "Major League Soccer" at http://www.mls.com, cited 22 February 2009; "National Basketball Association" at http://www.nba.com, cited 22 February 2009; "National Hockey League" at http://www.nhl.com, cited 22 February 2009.

Chapter 5

1. For legal aspects of the league and the NFLEP, see "Who Owns the NFL?" at http://www.funtrivia.com, cited 26 June 2009; "Limited Partnership" at http://www.quickmba.com, cited 29 June 2009; Michael E. Jones, *Sports Law* (Upper Saddle River, NJ: Prentice Hall, 1999). Besides legal issues in collegiate sports, *Sports Law* also includes chapters on labor and antitrust issues in professional sports, player agents, torts and sports, and the business of sports leagues, teams, relocations, and building stadiums.

2. The *Sports Business Resource Guide & Fact Book 2006* (Charlotte, NC: *Street & Smith's Sports Business Journal*, 2006) reports the media, executives, divisions, and sponsors with respect to the league while some of them appear in "NFL Organization" at http://www.nfl.com, cited 27 June 2009. Other officials are included in *NFL International: A Winning Partnership* (New York: National Football League, 2002). For a scholarly study, see Carol Marie Oeth, "Leadership in the National Football League," Ph.D. diss., University of Akron, 1996.

3. The year NFL Properties and other subsidiaries became established, and highlights of the NFL during 1920–2008 inclusive, are each contained in the *2008 NFL Record & Fact Book* (New York: Time Inc. Home Entertainment, 2008).

4. As reported in a blog, "An appropriate decision for football decision; the Court of Appeals for the 7th Circuit has affirmed, in an antitrust case, that the exclusive licensing of all professional football teams marks to one vendor is not a violation of the Sherman Act." See Pamela Chestek, "The NFL is One Entity — For Trademark Licensing Anyway" at http://www.propertyintangible.com, cited 1 July 2009.

5. For more details about the trademark and this NFL team, see Linda A. Sharp, "Baltimore Ravens Lose in Logo Dispute," *Sport Marketing and the Law* (2001), 112–113, and Clark C. Griffith, "Sports Licensing," *The Licensing Journal* (September 2003), 26–27.

6. Two readings discuss this case. These are Steve M. McKelvey, "Dawg Pound Decision Provides Guidance For Fan Group-Related Trademarks," *Sport Marketing Quarterly*

(2006), 181–183, and "Browns Score Patent Victory," *Inside Counsel* (April 2006), 96.

7. These readings are, respectively, Mark Hyman, "Patriots' Perfection: Patent Pending," *Business Week* (12 May 2008), 17; "PLB to Develop NFL Licensed Food," *Amusement Business* (24 January 2000), 14; Anna Wilde Matthews, "NFL Nears Web-Properties Deal With AOL, Viacom, SportsLine," *Wall Street Journal* (9 July 2001), B4; *Idem.*, "Sports Leagues Tightening Grip on Web Content," *Wall Street Journal* (11 June 2001), B1.

8. General information about the NFLF is included in "NFL Films," at http://en.wiki pedia.org, cited 26 June 2009, and "NFL Films" at http://www.answers.com cited 26 June 2009. Also, see facts about this organization in the *2008 NFL Record & Fact Book*, 2008.

9. The history about how Ed Sabol and his son Steve developed and improved this organization is discussed in Reid Cherner, "Behind the Curtain at NFL Films, Where Football Was Born," at http://www.usatoday.com, cited 2 July 2009; "Q&A With Steve Sabol," *Roar* (June 2009), 11, 13; Fritz Quindt, "Why Old School Isn't in Session," *Sporting News* (23 July 2001), 7.

10. For the emergence, growth, and business of the NFLN, see Stuart Levine, "Sport Centered," *Sports & Entertainment* (14 July 2004), A2, and "About NFL Network," at http://www.nfl.com, cited 26 June 2009.

11. More and specific information about the *Playbook*, *NFL Replay*, *NFL Game Day*, and *Total Access* programs of the league are available in "NFL Network," at http://www.nfl.com cited 26 June 2009.

12. Information about the three events were reported in Mike Reynolds, "Challenges Await NFL Net, OLN," *Multichannel News* (6 February 2006), 8; Ben Grossman, "NFL Tackles Cable," *Broadcasting Cable* (31 July 2006), 3, 8; R. Thomas Umstead, "NFL Network Is Still Plugging Holes," *Multichannel News* (20 November 2006), 6.

13. For problems that involved the NFLN during 2007, see John Dempsey, "NFL Digs in vs. Comcast," *Daily Variety Gotham* (11 June 2007), 6, 36; "NFL Network Gaining Little Yardage," *Variety* (2 December 2007), 22–23; Thomas Umstead and Linda Haugsted, "Blitzing the Statehouses," *Multichannel News* (12 November 2007), 40.

14. Several articles discussed the broadcast of the Patriots-Giants game. These included Mike Reynolds, "NFL's Perfect Storm," *Multichannel News* (31 December 2007), 3; John Dempsey, "CBS, NBC Get Piece of Pats," *Daily Variety Gotham* (27 December 2007), 1, 8; Jonathan Hemingway, "Stations Cry Foul Over NFL Play," *Broadcasting & Cable* (31 December 2007), 3, 20.

15. During 2008, news about the NFLN's operations appeared in Linda Haugsted, "Scoring With Affiliates," *Multichannel News* (January 2008), 26; Nicole Urso, "NFL Leads Sports Marketers Kicking and Streaming on to the Web," *Response* (January 2008), 36–41; Alex Weprin, "NFL Chief Vows to Grow Network," *Broadcasting & Cable* (28 April 2008), 1; William Triplett, "FCC Backs NFL Play," *Daily Variety Gotham* (14 December 2008), 4, 10; Greg Bishop, "In Letter, Goodell Blames Cable Operators For Impasse," *New York Times* (5 November 2008), 18; Mike Reynolds, "NFL Net Games Play Wider Field," *Multichannel News* (1 December 2008), 3, 22.

16. See Matthew Futterman, "Comcast-NFL Spat Over Viewer Access Intensifies," *Wall Street Journal* (15 April 2009), B7; John Eggerton, "Comcast 'Threatened' NFL," *Multichannel News* (20 April 2009), 6; Richard Sandomir, "Comcast and NFL Network Agree to 9-Year Deal" at http://www.nytimes.com cited 2 July 2009.

17. Various publications report the business of Super Bowls. For example, see Vanessa O'Connell, "Super-Bowl Spots Aren't Easy Sell For Fox," *Wall Street Journal* (21 January 2002), B5; Brett Nelson, "Super Bowls Don't Equal Super-Sized Profits" at http://www.forbes.com, cited 17 March 2009; Kurt Badenhausen, "A Super Bowl of Financial Champs" at http://www.forbes.com, cited 17 March 2009; Mark Yost, "Will Detroit Be the Loser?" *Wall Street Journal* (28–29 January 2005), 12; Skip Wollenberg, "Buyers Say ABC Getting $2 Million For 30-Second Super Bowl Ads" at http://sports.yahoo.com, cited 22 September 1999; "New Orleans Gets Super Bowl," *Charlotte Observer* (20 May 2009), 2C. To host a Super Bowl in 2012, organizers in Indianapolis raised $25 million in private donations while city officials expand the convention center as a new hotel arises across the street from Victory Field, home of the AAA

Indianapolis Indians. According to Ball State University's Bureau of Business Research, this event is "expected to generate a one-time economic boost of more than $300 million for the City including more than $30 million in state and local tax revenue." For more details, see "Indianapolis Ahead of Curve in Preparations For Super Bowl XLVI in 2012" at http://www.nfl.com, cited 23 July 2009.

18. Lake Forest College Professor of Economics Robert A. Baade and Williams College Professor of Economics Victor A. Matheson completed this study. It is "Super Bowl or Super (Hyper) Bowl?: Assessing the Economic Impact of America's Premier Sports Event," Working Paper (Ann Arbor, MI: University of Michigan (2003), 1–33).

19. Other readings on business of the Super Bowl include Kathy Babiak and Richard Wolfe, "More Than Just a Game? Corporate Social Responsibility and Super Bowl XL," *Sport Marketing Quarterly* (2006), 214–222; Ann Brown, "Black Entrepreneurs Tackle Super Bowl XL," *Black Enterprise* (January 2006), 28; Steve Feingold and Catherine Dugan O'Connor, "What's In a Name? Dispelling NFL's Super Bowl Myth," *Business Press* (19 November 2007), 17; Raymund Flandez, "Enterprise: NFL Helps Local Score Super Bowl Business; Focus is on Firms Owned by Women and Minorities," *Wall Street Journal* (29 January 2008), B5; Brian Morrissey, "Super Bowl Spots: Who Needs an Ad Agency?" *Adweek* (16 October 2006), 6–9.

20. Douglas Quinn's statement appeared in the *NFL International: A Winning Partnership* (New York: National Football League, 2002).

21. Much information about NFL International and the NFL's strategies in these na-

tions is contained on pages 76–88 of Frank P. Jozsa, Jr., *Sports Capitalism: The Foreign Business of American Professional Leagues* (Aldershot, England: Ashgate, 2004). Other readings are "History of NFL in Canada" at http://www.nflcanada.com, cited 27 June 2009; "NFL Ponders Second UK Game Option" at http://articles.latimes.com, cited 27 June 2009; Michael O'Boyle, "Mexico's Futbol Fans Embrace NFL," *Daily Variety Gotham* (4 October 2005), 1–7; Peter Spiegel, "NFL Struggles to Gain Ground in China," *Los Angeles Times* (7 February 2009), A3; Marc Edelman and Brian Doyle, "Antitrust and 'Free Movement' Risks of Expanding U.S. Professional Sports Leagues Into Europe," *Northwestern Journal of International Law & Business* (Spring 2009), 403–438.

22. According to some sports reporters, the best Japanese athletes tend to play baseball or soccer, football lacks a star to attract attention from the nation's mainstream media, and the country's best athletes commit to only one sport. Nevertheless, Japan has a semipro football league, about 5,000 high school students play the sport there, and an American football magazine named *Touchdown* is published in Japan. For other perspectives regarding the growth of football in Japan especially at the college level, see Daisuke Wakabayashi, "Japan Takes on the Fighting Irish," *Wall Street Journal* (28 July 2009), D8.

23. See "American Bowl" at http://en.wikipedia.org, cited 27 June 2009, and "NFL International Historical Results" at http://www.nfl.com, cited 25 November 2002.

24. The history of this series appears in a few readings. One of them is "NFL International Series" at http://en.wikipedia.org, cited 27 June 2009.

Bibliography

Articles

Abboud, Leila. "NFL Huddles Include 'Life Skills' Class." *Wall Street Journal* (28 July 2002): A5.

Albergotti, Reed. "Snap Judgments in the NFL." *Wall Street Journal* (24 April 2009): W5.

Anderson, Roger. "Brand NFL: Making and Selling America's Favorite Sport." *Journal of American Cultures* (June 2008): 210–211.

Ash, Katie. "NFL Effort Builds Middle School Football Programs." *Education Week* (19 December 2007): 12–16.

Baade, Robert A. "Professional Sports as a Catalyst for Metropolitan Economic Development." *Journal of Urban Affairs* (18 January 1996): 1–17.

_____ and Victor A. Matheson. "Have Public Finance Principles Been Shut Out in Financing New Stadiums For the NFL?" *Public Finance & Management* (September 2006): 284–320.

Babiak, Kathy, and Richard Wolfe. "More Than Just a Game? Corporate Social Responsibility and Super Bowl XL." *Sport Marketing Quarterly* (2006): 214–222.

Ball, Jeffrey. "Hail Mary? Birmingham Dreams of a New Stadium." *Wall Street Journal* (14 January 1998): S1.

Barra, Allen."$400 For a Day at the Ballpark." *Wall Street Journal* (11 May 2009): A17.

Barrette, Amy. "Can Woody Make It in New York?" *Business Week* (16 August 2004): 48–49.

Barringer, Felicity. "Private Sector: Going a Mile High and Back Over an Unwanted Nickname." *New York Times* (8 July 2001): 2.

Battista, Judy. "Feeling Pinch, N.F.L. Will Cut About 150 Jobs." *The New York Times* (9 December 2008): B17.

_____. "Owners Agree to Steelers' Restructured Ownership." *New York Times* (18 December 2008): 15.

Beighley, Dan. "Developer Appeals to Anaheim, OC With NFL Plan." *Orange County Business Journal* (2 June 2008): 1–14.

Bernstein, Paula. "NFL Ent. Ups Two as Topper Bernard Exits." *Daily Variety Gotham* (9 May 2000): 8.

Bishop, Greg. "In Letter, Goodell Blames Cable Operators For Impasse." *New York Times* (5 November 2008): 18.

"Blog On." *Sporting News* (18 August 2008): 5.

Blum, Ronald. "Squeeze Play: Baseball Slammed by Recession." *Charlotte Observer* (3 March 2009): 1D, 3D.

Borghesi, Richard. "Weather Biases in the NFL Totals Market." *Applied Financial Economics* (July 2008): 947–953.

Breaux, Phil. "NFL Wrestles With Franchise Free Agency." *Greater Baton Rouge Business Report* (17 August 1999): A16–A17.

"Bridgestone Ties With NFL Series." *Marketing* (10 October 2007): 7.

"Briefs." *Charlotte Observer* (30 June 2009): 5C.

Bronson, Cory. "Que Sara, Que Sara: President of NFL Properties Leaves." *Sporting Goods Business* (14 April 2000): 19.

Brown, Ann. "Black Entrepreneurs Tackle Super Bowl XL." *Black Enterprise* (January 2006): 28.

Browne, Ray B. "Brand NFL: Making and Selling America's Favorite Sport." *Chronicle of Higher Education* (14 September 2007): A10.

"Browns Score Patent Victory." *Inside Counsel* (April 2006): 96.

Burke, Monte. "Lifting a Loser." *Forbes* (1 October 2007): 94–97.

_____. "Running Up the Score." *Forbes* (13 December 2004): 68–70.

Burton, L.J. "Brand NFL: Making and Selling America's Favorite Sport." *Choice* (1 May 2008): 1.

Buss, Dale. "The Business of Sports." [Review. *The Business of Sports*] *Kirkus Reviews* (1 September 2008): 6.

_____. [Review. *The Business of Sports*] *Reference & Research Book News* (1 November 2008): 1.

_____. [Review. *The Business of Sports*] *Reference & Research Book News* (1 May 2007): 82.

_____. "Football's Lean, Green Revenue-Generating Machine." *Wall Street Journal* (9 September 2004): D8.

Cameron, Dave. "Trade the Face of the Franchise? It Might Help." *Wall Street Journal* (11 May 2009): B8.

Cameron, Steve. "Politically Correct? Rarely When It Comes to Facilities." *Amusement Business* (February 2006): 35.

Carlino, Gerald A., and N. Edward Coulson. "Should Cities Be Ready For Some Football? Assessing the Social Benefits of Hosting an NFL Team." *Business Review* (2004): 7–15.

Casey, Nicholas, and Stu Woo. "Schwarzenegger Threatens to Sell California Icons." *Wall Street Journal* (15 May 2009): A5.

Casselman, Ben. "Luxury Strikes Out." *Wall Street Journal* (6 March 2009): W1, W5.

Chandler, Charles. "Divisive Selection Process For NFLPA Chief Nears End." *Charlotte Observer* (13 March 2009): 10C.

Choe, Stan. "NFL Playoffs Not a Financial Score." *Charlotte Observer* (12 January 2005): 1D, 2D.

Coates, Dennis, and Brad Humphreys. "The Economic Consequences of Professional Sports Strikes and Lockouts." *Southern Economic Journal* (January 2001): 737–747.

_____ and _____. "The Economic Impact of Post-Season Play in Professional Sports." *Journal of Sports Economics* (3 March 2002): 291–299.

_____ and _____. "Proximity Benefits and Voting on Stadiums and Arena Subsidies." *Journal of Urban Economics* (March 2006): 285–299.

Cohen, Andy, and Erin Strout. "Chalk Talk For Women." *Sales & Marketing Management* (September 1999): 15–17.

Cohen, Joyce. "PSINet/Ravens Title Deal Sets Industry Benchmarks." *Amusement Business* (1 February 1999): 1–2.

Colvin, Geoffrey. "Lessons From the Comish." *Fortune* (17 April 2006): 65.

Consoli, John. "NFL Paydirt Pays Off For Nets." *Adweek* (6 October 2008): 6–8.

_____. "NFL Sticks to the Game Plan." *MediaWeek* (23 April 2007): 4–5.

_____ and Anthony Crupi. "Client Interest Lifts All NFL Boats." *MediaWeek* (24 September 2007): 5–8.

Cote, Greg. "Stadium Name a Mistake by Dolphins Owner." *Charlotte Observer* (13 May 2009): 2C.

Crupi, Anthony, and John Consoli. "Early ESPN, NBC NFL Ratings Sag." *MediaWeek* (24 September 2007): 4–5.

Dempsey, John. "CBS, NBC Get Piece of Pats." *Daily Variety Gotham* (27 December 2007): 1, 8.

_____. "NFL Digs In Vs. Comcast." *Daily Variety Gotham* (11 June 2007): 6, 36.

Duerson, Adam. "TV Watch." *Sports Illustrated* (10 December 2007): 27.

Easterbrook, Gregg. "Why Congress Should Look at the NFL's TV Deal." *Wall Street Journal* (2 October 2002): D12.

Edelman, Marc, and Brian Doyle. "Antitrust and 'Free Movement' Risks of Expanding U.S. Professional Sports Leagues Into Europe." *Northwestern Journal of International Law & Business* (Spring 2009): 403–438.

Eggerton, John. "Comcast 'Threatened' NFL." *Multichannel News* (20 April 2009): 6.

Evans, Howie. "So You Want to Be the Commissioner." *New York Amsterdam News* (26 July 2007): 44–46.

Everson, Darren. "At $21 Billion in Revenue, It's More Than a Game." *Wall Street Journal* (6 May 2009): D8.

_____. "Yankee Stadium's Ugly Start." *Wall Street Journal* (15 May 2009): W5.

Faber, Jonathan. "A Licensing Parable." *License Magazine* (July 2007): 104–106.

Fatsis, Stefan. "The Battle for the NFL's Future: Team Owners Used to Share a Common Vision, But No More." *Wall Street Journal* (29 August 2005): R1–R3.

_____."Can New $220 Million NFL Deal Appease Restive Owners?" *Wall Street Journal* (16 December 2003): B1–B11.

_____. "Can Socialism Survive?" *Wall Street Journal* (20 September 2004): R1–R5.

_____. "NFL's Television Partners Scramble for Ad Dollars." *Wall Street Journal* (29 July 2001): B13.

_____ and Peter Grant. "Prior to Brawling, Jets, Cablevision Mulled Joint Stadium." *Wall Street Journal* (23 March 2005): B1–B2.

Feingold, Steve, and Catherine Dugan O'Connor. "What's in a Name? Dispelling NFL's Super Bowl Myth." *Business Press* (19 November 2007): 17.

Fickenscher, Lisa. "Marketer at the Goal Line." *Crain's New York Business* (28 November 2005): 57.

Flandez, Raymund. "Enterprise: NFL Helps Local Score Super Bowl Business; Focus Is on Firms Owned by Women and Minorities." *Wall Street Journal* (29 January 2008): B5.

Fort, Rodney, and James Quirk. "Rational Expectations and Pro Sports Leagues." *Scottish Journal of Political Economics* (July 2007): 374–387.

Futterman, Matthew. "Anheuser Will Sponsor Stadium's Second Corner." *Wall Street Journal* (19 June 2008): B9.

_____. "As Economy Weakens, Sports Feel a Chill." *Wall Street Journal* (14 October 2008): A12.

_____. "Boss Talk: NFL Chief Tackles Labor Strife, TV." *Wall Street Journal* (4 September 2008): B10.

_____. "Comcast-NFL Spat Over Viewer Access Intensifies." *Wall Street Journal* (15 April 2009): B7.

_____. "Druckenmiller Withdraws Bid for Steelers." *Wall Street Journal* (19 September 2008): B10.

_____. "Football Tries a New Play to Score Overseas." *Wall Street Journal* (9 October 2008): B5.

_____. "Jets to Auction Seats on eBay." *Wall Street Journal* (17 September 2008): B1, B6.

_____. "Mr. Smith Gets Down to Business." *Wall Street Journal* (1 July 2009: D8.

_____. "NFL Chief Tackles Labor Strife, TV, Discipline Issues." *Wall Street Journal* (4 September 2008): B10.

_____. "NFL Games Go Wireless." *Wall Street Journal* (6 November 2008): B6.

_____. "NFL Owners Curtail Labor Pact." *Wall Street Journal* (21 May 2008): B6.

_____. "NFL Players Seek Bigger Slice of League's Revenue." *Wall Street Journal* (20 May 2008): B9.

_____. "NFL, Players Trade Hits Over Finances." *Wall Street Journal* (31 January 2009): A4.

_____. "NFL Seeks Balance in Cable Fray." *Wall Street Journal* (12 November 2008): B6.

_____. "NFL to Cut Jobs in Face of Recession." *Wall Street Journal* (10 December 2008): B4.

_____. "A Safety for Giants as Clock Ticks Down on Stadium." *Wall Street Journal* (17 June 2009): B6.

Futterman, Matthew, and John R. Wilke. "Behind the Steel Curtain, a Rusty Bucket." *Wall Street Journal* (10 July 2008): B8.

Gibson, Richard. "The Franchise Decision." *Wall Street Journal* (11 May 2009): R9.

Gibson, Stan. "It Shares Team's Glory." *eweek* (28 February 2005): 20–21.

Gillespie, John W. "Do the Packers Have the N.F.L.'s Best Business Model." *New York Times Magazine* (14 September 2008): 50.

Gladden, James M., Richard L. Irwin, and William A. Sutton. "Managing North American Major Professional Sport Teams in the New Millennium." *Journal of Sport Management* (October 2001): 297–317.

Glennon, Sean. "Behind the New Pigskin Primacy." *The Boston Globe* (13 February 2005): F8.

Gloeckler, Geoff, and Tom Lowry. "Roger Goodell." *Business Week* (8 October 2007): 48–50.

Goff, Brian L., and Thomas O. Wisley. "Is There a Managerial Life Cycle? Evidence from the NFL." *Managerial & Decision Economics* (October 2006): 563–572.

Goldman, Lea. "No NFL Stars." *Forbes* (2 July 2007): 93–100.

Graber, Ken. "Arizona Cardinals' New State-of-the-Art Retractable Stadium Roof Employs Technology to Open and Close Giant Panels." *Cost Engineering* (June 2006): 17–19.

Greppi, Michele. "ABC and Affiliates Near NFL Pact." *Electronic Media* (7 October 2002): 2–3.

Griffith, Clark C. "Sports Licensing." *Licensing Journal* (September 2003): 26–27.

Grossman, Ben. "NFL Tackles Cable." *Broadcasting Cable* (31 July 2006): 3, 8.

_____. "'Sunday Night Football' Scores Big For NBA." *Broadcasting & Cable* (9 July 2007): 22–24.

Harris, Sloan. "America's Game: The Epic Story of How Pro Football Captured a Nation." *Publishers Weekly* (13 September 2004): 68.

Haugsted, Linda. "Scoring With Affiliates." *Multichannel News* (January 2008): 26.

Helliker, Kevin. "Loyal Fans Are Batting Cleanup." *Wall Street Journal* (30 April 2009): D1, D8.

Hemingway, Jonathan. "Stations Cry Foul Over NFL Play." *Broadcasting & Cable* (31 December 2007): 3, 20.

Herrick, Thaddeus, and Alex Frangos. "NFL Teams See Pay Dirt in Modern Stadium Designs." *Wall Street Journal* (3 January 2007): B1–B6.

Hoffer, Richard. "The King of Texas." *Sports Illustrated* (16 July 2007): 68–72.

Horick, Randy. "Business Bookshelf—Share and Share Alike: How the NFL Manages to Score Big." *Wall Street Journal* (18 January 2007): D7.

Hyman, Mark. "Did the Bengals Claw Taxpayers?" *Business Week* (6 October 2003): 96.

_____. "How to Lose Fans and Get Richer." *Business Week* (26 January 1998): 70.

_____. "In a League of Its Own." *Economist* (27 April 2006): 63–64.

_____. "A League of Their Own?" *Business Week* (15 June 1998): 66.

_____. "Patriots' Perfection: Patent Pending." *Business Week* (12 May 2008): 17.

Janoff, Barry. "Naming Rights Deals Near $1B." *Brandweek* (21 April 2008): 18–20.

_____. "NFL Accelerates Activation For Digital Media Marketing." *Brandweek* (23 April 2007): 16–18.

_____. "NFL Rookies Study at Brand U; Cisco Systems Plays the Field." *Brandweek* (12 May 2008): 16–18.

Johnson, Matthew. "NJ, Agency Reach Deal With Teams Over Stadium." *Bond Buyer* (3 April 2006): 34.

"Jurors Side With NFL in Oakland Raiders' Suit Over Lost Stadium Deal." *Wall Street Journal* (22 May 2001): B11.

Karp, Hannah. "The NFL Doesn't Want Your Bets." *Wall Street Journal* (16 June 2009): D16.

_____. "Why the NFL Spies on Its Players." *Wall Street Journal* (7 November 2008): W1, W4.

Kelley, Austin. "Taking a Stand in the Grandstands." *Wall Street Journal* (5 May 2009): D18.

Kenny, Jack. "The Never-Ending Season." *New Hampshire Business Review* (3 February 2006): 63.

Kenny, Tom. "NFL Films' Expansion." *Broadcasting Engineering* (January 2003): 32, 34.

Keough, Jack. "A Lesson From the Patriots." *Industrial Distribution* (May 2005): 11.

Lane, Randall. "Bread and Circuses." *Forbes* (6 June 1994): 62–65.

LaPointe, Joe. "At Meadowlands Stadium, Lots of Bells and Whistles." *New York Times* (31 October 2008): 15.

Lefton, Terry. "Sleet in Atlanta?: The Weather's Also Unpredictable at NFLP, Other Orgs." *Brandweek* (7 February 2000): 8A–11A.

Lentz, Philip. "Trip to Tampa Not Super Financially For NY Giants." *Crain's New York Business* (22 January 2001): 1–2.

Levine, Stuart. "Sport Centered." *Sports & Entertainment* (14 July 2004): A2.

Lowrey, Michael. "Benefits of Sports Subsidies Rarely Add Up." *Carolina Journal* (July 2009): 17.

Lukowsky, Wes. "America's Game: The Epic Story of How Pro Football Captured a Nation." *Booklist* (15 November 2004): 545.

Lunt, Perry. "The NFL Kicks Off a Digital Asset Management Drive." *Transform Magazine* (September 2003): 45.

Lyons, John. "The NFL Asks Soccer-Mad Mexicans If They're Ready For Some Football." *Wall Street Journal* (30 November 2006): B1–B8.

Maddox, Kate. "B-to-B Players Get Game in Sports Ads." *B-to-B* (10 October 2005): 14.

Mader, Robert P. "Texans Open Deluxe Digs." *Contractor Magazine* (September 2002): 1–2.

Maher, Kris. "'Hail, Mary': Steelers Fans Face Realities of a Sale." *Wall Street Journal* (9 July 2008): A2.

Mahmud, Shahnaz. "Farther Afield." *Adweek* (7 April 2008): 11–12.

_____. "The New Rule Book." *Adweek* (22 September 2008): 10–13.

"Major Television Rights Deals in Place." In *Sports Business Resource Guide & Fact Book 2006* (Charlotte, NC: Street & Smith's Sports Business Journal, 2006): E-120.

Matthews, Anna Wilde. "NFL Nears Web-Properties Deal With AOL, Viacom, Sports-Line." *Wall Street Journal* (9 July 2001): B4.

_____. "Sports Leagues Tightening Grip on Web Content." *Wall Street Journal* (11 June 2001): B1.

Maxymuk, John. "America's Game: The Epic Story of How Pro Football Captured a Nation." *Library Journal* (1 October 2004): 90.

McCarthy, Michael, and Judy Warner. "Meet 'the Danny.'" *Adweek* (8 November 1999): 74.

McCullough, Michael. "Football Stadiums: Sports Palaces." *School Library Journal* (1 April 2001): 166–167.

McEachern, Martin. "The Only Game in Town." *Computer Graphics World* (October 2005): 16–17.

McGee, Sherri A. "NFL Manager of On-Field Operations." *Essence* (November 2004): 112.

McKelvey, Steve M. "Dawg Pound Decision Provides Guidance for Fan Group-Related Trademarks." *Sport Marketing Quarterly* (2006): 181–183.

"Meritocracy Only Goes So Far in Professional Football." *Wall Street Journal* (6 January 2009): A14.

Metz, Cade. "The NFL's Wireless Game Plan." *PC Magazine* (23 August 2005): 74.

Miller, Michael. "The Rationalization of the Irrational." *International Journal of Politics, Culture & Society* (Fall 1997): 101–127.

Mollenkamp, Carrick, and Jeffrey Ball. "Midsize Cities Scramble to Woo Stadium Sponsors." *Wall Street Journal* (13 May 1998): S1, S3.

Mondello, Mike, and Joel Maxcy. "The Impact of Salary Dispersion and Performance Bonuses on NFL Organizations." *Management Decision* (December 2008): 110–123.

Moore, Thomas. "It's 4th & 10—The NFL Needs the Long Bomb." *Fortune* (4 August 1986): 160–166.

Morrell, John. "NFL Teams Profiting from New Venues." *Amusement Business* (21 May 2001): 1–2.

Morrissey, Brian. "Super Bowl Spots: Who Needs an Ad Agency?" *Adweek* (16 October 2006): 6–9.

Mueller, Randy. "TSN NFL Executive of the Year." *Sporting News* (2 April 2001): 59–60.

Muret, Don. "Baseball, NFL Teams Terms All Over the Playing Field." *Amusement Business* (4 August 2007): 3–5.

"The New Cathedrals: Politics and Media in the History of Stadium Construction." *Choice* (1 July 2007): 1948–1949.

"New Orleans Gets Super Bowl." *Charlotte Observer* (20 May 2009): 2C.

"NFL.Com." In *Sports Business Resource Guide & Fact Book 2006* (Charlotte, NC: Street & Smith's Sports Business Journal, 2006): E-84.

"NFL Films." In *Sports Business Resource Guide & Fact Book 2006* (Charlotte, NC: Street & Smith's Sports Business Journal, 2006): E-88.

"NFL Marketing Game Plan: Highlight Connection Fans Have with Football." *Brandweek* (21 January 2002): 14–16.

"NFL Network." In *Sports Business Resource Guide & Fact Book 2006* (Charlotte, NC: Street & Smiths' Sports Business Journal, 2006): E-6, E-7.

"NFL Network Gaining Little Yardage." *Variety* (2 December 2007): 22–23.

"NFL Not That Strict on Drug Abuse." *Wall Street Journal* (18 October 2008): A12.

O'Boyle, Michael. "Mexico's Futbol Fans Embrace NFL." *Daily Variety Gotham* (4 October 2005): 1, 7.

O'Brien, Tim. "Work Begins on Houston's New Stadium." *Amusement Business* (27 March 2000): 18–19.

O'Connell, Vanessa. "Super-Bowl Spots Aren't Easy Sell for Fox." *Wall Street Journal* (21 January 2002): B5.

Ozanian, Michael K. "Selective Accounting." *Forbes* (14 December 1998): 124–134.

Paluta, Roman. "A League of Our Own." *Adweek* (28 February 2005): 22.

Paul, Alan. "The Year of the Pigskin." *Wall Street Journal* (19 January 2007): W1, W6.

"Paul Tagliabue." *Business Week* (12 January 2004): 66–71.

Peter, Josh. "Building NFL Fortunes." *The Times-Picayune* (14 July 2002): 1.

Phelan, Carolyn. "Football Stadiums: Sports Palaces." *Booklist* (1 April 2001): 5–8.

"PLB to Develop NFL Licensed Food." *Amusement Business* (24 January 2000): 14.

"A Political Football." *Broadcasting & Cable* (10 December 2007): 32–34.

Pompei, Dan. "Giving Coaches More Say Has Become the Rule Today." *Sporting News* (9 April 2001): 41–42.

_____. "Roll Tape." *Sporting News* (10 March 2003): 14.

_____. "Speed Reads." *Sporting News* (16 December 2005): 31–38.

Powers, Steve. "Sacks of Cash." *Business 2.0* (October 2006): 30.

Prasso, Sheridan. "Lost Backers." *Business Week* (3 February 2003): 14–16.

"Pro Football; N.F.L. to Play in Tokyo." *New York Times* (18 December 1988): 4.

"Q & A With Steve Sabol." *Roar* (June 2009): 11, 13.

Quindt, Fritz. "Why Old School Isn't in Session." *Sporting News* (23 July 2001): 7.

"Rams Release Leading Tackler." *Charlotte Observer* (9 May 2009): 9C.

Reese, James T., and Robin D. Mittelstaedt. "An Exploratory Study of the Criteria Used to Establish NFL Ticket Prices." *Sport Marketing Quarterly* (2001): 223–230.

Reiss, S.A. "America's Game: The Epic Story of How Pro Football Captured a Nation." *Choice* (1 March 2005): 1.

Renaud, Gilles. "Brand NFL: Making and Selling America's Favorite Sport." *Library Journal* (July 2007): 97.

Reynolds, Mike. "Challenges Await NFL Net, OLN." *Multichannel News* (6 February 2006): 8.

_____. "NFL Net Games Play Wider Field." *Multichannel News* (1 December 2008): 3, 22.

_____. "NFL's Perfect Storm." *Multichannel News* (31 December 2007): 3.

Richards, Don, III. "Stadium Savvy." *Consulting-Specifying Engineer* (July 2002): 53–55.

Robinson, Alan. "100 Years Ago, Forbes Was First Place." *Charlotte Observer* (30 June 2009): 4C.

Rogers, R. Scott. "U.S., European Leagues Tell a Tale of Two Footballs." *Corporate Legal Times* (December 2001): B15–B17.

Romer, David. "Do Firms Maximize? Evidence from Professional Football." *Journal of Political Economy* (April 2006): 340–365.

Ross, Chuck. "Comfort, Diversity Hallmarks of New NFL Stadiums." *Building Design & Construction* (September 2002): 12–14.

St. Onge, Peter. "Major League Sports Franchises Eye Future Uneasily." *Charlotte Observer* (7 March 2009): 10A.

Sanderson, A.R. "The Business of Sports." *Choice* (1 November 2008): 1.

Sandomir, Richard. "The Real National Pastime." *New York Times Book Review* (7 November 2004): 20.

Sappenfield, Mark. "L.A. Fans Tell NFL, It's Our Way or the Highway." *Christian Science Monitor* (11 August 1999): 2.

Schaffer, Athena. "FedEx Gives $205 Million to Name Redskins Stadium." *Amusement Business* (29 November 1999): 13.

"Scholastic/NFL Deal Latest in Sting of Licensing Agreements." *Book Publishing Report* (1 November 2004): 4.

Scott, David. "Goodell Wants to 'Grow the Game.'" *Charlotte Observer* (13 May 2009): 2C.

Sharp, Linda A. "Baltimore Ravens Lose in Logo Dispute." *Sport Marketing and the Law* (2001): 112–113.

Shields, Mike. "Sprint Nextel Calls Mobile Content Play with NFL." *Media Week* (22 August 2005): 6.

Shook, David. "Lessons from the NFL Playbook." *Business Week Online* (23 September 2002): N1.

Siegfried, John, and Andrew Zimbalist. "The Economics of Sports Facilities and Their Communities." *Journal of Economic Perspectives* (Summer 2000): 95–114.

_____ and _____. "A Note on the Local Economic Impact of Sports Expenditures." *Journal of Sports Economics* (3 April 2002): 361–366.

Smith, Mark R. "Super, Indeed: Capturing the NFL's Great Event in Tampa." *Digital Television* (February 2001): 63–65.

Snyder, Eldon E. "Football and American Identity." *The Journal of American Culture* (March 2006): 70–71.

Solomon, John. "Whose Game Is It, Anyway?" *Washington Monthly* (December 1999): 31–34.

Spiegel, Peter. "NFL Struggles to Gain Ground in China." *Los Angeles Times* (7 February 2009): A3.

Staudohar, Paul D. "The Scope of Pro Football's Antitrust Exemption." *Labor Law Journal* (Spring 1999): 34–42.

Stellino, Vito. "To Live and Die in L.A." *Football Digest* (August 1999): 52–55.

Stone, David. "New Homes Abound For NFL Teams." *Football Digest* (April 2001): 12–14.

Sullivan, Tom. "Political Football: A New Stadium Is Low on the List for New Orleans." *Wall Street Journal* (9 November 2005): C9.

"Tagliabue on the NFL Today." *Business Week* (25 October 1999): 160, 162.

Taylor, Susan Lee, and Marilyn Young. "A Preliminary Investigation of NFL Games and Self-Driven Tourism: Marketing Opportunities For Accommodation Providers." *International Journal of Hospitality & Tourism Administration* (2005): 47–63.

"Teamwork." *Economist* (29 January 2000): 72–74.

Thomas, Jim. "The Right Ingredients." *Sporting News* (5 March 2001): 34–35.

Thomaselli, Rich. "Collins Sets Out to Reclaim 'Sweet Spot' for NFL Sponsors." *Advertising Age* (1 September 2003): 19–20.

Thompson, Adam. "Sports Leagues Impose More Rules on Coverage." *Wall Street Journal* (16 July 2007): B1–B2.

_____ and Brian Steinberg. "At Rams' Field, Two Sponsors for One Night Only." *Wall Street Journal* (8 December 2006): B3.

Triplett, William. "FCC Backs NFL Play." *Daily Variety Gotham* (14 December 2008): 4, 10.

Tse, Eliza Ching-Yick, and Suk-Ching Ho. "Targeting Sports Teams." *Cornell Hotel & Restaurant Administration Quarterly* (February 2006): 49–60.

Turner, Katherine. "US Insurer Briefs McCann Erickson." *Marketing Week* (29 March 2007): 12.

"The 2004 Team Valuations." *Forbes* (20 September 2004): 138.

Umstead, R. Thomas. "NFL Network Is Still Plugging Holes." *Multichannel News* (20 November 2006): 6.

_____. "Showtime Will Tackle NFL, Spielberg Sitcom." *Multichannel News* (9 June 2008): 6–10.

_____, and Linda Haugsted. "Blitzing the Statehouses." *Multichannel News* (12 November 2007): 40.

Urso, Nicole. "NFL Leads Sports Marketers Kicking and Screaming on to the Web." *Response* (January 2008): 36–41.

"U.S. Digital Media Rights." In *Sports Business Resource Guide & Fact Book 2006* (Charlotte, NC: *Street & Smith's Sports Business Journal*, 2006): E-116, E-118.

"U.S., European Leagues Tell a Tale of Two Footballs." *Corporate Legal Times* (December 2001): BWB15–17.

Vogan, Travis. "Brand NFL: Making and Selling America's Favorite Sport." *Journal of Popular Culture* (October 2008): 908–909.

Vrooman, John. "Franchise Free Agency in Professional Sports Leagues." *Southern Economic Journal* (July 1997): 191–219.

_____. "Theory of the Perfect Game: Competitive Balance in Monopoly Sports Leagues." *Review of Industrial Organization* (February 2009): 5–44.

Waddell, Ray. "Public/Private Ownership Ventures Grow in Popularity." *Amusement Business* (14 June 1999): 19–20.

Wade, Will. "Blackhawk to Offer NFL Gift Products." *American Banker* (6 November 2007): 8.

Wakabayashi, Daisuke. "Japan Takes on the Fighting Irish." *Wall Street Journal* (28 July 2009): D8.

Walker, Sam. "Gridiron Godfathers." *Wall Street Journal* (20 January 2006): W4.

_____. "A No-Win Situation." *Wall Street Journal* (26 January 2001): W1.

_____. "The People vs. NFL." *Wall Street Journal* (5 October 2001): W6.

_____. "Pro Football: Scoring in a Slow Economy." *Wall Street Journal* (7 September 2001): W1, W6.

Watson, Noshua. "The Amazing Predictive Power of Pigskin." *Fortune International* (24 December 2001): 98–100.

Watts, Jim. "Arizona: Up Nabs Naming Rights." *Bond Buyer* (3 October 2006): 33–40.

Welki, Andrew M., and Thomas J. Zlatopen. "U.S. Professional Football Game-Day Attendance." *Atlantic Economic Journal* (September 1999): 285–298.

Weprin, Alex. "NFL Chief Vows to Grow Network." *Broadcasting & Cable* (28 April 2008): 1.

Wilke, John R. "Pittsburgh's Rooney Family Quietly Shopping the Steelers." *Wall Street Journal* (8 July 2008): A1, A17.

Wilson, Beverly. "The Georgia Dome." *Broadcast Engineering* (January 2004): 32–34.

Wilson, Duff. "N.F.L. Executives Hope to Keep Salaries Secret." *The New York Times* (12 August 2008): 10.

Yost, Mark. "Loutish Fans Disgrace the NFL." *Wall Street Journal* (16 October 2007): D6.

_____. "NFL's Eagles Tackle Drunken, Rowdy Fans." *Wall Street Journal* (14 October 2007): D7.

_____. "Will Detroit Be the Loser?" *Wall Street Journal* (28–29 January 2005): 12.

Zaretsky, Adam M. "Should Cities Pay for Sports Facilities?" *The Regional Economist* (April 2001): 5–9.

Books

Bennett, Tom. *The Pro Style: The Complete Guide to Understanding National Football League Strategy.* Upper Saddle River, NJ: Prentice Hall, 1976.

Carroll, Bob. *Total Football II: The Official Encyclopedia of the National Football League.* New York: HarperCollins, 1999.

Carroll, John. *Red Grange and the Rise of Modern Football.* Urbana: University of Illinois Press, 1999.

Chipman, Donald, Randolph Campbell, and Robert Cavert. *The Dallas Cowboys and the NFL.* Norman: University of Oklahoma Press, 1970.

Davis, Jeff. *Rozelle: Czar of the NFL.* New York: McGraw-Hill, 2008.

Delaney, Kevin, and Rick Eckstein. *Public Dollars, Private Stadiums: The Battle Over Building Sports Stadiums.* New Brunswick, NJ: Rutgers University Press, 2003.

Didinger, Ray. *The Super Bowl: Celebrating a Quarter-Century of America's Greatest Game.* New York: Simon & Schuster, 1990.

Downward, Paul, and Alistair Dawson. *The Economics of Professional Team Sports.* New York: Routledge, 2000.

Eisen, Rich. *Total Access: A Journey to the Center of the NFL Universe.* New York: Thomas Dunne Books, 2007.

Falk, Gerhard, Frank Hoffman, and Martin Manning. *Football and American Identity.* New York: Haworth Press, 2005.

Felser, Larry. *The Birth of the New NFL: How the 1966 AFL/NFL Merger Transformed Pro Football.* Guilford, CT: Lyons Press, 2008.

Fizel, John, ed. *Handbook of Sports Economics Research.* Armonk, NY: M.E. Sharpe, 2006.

Fleder, Rob. *Sports Illustrated: The Football Book.* New York: Sports Illustrated, 2005.

Ganz, Howard L., and Jeffrey L. Kessler. *Understanding Business & Legal Aspects of the Sports Industry, 2001.* New York: Practicing Law Institute, 2001.

Gillette, Gary, ed. *The ESPN Pro Football Encyclopedia.* New York: Sterling Publishing, 2006.

Harris, David. *The League: The Rise and Decline of the NFL.* New York: Bantam Books, 1986.

Higgs, Ben. *Sidelines: Behind the Scenes of America's Favorite Game.* Richmond, VA: Cadmus Publishing, 1992.

Humphreys, Brad R., and Dennis R. Howard, eds. *The Business of Sports.* Westport, CT: Praeger, 2008.

Jones, Michael E. *Sports Law.* Upper Saddle River, NJ: Prentice Hall, 1999.

Jozsa, Frank P., Jr. *American Sports Empire: How the Leagues Breed Success.* Westport: CT: Praeger, 2003.

_____. *Big Sports, Big Business: A Century of League Expansions, Mergers, and Reorganizations.* Westport, CT: Praeger, 2006.

_____. *Global Sports: Cultures, Markets and Organizations.* Singapore: World Scientific, 2009.

_____. *Sports Capitalism: The Foreign Business of American Professional Leagues.* Aldershot, England: Ashgate, 2004.

_____ and John J. Guthrie, Jr. *Relocating Teams and Expanding Leagues in Professional Sports: How the Major Leagues Respond to Market Conditions.* Westport, CT: Quorum Books, 1999.

King, Peter. *Football: A History of the Professional Game.* Birmingham, AL: Oxmoor House, 1993.

_____. *75 Seasons: The Complete Story of the National Football League, 1920–1995.* Atlanta: Turner Publishing, 1994.

MacCambridge, Michael. *America's Game: The Epic Story of How Football Captured a Nation.* New York: Random House, 2004.

Maher, Tod, and Bob Gill, eds. *The Pro Football Encyclopedia: The Complete and Definitive Record of Professional Football.* New York: Macmillan, 1997.

Maltby, Marc. *The Origins and Early Development of Professional Football.* New York: Garland Publishing, 1997.

McClellan, Keith. *The Sunday Game: At the Dawn of Professional Football.* Akron, OH: University of Akron Press, 1998.

McDonough, Will. *The NFL Century: The Complete Story of the National Football League, 1920–2000.* New York: Smithmark Publishers, 1999.

Morgan, Jon. *Glory for Sale: Fans, Dollars and the New NFL.* Baltimore: Bancroft Press, 1997.

Neft, David S., and Richard M. Cohen. *The Sports Encyclopedia: Pro Football.* 5th ed. New York: St. Martin's Press, 1997.

Noll, Roger G. ed. *Government and the Sports Business: Studies in the Regulation of Economic Activity.* Washington, D.C.: Brookings Institution, 1974.

Oriard, Michael. *Brand NFL: Making and Selling America's Favorite Sport.* Chapel Hill: University of North Carolina Press, 2007.

Owens, Thomas. *Football Stadiums: Sports Palaces.* Brookfield, CT: Millbrook Press, 2001.

Palmer, Pete, ed. *The ESPN Pro Football Encyclopedia.* 2nd ed. New York: Sterling Publishing, 2007.

Paolantonio, Sal. *How Football Explains America.* Chicago: Triumph Books, 2008.

Peterson, Robert W. *Pigskin: The Early Years of Pro Football.* New York and London, England: Oxford University Press, 1996.

Quirk, James, and Rodney D. Fort. *Pay Dirt: The Business of Professional Team Sports.* Princeton, NJ: Princeton University Press, 1992.

Ross, Charles K. *Outside the Lines: African Americans and the Integration of the National Football League.* New York: NYU Press, 2001.

Schaaf, Phil. *Sports, Inc.: 100 Years of Sports Business.* Amherst, NY: Prometheus Books, 2004.

Smith, Ron. *NFL Football: The Official Fans' Guide.* Chicago: Triumph Books, 1997.

Sports Business Resource Guide & Fact Book 2006 . Charlotte, NC: Street & Smith's Sports Business Journal, 2006.

The World Almanac and Book of Facts. New York: World Almanac Books, 1930–2007.

Trumpbour, Robert. *The New Cathedrals: Politics and Media in the History of Stadium Construction.* Syracuse, NY: Syracuse University Press, 2006.

Willis, Chris. *Old Leather: An Oral History of Early Pro Football in Ohio, 1920–1935.* Lanham, MD: Scarecrow Press, 2005.

Yost, Mark. *Tailgating, Sacks, and Salary Caps: How the NFL Became the Most Successful Sports League in History.* Chicago: Kaplan Business, 2006.

Dissertations

Coenen, Craig R. "Little Cities That Led Them: Civic Responses to National Football League Franchises, 1920–1966." Ph.D. diss., Lehigh University, 2001.

Drayer, Juris. "An Analysis of the Primary and Secondary Ticket Markets for a National Football League Team: A Case Study of the Denver Broncos." Ph.D. diss., University of Northern Colorado, 2007.

Dzikus, Lars. "From Violence to Party: A History of the Presentation of American Football in England and Germany." Ph.D. diss., Ohio State University, 2005.

Jozsa, Frank P., Jr. "An Economic Analysis of Franchise Relocation and League Expansion in Professional Team Sports, 1950–1975." Ph.D. diss., Georgia State University, 1977.

Latham, Donald R. "An Analysis of the Organizational Structures of National Football League Teams." Ph.D. diss., University of Arkansas, 1979.

Maltby, Marc. "The Origin and Early Development of Professional Football, 1890–1920." Ph.D. diss., Ohio University, 1987.

Oeth, Carol Marie. "Leadership in the National Football League." Ph.D. diss., University of Akron, 1996.

Simons, Nancy. "The Future of the National Football League: Trends Identified in a Delphi Study." Ph.D. diss., Walden University, 1995.

Internet Sources

"About NFL Network." http://www.nfl.com cited 26 June 2009.

"American Bowl." http://en.wikipedia.org cited 27 June 2009.

"Anthony Joins Estefans as Musicians Who Are Dolphins Minority Owners." http://www.nfl.com cited 23 July 2009.

"Atlanta Falcons." http://www.nfl.com cited 18 March 2009.

Badenhausen, Kurt. "Cardinal Red." http://www.forbes.com cited 17 March 2009.

_____. "A Super Bowl of Financial Champs." http://www.forbes.com cited 17 March 2009.

_____, Michael K. Ozanian, and Christina Settimi. "The Business of Football." http://www.forbes.com cited 9 February 2009.

_____, _____ and _____. "The Richest Game." http://sports.yahoo.com cited 27 May 2009.

"Ballparks." http://www.ballparks.com cited 12 March 2009.

"Best Coaches in the NFL." http://www.forbes.com cited 17 March 2009.

"Birth of Pro Football." http://www.profootballhof.com cited 18 March 2009.

Bloom, Howard. "In 2006: Titans of Industry—The National Football League." http://www.sportsbusinessnews.com cited 1 January 2007.

_____. "The National Football League—A Business Getting It Right." http://www.sportsbusinessnews.com cited 7 September 2006.

_____. "The National Football League Does What It Does Best—Makes More Money." http://www.sportsbusinessnews.com cited 23 May 2007.

_____. "The National Football League—Sports Socialism at Its Very Best." http://www.sportsbusinessnews.com cited 29 March 2007.

_____. "The Nationalization of the National Football League." http://www.sportsbusinessnews.com cited 17 July 2007.

_____. "NFL Expansion to Canada Will Not Include the Peanuts Cartoon Gang." http://www.sportsbusinessnews.com cited 12 October 2007.

_____. "NFL Heading to Canada, Not to Los Angeles." http://www.sportsbusinessnews.com cited 26 October 2006.

_____. "United Football League—How to Lose Tens, Hundreds of Millions of Dollars." http://www.sportsbusinessnews.com cited 31 May 2007.

"Brand NFL: Making and Selling America's Favorite Sport." http://www.publishersweekly.com cited 17 February 2009.

Brenner, Adam. "Welcome to the Club." http://www.forbes.com cited 17 March 2009.

Burke, Monte. "Running Up the Score." http://www.forbes.com cited 17 March 2009.

"Carolina Panthers." http://www.nfl.com cited 18 March 2009.

Cherner, Reid. "Behind the Curtain at NFL Films, 'Where Football Was Born.'" http://www.usatoday.com cited 2 July 2009.

Chestek, Pamela. "The NFL Is One Entity—For Trademark Licensing, Anyway." http://www.propertyintangible.com cited 1 July 2009.

Christl, Cliff. "Texans Have a Headstart Over Other Expansion Teams." http://www.jsonline.com cited 12 July 2005.

Clayton, John. "NFL Owners' Timetable for Team in L.A. Remains Uncertain." http://www.sportsbusinessnews.com cited 23 May 2006.

"Cleveland Bulldogs." http://www.ohiohistorycentral.org cited 6 March 2009.

"Cleveland Indians (American Professional Football Association) (1921)." http://www.ohiohistorycentral.org cited 6 March 2009.

"The Cowboys New Stadium All That and a Great Deal More." http://www.sportsbusinessnews.com cited 13 December 2006.

"Dallas Cowboys." http://www.nfl.com cited 18 March 2009.

"Deal That Would Keep Saints in New Orleans Through 2025 Nearly Done." http://www. nfl.com cited 23 July 2009.

Desai, Anuj. "Is the Football Cardinals New Crib Going to Impact the Sports Industry?" http://www.sportsbusinessnews.com cited 3 September 2006.

"Developer Abandons Plan to Build New Chargers Stadium." http://www.nfl.com cited 23 July 2009.

"Estefans' Minority Ownership of Dolphins Is Music to the Team's Ears." http://www.nfl. com cited 23 July 2009.

Evans, Simon. "Dolphin Stadium Renamed Land Shark Stadium." http://www.reuters.com cited 18 June 2009.

"Expanding Possibilities: New Stadium Plans Developed to Save L.A. Expansion Bid." http://www.cnnsi.com cited 30 July 1999.

"Fan Cost Index." http://www.teammarketing.com cited 26 February 2009.

Forde, Pat. "Tough Days for Those Managing Sports Leagues." http://www.sportsbusiness news.com cited 27 July 2007.

"Franchise History: Atlanta Falcons." http://en.wikipedia.org cited 3 March 2009.

"Franchise History: Carolina Panthers." http://en.wikipedia.org cited 3 March 2009.

"Franchise History: Dallas Cowboys." http://en.wikipedia.org cited 3 March 2009.

"Franchise History: Houston Texans." http://en.wikipedia.org cited 3 March 2009.

"Franchise History: Jacksonville Jaguars." http://en.wikipedia.org cited 3 March 2009.

"Franchise History: Minnesota Vikings." http://en.wikipedia.org cited 3 March 2009.

"Franchise History: New Orleans Saints." http://en.wikipedia.org cited 3 March 2009.

"Franchise History: Philadelphia Eagles." http://en.wikipedia.org cited 3 March 2009.

"Franchise History: Pittsburgh Steelers." http://en.wikipedia.org cited 3 March 2009.

"Franchise History: Tampa Bay Buccaneers." http://en.wikipedia.org cited 3 March 2009.

"Giants, Jets Will Wait for Right Price for New Stadium Naming Rights." http://www.nfl. com cited 23 July 2009.

"Goodell Wants to Expand Season." http://www.si.com cited 26 March 2009.

Goodman, Jeff. "Expansion Candidates Meet With NFL in New York." http://sports. yahoo.com cited 14 September 1999.

Gretz, Adam. "Welcome to Land Shark Stadium, Home of the Miami Dolphins." http:// nfl.fanhouse.com cited 18 June 2009.

Harrow, Rick. "Are You Ready for Some Football Biz Related News (Of Course You Are)." http://www.sportsbusinessnews.com cited 1 August 2006.

_____. "Marketing and the National Football League." http://www.sportsbusinessnews. com cited 23 August 2005.

Harry, Chris. "NFL Continues to Thrive by Dividing Profits Among Teams." http://www. sportsbusinessnews.com cited 27 March 2006.

Hasett, Kevin. "The Economics of Managing an NFL Franchise." http://www.sports businessnews.com cited 17 December 2006.

"History of NFL in Canada." http://www.nflcanada.com cited 27 June 2009.

"History of the Pro Bowl." http://www.nfl.com cited 5 March 2009.

Hoffmann, Leah. "The NFL Playoffs: Rich Team, Poor Team." http://www.forbes.com cited 17 March 2009.

"Houston Texans." http://www.nfl.com cited 18 March 2009.

"Indianapolis Ahead of Curve in Preparations for Super Bowl XLVI in 2012." http://www. nfl.com cited 23 July 2009.

"Jacksonville Jaguars." http://www.nfl.com cited 18 March 2009.

"Jaguars Introduce Half-Season Ticket Packages to Boost Sales." http://www.nfl.com cited 23 July 2009.

"Limited Liability Company (LLC)." http://www.irs.gov cited 29 June 2009.

"Limited Partnership." http://www.quickmba.com cited 29 June 2009.

"List of NFL Franchise Owners." http://en.wikipedia.org cited 25 February 2009.

Lubinger, Bob. "NFL Tickets: Where Does the Money Go?" http://www.cleveland.com cited 3 April 2009.

Lutz, Michael A. "McNair's Determination Rewarded with NFL Franchise." http://sports.yahoo.com cited 6 October 1999.

Macmillan, Kate. "NFL Stadiums: What's in a Name?" http://sports.yahoo.com cited 27 May 2009.

"Major League Baseball." http://www.mlb.com cited 22 February 2009.

"Major League Soccer." http://www.mls.com cited 22 February 2009.

"Minnesota Vikings." http://www.nfl.com cited 18 March 2009.

"Naming Rights Online." http://www.namingrightsonline.com cited 27 May 2009.

"National Basketball Association." http://www.nba.com cited 22 February 2009.

"National Football League." http://www.nfl.com cited 22 February 2009.

"National Football League Franchise Histories." http://www.profootballhof.com cited 18 March 2009.

"National Football League (NFL) History." http://www.rauzulusstreet.com cited 12 August 2005.

"National Hockey League." http://www.nhl.com cited 22 February 2009.

"NBA Standings, 2008–2009 Season." http://sports.espn.go.com cited 30 May 2009.

Nelson, Brett. "Super Bowls Don't Equal Super-Sized Profits." http://www.forbes.com cited 17 March 2009.

"New Orleans Saints." http://www.nfl.com cited 18 March 2009.

"New York Giants." http://www.nfl.com cited 18 March 2009.

"NFL Attendance." http://sports.espn.go.com cited 24 April 2009.

"NFL Charities." http://www.answers.com cited 26 June 2009.

"NFL Coverage Going Global." http://www.sportsbusinessnews.com cited 23 September 2007.

"NFL Expansion Fees." http://www.profootballhof.com cited 18 March 2009.

"NFL Films." http://en.wikipedia.org cited 26 June 2009.

_____. http://www.answers.com cited 26 June 2009.

"NFL Franchise Chronology." http://www.hickoksports.com cited 27 August 2005.

"NFL Franchise Year-by-Year Genealogy." http://www.nflteamhistory.com cited 9 March 2009.

"NFL International Historical Results." http://www.nfl.com cited 25 November 2002.

"NFL International Series." http://en.wikipedia.org cited 27 June 2009.

"NFL Network." http://www.nfl.com cited 26 June 2009.

"NFL Organization." http://www.nfl.com cited 27 June 2009.

"NFL Ponders Second UK Game Option." http://articles.latimes.com 27 June 2009.

"NFL Stadium Rankings." http://sportsillustrated.cnn.com cited 25 May 2005.

"NFL Team History." http://www.nflteamhistory.com cited 9 March 2009.

"NFL Team Valuations." http://www.forbes.com cited 9 February 2009.

"NFL Team Valuations (2004)." http://www.forbes.com cited 17 March 2009.

"NFL Teams Playoff Histories." http://www.sportsencyclopedia.com cited 3 March 2009.

"The NFL—The Ideal Business Model." http://www.sportsbusiness.com cited 7 May 2006.

"Niners Show Santa Clara Officials Their Plans for New $937 Million Stadium." http://www.nfl.com cited 23 July 2009.

Ozanian, Michael K. "Football Fiefdoms." http://www.forbes.com cited 17 March 2009.

Peters, Ken. "Houston Rejoins NFL with Expansion Team." http://sports.yahoo.com cited 6 October 1999.

"Philadelphia Eagles." http://www.nfl.com cited 18 March 2009.

"Pittsburgh Steelers." http://www.nfl.com cited 18 March 2009.

Poling, Travis. "Is San Antonio Big Enough to Play in the Economic NFL Game(s)." http://www.sportsbusinessnews.com cited 26 September 2005.

"Portsmouth Spartans." http://www.football-almanac.com cited 20 March 2009.

"Professional Sports Leagues." http://www.hickoksports.com cited 22 February 2009.

_____. http://en.wikipedia.org cited 22 February 2009.

Pulley, Brett. "The $1 Billion Team." http://www.forbes.com cited 17 March 2009.

"Representative NFL Stadium Public/Private Partnerships." http://www.sandiego.gov cited 4 June 2009.

Sandomir, Richard. "Comcast and NFL Network Agree to 9-Year Deal." http://www.nytimes.com cited 2 July 2009.

Shook, David. "Lessons From the NFL Playbook." http://www.businessweek.com cited 23 September 2002.

Simers, T.J. "Ovitz Confident LA Will Win NFL Expansion Bid." http://sports.yahoo.com cited 30 September 1999.

"Specter of Change: NFL Leaders Oppose Legislation on Financing New Stadiums." http://www.cnnsi.com cited 28 June 1999.

"Sports Business Data." http://www.rodneyfort.com cited 27 February 2009.

"Stadiums." http://www.football.ballparks.com cited 25 February 2009.

"Super Bowl." http://en.wikipedia.org cited 5 July 2009.

"Tampa Bay Buccaneers." http://www.nfl.com cited 18 March 2009.

"Team Games & Schedules." http://www.pro-football-reference.com cited 11 June 2009.

"Team History: New York Giants." http://en.wikipedia.org cited 3 March 2009.

"Team Marketing Report: 1991–2008." http://www.teammarketing.com cited 9 February 2009.

Thomas, G. Scott. "Who Are the Most Loyal Fans in the NFL?" http://milwaukee.bizjournals.com cited 1 June 2009.

"23 NFL Teams Freeze Ticket Prices as Global Economic Meltdown Takes a Toll." http://www.google.com cited 3 April 2009.

"2008 Major League Soccer Season." http://en.wikipedia.org cited 30 May 2009.

Van Riper, Tom. "The Super Bowl, Super Business?" http://www.newsweek.com cited 5 July 2009.

"What's in a Name?" http://www.forbes.com cited 27 May 2009.

"Who Owns the NFL?" http://www.funtrivia.com cited 26 June 2009.

Wieberg, Steve. "New Pro League to Be Built on College Football Ties." http://www.usatoday.com cited 2 July 2007.

Wilson, Bernie. "18? NFL Commissioner Wants Longer Regular Season." http://www.fanhouse.com cited 26 March 2009.

Wollenberg, Skip. "Buyers Say ABC Getting $2 Million for 30-Second Super Bowl Ads." http://sports.yahoo.com cited 22 September 1999.

Media Guides

Boss, David, and Bob Oates, Jr. *First Fifty Years: A Celebration of the National Football League in Its Fiftieth Season.* New York: Ridge Press/Benjamin, 1969.

NFL International: A Winning Partnership. New York: National Football League, 2002.

2008 NFL Record & Fact Book. New York: Time Inc. Home Entertainment, 2008.

Working Paper

Baade, Robert A., and Victor A. Matheson. "Super Bowl or Super (Hyper) Bowl?: Assessing the Economic Impact of America's Premier Event." Ann Arbor, MI: University of Michigan (2003), 1–33.

Index